Upon Further Review

Power Line Books

Upon Further Review

Books and Arts, 1983 – 2024

Steven F. Hayward

To Power Line readers everywhere

Contents

Chapter 1

Spaced Out

Lost in the Cosmos: The Last Self-Help Book, by Walker Percy

It is a disastrous discovery, according to Emerson, that we exist: disastrous, because our own consciousness comes as such a puzzle at times. It is the gift of consciousness that marks man's distinctiveness from all other animals, but the exact nature of that distinctiveness is elusive. Man is the only animal who laughs and smokes, a cheerful observer might point out, while the dour-minded Dostoyevsky remained transfixed by his perception that man is the only animal bent on his own self-destruction.

That man is a complex creature-poised halfway between the beasts and the gods, endowed with speech and reason-is of course not a new observation. Modern literature has developed a new genre that takes as its subject the "alienation" of man. Alienation, man's homelessness in his own world, has become the bane of literature and the cornerstone of many modern ideologies. Walker Percy takes alienation as the focus of his writing, but not in the reductionist sense of the Marxists or Freudians, nor in the gratuitous manner of New York parlor existentialists who bemoan their lack of meaning while getting rich on their second-rate novels. Percy's jaundiced view of popular trends and run-of-the-mill "alienation" set him apart from most modern writers whose overblown seriousness prevents the least admission of humor. Indeed, Percy's latest, *Lost in the Cosmos: The Last Self-Help Book,* combines serious themes with some well-aimed jibes at the "naive scientism" of Carl Sagan as well as the entire self-help industry, with its guides to surviving "mid-life crises" and other passages of life.

For Percy, man feels homeless in his own world not for materialist reasons (Marx), or because of fragmented consciousness (Freud), or because of the meaninglessness of the abyss (Sartre), but because each of us does not understand himself. The modern scientific enterprise of the "relief of man's estate" is not at hand, nor is it on the horizon. Modernity's quest to conquer nature, it seems, has failed on the simplest level. Man is not, as was hoped, better for modern science, rather he is miserable. Percy takes the epigram to *Lost in the Cosmos* from Nietzsche, "We are unknown, we knowers, to ourselves. . . . Of necessity we remain strangers to ourselves. . . ." As a result, the course of modernity is toward not greater self-knowledge but toward even less self-knowledge. In fact, modern scientific method-Percy calls it the "objective-empirical method"-is itself a force for increased alienation. "Every advance in an objective understanding of the Cosmos," he writes, "and in its technological control further distances the self from the Cosmos precisely in the degree of the advance-so that in the end the self becomes a space-bound ghost which roams the very Cosmos it understands perfectly" (p. 12).

Percy goes to great lengths to assure the reader that he is not a neo-Luddite out to make a frontal assault on science and technology. (Recall that Percy was an M.D. before he began writing.) Percy protests the necessary abstraction of the scientist from the natural phenomenon studied: Modern science tries to conquer human nature through the same means it uses toward the rest of nature, by objectifying man, but it has only resulted in controverting reality and denying consciousness. When the psychologists and therapists study the human psyche and break it down into so many "needs," the result is not greater self-knowledge but increased abstraction, or alienation, from the self. Percy suggests in his essay "The Man on the Train" that there is no more ideal candidate for suicide than someone who attempts to follow the prescriptions of the mental health savants.

This irony within triumphant modernity forms the subject matter for Percy's fiction: technology has largely succeeded in conquering nature and meeting man's basic needs, yet man feels more homeless than ever. The protagonists of Percy's novels (Binx Bolling, Tom More, Will Barrett) are always extreme caricatures of alienated man and, borrowing from Flannery O'Connor, Percy points out that when writing for the near-blind one must draw very large caricatures.

Percy's characters and plots are not simply large; they are outrageous. The protagonist of *Love in the Ruins*, Thomas More-yes, a descendant of Sir Thomas More, author of *Utopia*-is the confident inventor of the "Ontological Lapsometer," a "stethoscope of the human spirit" that can diagnose and cure the troubled patches of our

2

brain that divide and disorient our consciousness. Never mind that Dr. More is himself a basket case, both an outpatient and a resident psychiatrist at the same mental institution. Published in 1971, *Love in the Ruins* is set in 1983 and invokes the specter of the Orwellian year, with its connotations of heightened order and rigid bureaucratization. But *Love in the Ruins* pulls a reversal on 1984; rather than strict order, there is complete chaos. The auto age is over, vines sprout on the streets and buildings of our major cities, and wolves have been seen in downtown Cleveland, "like Rome during the Black Plague." The United States is divided along sectional and factional lines.

Life, however, goes on much as usual for most Americans. Golf continues in suburbia, while Left and Right have become more psychological types than political persuasions. The end may be at hand: potentially toxic fallout clouds are drifting about in the atmosphere. And here stands Tom More with his Ontological Lapsometer ready to cure all manner of neurosis and phobia and finally usher in the Utopia that eluded his distinguished ancestor. Yet, no one seems to take much notice of either the chaos around them or the need of Ontological wholeness that More offers to fulfill.

It is not so much that More, the scientific Utopian who cannot understand himself in the end, resembles Chicken Little as much as the fact that Percy's peripheral characters seem so lifeless. His main characters are always more aware of their predicament, and being aware of their alienation, they achieve a measure of transcendence. Most, however, are unaware of their estrangement from themselves. The epigraph to *The Moviegoer* comes from Kierkegaard: ". . . the special character of despair is precisely this: it is unaware of being despair." There, Binx Bolling, recognizing his despair, confesses that "for a long time now the impression has been growing upon me that everyone is dead. . . . It happens when I speak to people. In the middle of a sentence it will come over me; yes, beyond a doubt this is death."

Will Barrett (*The Last Gentleman; The Second Coming*) comes to the same perception in the latter novel:

In a strange new mood he made the following observation: people notice very little indeed, ghost-ridden as they are by themselves. You have to be bleeding from the mouth or throwing a fit for them to take notice. Otherwise, anything you do is no more or less than another part of the world they have to deal with, poor souls.

3

Most of us, Percy suggests, have dead souls at best; not even the appearance of Christ Himself would cause a shock. The more adept among us drift along in the grip of "everydayness," while the more acute, like Percy's heroes, recognize their alienation and are, as it were, in perpetual crisis.

To be sure, Percy makes it clear that this alienation is largely unique to modern, affluent, profanized man. Recalling Steinbeck, Percy observes that "the Okies were too hungry to have 'identity crises.'" But, "what happens to the Okie who succeeds in Pomona and now spends his time watching Art Linkletter? Is all well with them or are they in deeper trouble than they were . . . in the dust bowl?" (*The Message in the Bottle*).

The problem of modernity as Percy sees it is that the moment of man's conquest of nature is also the moment he runs completely out of meaning; man arrives at the ultimate estrangement from his own nature because his own nature cannot be explained and manipulated in the same technological manner as the rest of nature. To explain this difference between human nature and the nature of everything else, Percy has come to embrace semiotic theory. His first nonfiction collection, *The Message in the Bottle* (1975), contained several essays on semiotic theory. *Lost in the Cosmos* contains a short, simple introduction to semiotics, a study of signs and symbols as they impart meaning.

Developed by Ernst Cassirer, Charles Pierce, Susanne Langer and others, semiotics can be vastly complicated, but for Percy this is crucial: While the signs and symbols for objects in nature have an intrinsically understood commonality (essentially the Aristotelian notion of the "common noun"), the "self" as symbol has no such corresponding commonality. As Percy puts it: "This is a chair for you and me, that is a tree, everything is something, you are what you are, but *what am I?*" (*The Message in the Bottle*, p. 284).

The twenty extended questions of the "self-help" section of *Lost in the Cosmos* are designed to illuminate the various facets of selfhood, the assorted modes people tend to assume in answering the question "What am I?"-all of them, Percy insists, are unsuccessful. Many of the answers Percy supplies show rare insight; many others are overwrought and exaggerated. This and the whole "twenty questions" format tend to make the book a bit uneven, though it is still well worth reading. The reader will laugh out loud at his send-up of Phil Donahue, and his cosmic space adventures, inspired by Carl Sagan's search for extraterrestrial intelligence, are first-rate satire. C.

S. Lewis once speculated that the vast distances between objects in the universe might be God's quarantine against sinful man. Pursuing the same thought, Percy suggests that any superior extraterrestrial intelligence will avoid us like the plague.

Percy offers no remedies. For him, Christendom and modernity alike have run their course and are equally bankrupt. There is seemingly no going "forward" or "back." All choices are bleak. But for Percy, who joined the Roman Catholic church, there is Grace. Mysteriously enough, it is Grace that Percy holds out to us in his novels and in the end of *Lost in the Cosmos*. And because Grace is a divine mystery, Percy does not presume to explain it.

—*Claremont Review of Books*, Fall 1983

Chapter 2

The Elusive Lincoln

Freedom: A Novel of Abraham Lincoln and the Civil War, by William Safire, New York: Doubleday, 1123 pages, $24.95

William Safire has written an enormous book. It offers the reader a 975-page narrative, along with a 147-page "underbook" of "sources and commentary" and a bibliography of 320 books that Safire consulted. The narrative is divided into nine parts; Safire uses each to alter the focus slightly as the story proceeds. His narrative, which covers the time period from July 1861 to the signing of the Emancipation Proclamation on January 1, 1863, encompasses virtually the whole array of important (and unimportant) historical characters and viewpoints.

From the earliest pages, the largest issues loom. What is the war primarily about? Is Lincoln justified in his use of "extraconstitutional" measures to "preserve" the union? Safire's rich sweep of events devotes major attention to a wide cast of characters with widely diverging views. Kentucky Senator John Breckinridge, who preferred peaceful separation by the southern states rather than a war that undermined certain constitutional liberties, provides a compelling contrast to abolitionists like Senator Benjamin Wade or pro-unionists, including pamphleteer Anna Ella Carroll and the prominent Washington family headed by Francis Prescott Blair. Depictions of General George McClellan elucidate the military dilemmas of conducting a successful war in the face of politicians hungering for immediate action. Amidst this cast, Abraham Lincoln is still at the center of every part of the book. As he must be.

"The Lincoln legend," historian Richard Hofstadter wrote in his famous essay in *The American Political Tradition,* "has come to have a hold on the American imagination that defies comparison with anything else in political mythology." A tall thing to say, indeed, but a moment's reflection will validate Hofstadter's view. It is perhaps the case that more has been written about Lincoln than any other statesman in history. He continues to fascinate and compel attention because of his elusiveness. The real Lincoln is hard to identify and understand. The same man who was a student of Shakespeare and the classics, who brought formidable dialectical skills to public debate, was also given to telling folksy stories and cornball jokes to important people at important moments.

It requires a very keen political mind to discern the unity of thought and purpose in Lincoln's words and deeds. A vast horde of historians, many of them unequal to the task, has flogged every imaginable source and offered every plausible vision and revision. Fiction has now taken up the challenge. Historical fiction has an advantage over standard history. As Safire tells it in his commentary, historical fiction can make use of "informed guesswork to come to conclusions that the known facts alone cannot fully sustain." Fiction, in other words, can get at the truth, even if it lacks "historical" veracity. Safire justifies this enterprise by citing the 19th-century German historian Leopold von Ranke: "Fact has a spiritual content....It is our job to recognize how it really took place....intuition is required."

Gore Vidal attempted this same project recently, and failed. Vidal raised the ire of historians who found his speculations wholly implausible or even outrageous, and the political Lincoln he presented was largely disconnected from the principles and ideas expressed in Lincoln's many speeches and writings. Safire is much more scrupulous, offering factual or circumstantial justifications for his interpolations. Where none is possible, he admits to fiction without apology. But Safire, like Vidal, has an argument to make about Lincoln, an argument with some resonance for today's debate about executive prerogative. Despite his painstaking research and caution, however, the real Lincoln eludes Safire's account in the same way he eluded Vidal's, and for the same reason.

Lincoln had a serious and carefully thought out political teaching. But because he wrote no systematic account, and because as a practical politician his political ideas had to be subsumed to circumstances, his political teaching often remains obscure, even to a mind as fine as Safire's. Safire's Lincoln is divorced from his rich political teaching. Safire fails to grasp the vital relationship between the Declaration of Independence and the Constitution—a relationship that was absolutely central to Lincoln's teaching and statecraft.

For instance, Safire has Anna Carroll wondering "if it was such a good idea for Lincoln to invoke the days of the Declaration of Independence, with its radical 'all men are created equal,' soon set aside by the more conservative framers of the Constitution." We might let this un-Lincolnian understanding pass by were it limited to observers such as Anna Carroll or Lincoln's secretary, John Hay; but Safire ascribes this understanding to Lincoln himself on the final page, when Lincoln signs the Emancipation Proclamation: "Its roots were not in the cool

8

compromises of the Constitution, but in the heat and fervor of the Declaration of Independence. *He was in the end at one with the revolutionaries of 1776, at odds with the cool compromisers of 1787."* (Emphasis added.)

Far from being a sentence that just slipped out, Safire shows this to be his considered judgment when, in the middle of the book, he wonders: "Lincoln was a man of the Declaration of Independence, with its radical 'all men are created equal,' while [Breckinridge] was a man of the Constitution, with its compromises, balances, and conservatism. Which was more American?"

Wrong question. To be faithful to Lincoln, and therefore to be able to comprehend his statecraft, one must understand his view of the relation between the Declaration of Independence and the Constitution. True it is that Lincoln said, "I have never had a feeling politically that did not spring from the sentiments embodied in the Declaration of Independence." But Lincoln understood the Constitution to be an instrument complementary, not contradictory, to the Declaration. The Declaration set out the ends of free government—equal rights—and the Constitution was the means to secure those ends.

Lincoln's most memorable formulation of the natural harmony between the two documents was his invocation of Proverbs 25:11, about how a word "fitly spoken" was like "an apple of gold within a picture of silver." The Declaration was the apple of gold, and the Constitution the picture of silver. "The picture was made, not to conceal, or destroy the apple," Lincoln wrote, "but to adorn, and preserve it. The picture was made for the apple—not the apple for the picture."

Lincoln understood, and accepted, the necessity for compromise over slavery when the Constitution was written in 1787. He frequently cited Henry Clay—a slave owner—on the necessity of the slavery compromise and the awful dilemma it posed for future American statesmen. In his Eulogy to Clay, Lincoln noted with prescience: "Cast into life where slavery was already widely spread and deeply seated, he did not perceive, as I think no wise man has perceived, how it could be at once eradicated, without producing a greater evil, even to the cause of human liberty itself."

We can see in Lincoln's rhetoric the balance of principle and moderation. He often compared slavery to cancer. It is not always possible to excise the malignancy without causing the patient to bleed to death, but neither is it possible for it to spread without causing death. Lincoln understood before he was president that he could not rightly threaten slavery where it existed, without violating the principle of the

9

very "Charter of Freedom" he sought to uphold. That is why Lincoln was never an abolitionist. But Lincoln understood that slavery could not be permitted to spread to the Western territories, without also violating the central principle the Constitution was intended to establish.

The goal of the Republican Party at its founding was to place slavery "in the course of ultimate extinction" by preventing its spread. If the Union could be held intact and slavery prohibited in the Western territories, slavery would be in the course of ultimate extinction. This the South could not accept. One observer, apparently not consulted by Safire, who understood the situation with great clarity was John Stuart Mill, who wrote in December 1861: "The day when slavery can no longer extend itself, is the day of its doom. The slave-owners know this, and it is the cause of their fury."

Safire's book is largely oblivious to the substantive view guiding Lincoln's statecraft. Instead, for Safire, Lincoln's central purpose is majority rule: "If the experiment of this republic was to work, the majority had to rule—all the time, with no exceptions." Nowhere does Safire offer an account of how Lincoln's idea of majority rule differed from that of Stephen Douglas's majoritarianism of "popular sovereignty." It was over precisely this point that Lincoln and Douglas clashed in 1858.

Lincoln understood that majority rule was merely a practical substitute for the unanimous consent over first principles, the principles spelled out in the Declaration of Independence. Majority rule made no sense without reference to those principles. A majority cannot, in Lincoln's view, vote to enslave itself—or others—and remain consistent with democratic principles. The secession of the South was much more than a defiance of simple majority rule; it was a repudiation of the unanimous consent over the founding principles of America.

Thus Lincoln's opposition to slavery and his dedication to preserving the Union rested on the same ground, which is why for Lincoln the war to preserve the Union and the war to abolish slavery quickly became one and the same struggle. Safire, following Stephen Douglas, interprets majority rule simply, and misses entirely Lincoln's understanding, thus distorting the meaning of events and doing a grave disservice to the reader. Safire describes Lincoln's thoughts on emancipation as a "newly embraced cause—not his original, central cause of majority rule."

Safire portrays Lincoln's gradual move toward the Emancipation Proclamation primarily as an expediency to boost the war effort. This function it certainly achieved, and Safire excellently captures this dimension. But the apple of gold is missing from Safire's picture of silver. Again, John Stuart Mill provides a better guide: "The Republicans well know that if they can reestablish the Union, they can gain everything for which they originally contended; and it would be a plain breach of faith with Southern friends of the Government, if, after rallying them round its standard for a purpose of which they approve, it were suddenly to alter its terms of communion without their consent."

Mill saw from a distance what Lincoln knew, that the middle ground that marked the clearest common denominator of Union opinion could not long remain the ground of policy. Mill wrote: "I at least have foreseen and foretold from the first, that if the South were not promptly put down, the contest would become distinctly an anti-slavery one." Mill, writing in December 1861, gave the end of summer 1862 as the time for this transformation to take place—exactly as it occurred.

And so Safire's book ends with the signing of the Emancipation Proclamation on January 1, 1863. The book cannot continue after this point. For Safire, this was the ultimate moment of the Civil War. But for Lincoln, this was the penultimate moment. The ultimate moment came at Gettysburg, when, in the most important political speech in American history, Lincoln defined the meaning of the present struggle—to complete "a new birth of freedom." In the end it is fortunate that Safire's book closes where it does. It is worrisome to contemplate, had the narrative continued, how he would have handled the Lincoln of Gettysburg.

There is much to commend in Safire's book. It is rich in detail and vivid in its portrayal. But on its central character, Lincoln, Safire is wrong. And it is on the understanding of the central figure that such an enterprise stands or falls. Safire has given us a fragmentary Lincoln, who might well say of this effort: "A book divided against itself cannot stand."

—*Reason*, December 1987

Chapter 3

The Children of Abraham

The Civil War, a documentary by Ken Burns

The astonishing success Of Ken Burns's Civil War documentary on PBS last fall has touched off a full-scale fad among the public and has revived the quarrels about the lasting significance of the Civil War. It seems the Civil War won't go quietly into the history books. We keep coming back to the Civil War because it is the fundamental conflict about what America means, and what America's principles are. The Civil War has serious lessons for contemporary American politics and may shape the debates of the 1990s over equality, civil rights, and federalism.

Historian Dwight Lowell Dumond called the Civil War "the most interesting war in all history." There have been over 90,000 books and articles published on Abraham Lincoln and the Civil War, including even the unlikely *Lincoln and the Coming of the Caterpillar Tractor*. Each generation seems to go through its own Civil War fad, often spurred by a new epic treatment of the subject, such as Carl Sandburg's several volumes back in the 1920s. The Burns film surely ranks as one of the most ambitious and stunning treatments ever, capturing the Homeric and paradoxical character of the Civil War. The Civil War can be considered the first "total war"—a preview of the mass slaughter of World War I. Even so, Winston Churchill's judgment is equally true that the American Civil War was the last war fought between gentlemen.

But the enduring importance of the Civil War lies in its political dimension, in its legacy to the subsequent political thought of America. In his afterword to the film, Burns says, "Our consideration of the Civil War *now* raises all of the questions that it did *then*." This implies that some of the questions were not settled, or at least have become unsettled. Early in the first episode, historian Shelby Foote, the author of a multivolume narrative of the Civil War who serves as the principal commentator in the Burns film, frames the task rightly:

Any understanding of this nation has to be based, and I mean really based, on an understanding of the Civil War. I believe that firmly. It defined us....The Civil War defined us as what we are and it opened us to what we became, good and bad things. And it is very necessary, if you're going to understand the American character in the 20th century, to learn about this enormous catastrophe of the 19th century. It was the crossroads of our being, and it was a hell of a crossroads.

Everyone agrees with Foote that the Civil War defined America, but they disagree about what that definition means and whether it is for good or ill. Depending on whom we consult, the Civil War was either a noble struggle to complete the unfinished work of the Founding Fathers and to enhance equality as the central idea of American politics or a desperate struggle to check the expansion and centralization of power in the federal government. Hence the controversy over the central figure of the Civil War: Abraham Lincoln.

The right is especially divided over Lincoln. His critics say that he was America's Cromwell, that Lincoln's insistence on equality was a cornerstone for today's radical egalitarianism, and that the Civil War was a crucial step on the road to today's federal leviathan. Lincoln's defenders say he resolved the inherent contradiction of the Founding—slavery—through a principled understanding of free government that should be rearticulated today.

The chief issue raised by the Burns film is equality. "Every nation has a central idea from which all its minor thoughts radiate," Lincoln said. At Gettysburg, Lincoln concisely summarized the central idea of America as "the proposition" that "all men are created equal." Lincoln viewed the Declaration of Independence and the Constitution as harmonious and complementary political charters. The Declaration abstractly set out the just ends of government—to secure the natural rights of life, liberty, and the pursuit of happiness—and the Constitution set out the means to these ends. The rule of law, Lincoln thought, could not make sense without reference to these ends, which are based, remember, on the "self-evident truths" derived from the laws of nature. For Lincoln, as for the Founders, equality and liberty were *complementary* doctrines. Our liberties were based on our equal right not to be governed without our consent.

The Burns film reveals the problematic character of equality in the American political tradition, especially as it relates to the Civil War. At one point, for example, Burns says that Lincoln at Gettysburg "probably said more than he knew," suggesting that Lincoln foreshadowed an understanding of the meaning of the war that he didn't comprehend.

Burns and one of his commentators, historian Barbara Fields, supply this understanding in the final episode of the film. Burns says that America is "constantly trying to enlarge the definition and deepen the meaning of 'all men are created equal'" and that "we have not fulfilled the promises that we made at the end of the war." Burns endorses with enthusiasm Fields's "struggle" over the meaning of the war in her commentary, in which she says that the war "established a standard that will not mean anything until we have finished the work....If some citizens live in houses and others live on the street, the Civil War is still going on. It is still to be fought, and...it can still be lost."

It is deliciously ironic that Fields would try to appropriate Lincoln and the Civil War for today's homeless, given Lincoln's injunction "let not him who is houseless pull down the house of another." This is, of course, precisely what today's egalitarians wish to do. Yet Burns and Fields's comments make explicit how the meaning of equality has changed. Fields presumes the legitimacy of contemporary radical egalitarianism—the leveling kind that requires massive government power. Clearly this kind of equality opposes liberty, which is why libertarians have rightly attacked equality as it is manifested today. What is less clear is how much of the blame for modem egalitarianism should be assigned to Lincoln and the Civil War.

When the question is framed this way, one soon discovers that arguing about Lincoln and the Civil War entails arguing about the meaning of the American Founding. Lincoln followed the Founders in believing that equality is the basis of individual natural rights. James Madison, in the famous *Federalist 10*, wrote that the first duty of a government founded on equal rights and individual liberty is to safeguard the *unequal results* such a regime will inevitably produce. Humans are not equal in natural attributes such as strength and intelligence, but they are equal in the decisive political respect that they cannot be *governed* without their consent and that their rights are inviolable by government, no matter how large the majority that wishes to violate their rights. This distinction, though subtle, was clear to the Founders and to Lincoln, but it is largely lost today.

Lincoln explicitly rejected the idea that the standard of equality is meaningless unless perfectly and comprehensively achieved. Lincoln knew what today's egalitarians refuse to see, that the drive to have equality comprehensively and "perfectly attained" is a formula for tyranny. In criticizing the "obvious violence" done to the "plain unmistakable language" of the Declaration of Independence by the Supreme Court's *Dred Scott* decision in 1857 (which held that the black man had no rights that the white man was bound to respect), Lincoln said:

"I think the authors of the notable instrument intended to include *all* men, but they did not intend to declare men equal *in all respects*. This did not mean to say that all were equal in color, size, intellect, moral developments, or social capacity. They defined with tolerable distinctness, in what respects they did consider all men created equal—equal in 'certain inalienable rights, among which are life, liberty, and the pursuit of happiness'....They did not mean to assert the obvious untruth that all were then actually enjoying that equality, nor yet, that they were about to confer it immediately upon them. In fact they had no power to confer such a boon. They meant simply to declare the *right*, so that the *enforcement* of it might follow as fast as circumstances should permit. They meant to set up a standard maxim for free society, which should be familiar to all, and revered by all; constantly looked to, constantly labored for, and even though never perfectly attained, constantly approximated, and thereby constantly spreading and deepening its influence."

What is important to note about the Burns and Fields view of equality is not just that it is historically and philosophically wrong, but that it is based on a wholly different premise than the view of Lincoln and the Founders. In their efforts to "enlarge the definition" of equality, Burns and Fields are essentially saying that we are duty bound to understand equality (and other political principles) according to the sentiment of the moment. This sort of historicism (or Progress with a capital *P*), which has become so commonplace as to be beyond controversy among our intellectual elites, holds that the words in our nation's political charters are without any fixed meaning and are merely empty vessels into which we are free to pour our own meaning. Call it the deconstructionist view of equality and the Civil War.

It would be mistaken to attribute the radicalization of equality in America to Lincoln, or even to Karl Marx. The Progressive movement was the real culprit. Within Progressive thought, "progress" replaces nature as the ground of politics. Hence, Progressivism rejects natural rights. For example, Richard Hoftstadter wrote in *The American Political Tradition* that "no man who is as well abreast of modern science as the Fathers were of eighteenth century science believes any longer in unchanging human nature. Modem humanistic thinkers who seek for a means by which society may transcend eternal conflict and rigid adherence to property rights as its integrating principles can expect no answer in the philosophy of balanced government as it was set down by

16

the Constitution makers of 1787." And Carl Becker, in his otherwise fine 1922 book *The Declaration of Independence*, wrote that "To ask whether the natural rights philosophy of the Declaration of Independence is true or false is essentially a meaningless question."

Progressive thought begins with the premise that the revolution in natural science makes necessary a revolution in political science as well. Certainly Woodrow Wilson thought so. Wilson wrote that American government "was constructed upon the Whig theory of political dynamics, which was a sort of unconscious copy of the Newtonian theory of the universe." But Darwin had eclipsed Newton; thus, Wilson thought, "Living political constitutions must be Darwinian in structure and in practice." Nature cannot tell us anything definite about the rights of man or the limits of government because nature is changeable.

Indeed, Progressives such as Herbert Croly saw the idea of individual rights as an irrational impediment to progress, and Woodrow Wilson sought to overcome the separation of powers in the American scheme of government for the same reason. Modern government, Progressives thought, requires visionary leaders, expert elites, and enhanced (and in principle unlimited) government power to direct and promote the grand unfolding of human progress.

One of the less understood implications of the Progressive view is that equality is really a subsidiary principle. If some people aren't "equal" to their fellow citizens, it isn't because their rights have been violated. Rather, it is because progress hasn't caught up with them yet. Equality actually has a very small place in most Progressive tracts. It is important to note, for instance, that the rhetoric employed by the "multiculturalists" in academia today emphasizes not equality but "empowerment" for the "disenfranchised." At bottom, the "empowerment" theme isn't based on an argument for equality and genuine diversity (despite the many rhetorical bows to "diversity"), but on the view that white, Eurocentric "culture" is illegitimate and must be overthrown. In the end, the "empowerment" rhetoric reveals itself to be a manifestation of the Nietzschean will to power.

When one sees that the explicit goal of Progressivism was to refound the nation on new principles, substituting progress for nature and rejecting the Founders' understanding of equality and natural rights, it helps put the contemporary Civil War dispute, and the revisionism that preceded it, in a new light. "The endless cycles of wheel-spinning revisionism," as historian Lee Benson calls it, took two distinctive forms.

First, historians began to deny that the Civil War was an "irrepressible conflict," the phrase William Seward made famous before the war. Rather, it was bumbling political leadership, or Lincoln's ruthless ambition, that led to a "needless war." The second and sometimes subsidiary strain was that the war's real cause wasn't political but economic. The cause wasn't slavery or constitutional principle, but rather Northern industrial capitalism. (Yup, the Marxists are grinning in the background.) A closely related argument held that slavery had already reached its natural limits, was becoming less productive and economical, and therefore was probably on its way out. Remember, the original goal of Lincoln and the new Republican Party was to place slavery "in the course of ultimate extinction." The revisionists said it was on this course anyway; therefore, it was a needless war begun for bad motives.

Much of the revisionist scholarship reflected the new Progressive view that since nature is changeable, wars are an unnecessary phenomenon. James G. Randall, for instance, in his 1945 book *Lincoln the President* wrote that "one of the most colossal misconceptions is the theory that fundamental motives produce war." But revisionism also well served the partisan motives of the Progressive movement. Just as the Progressives, beginning with Charles Beard, challenged the disinterestedness of the Framers of the Constitution to buttress the Progressive view that American government needed to be refounded on new principles, so too they needed to overcome Lincoln's interpretation of the Civil War and his position about the eternal sufficiency of the American Founding (even as they admired Lincoln as a strong, activist president). And revisionism as a whole tended to support the Southern line that the Civil War had been "a war of Northern aggression."

The early reaction to the revisionists was based almost wholly on categorical moral grounds. In 1945 Arthur Schlesinger, Jr., attributed the "vogue of revisionism" to "the modem tendency to seek in optimistic sentimentalism an escape from the severe demands of moral decision...it is the offspring of our modem sentimentalism." Taking issue directly with Randall and another leading revisionist, Avery Craven, Schlesinger wrote that "To reject the moral actuality of the Civil War is to foreclose the possibility of an adequate account of its causes." The Dutch historian Pieter Geyl wrote in 1951 that the "vision of a 'blundering generation' does not do justice to the past. That vision belittles what had real greatness." But there wasn't much new historical investigation and evidence offered by the counter-revisionists. Surveying the scene of revision and counter-revision in 1959, Kenneth Stampp wrote that it can be "discouraging...that twentieth-century historians often merely go back to interpretations advanced by partisans while the war was still in progress."

The subsequent generation of counter-revisionist scholarship delivered the hard goods. Harry Jaffa's *Crisis of the House Divided* and Don Fehrenbacher's *Prelude to Greatness: Lincoln in the 1850s* did much to sort out the mangled political interpretations revisionists held. Jaffa and Fehrenbacher defended Lincoln from the charge that he was purely an opportunist and argued that the legal and practical tendencies toward the continued expansion of slavery were genuine. A major breakthrough came in 1974, with Robert William Fogel and Stanley Engerman's *Time on the Cross: The Economics of American Negro Slavery*, which painstakingly analyzed economic and demographic data about the slave economy of the South. Their findings scotched the revisionist line that slavery was a less efficient mode of production that would eventually resolve itself of its own accord.

Fogel has revisited and expanded the analysis in his 1989 book *Without Consent or Contract: The Rise and Fall of American Slavery*. Fogel convincingly demonstrates the economic viability of the slave economy (slave farms often outproduced Northern farms), along with its gradual spread to the West. Fogel's evidence shows that the political dispute over the expansion of slavery to the Western territories wasn't in the least artificial or contrived. The "new synthesis of scholarship," Fogel concludes, is that "if the foes of slavery had waited for economic forces to do their work for them, America might still be a slave society, and democracy, as we know it, might have been a subject only for the history books." Other recent books that reinforce the older view of the political causes of the Civil War, and its inevitability, include Kenneth Stampp's *America in 1857: A Nation on the Brink* and William Freehling's *The Road to Disunion: Secessionists at Bay 1776–1854*.

Even if Lincoln isn't held responsible for the radicalization of equality, and even if recent scholarship tends to buttress the case that the Civil War was a fundamental and unavoidable conflict, it doesn't immediately follow that Lincoln and the Civil War should be celebrated by libertarians. There are many other aspects of the problem, such as states' rights and the centralization of government, that must be considered. Notwithstanding Lincoln's defenders on the right, it is easily understandable why libertarians and conservatives would be uncomfortable with, if not hostile to, Lincoln.

The broad case against Lincoln is easily made. As Llewellyn Rockwell put it recently, "he fastened the federal leviathan on the body of the old republic." Lincoln and the Civil War led to the aggrandizement of executive power and the centralization of government. The Civil War provided the precursor to the national income tax and was the precedent for the New Deal. Clinton Rossiter, in his famous textbook on the presidency, argues that Lincoln "pushed the powers of the Presidency to a new plateau high above any conception of executive authority hitherto imagined in this country." In fact, Don Fehrenbacher adds, "serious scholars have applied the word 'dictator' more often to Lincoln than any other president." In *Patriotic Gore*, Edmund Wilson compared Lincoln to Lenin. Some now compare Mikhail Gorbachev's crackdown on the secessionist-minded Baltic republics to Lincoln's war against secession—never mind the crucial distinction that the Baltic states never consented to join the Soviet Union in the first place.

More fundamental is the criticism of Wilmoore Kendall and George Carey, who argued in their persuasive book *The Basic Symbols of the American Political Tradition* that Lincoln's emphasis on equality had "derailed" our authentic political heritage, which Kendall thought was a compact-oriented majoritarianism. Not to be outdone, M.E. Bradford, in his *A Better Guide Than Reason*, even suggests Hitler ("a firm higher law man") as a "useful analogue" to Lincoln. (On the other hand, we should note that Hitler said that the victory of the Union was the great tragedy of American history.)

As if the direct attacks on Lincoln weren't enough, it is equally disconcerting to note some of his admirers. Herbert Croly heaps lavish praise on Lincoln in his notorious blueprint for the Progressive movement, *The Promise of American Life*. Croly wrote that "the life of no other American has revealed with anything like the same completeness the peculiar moral promise of genuine democracy."

On the contemporary scene, the book that arrests one's attention is a collection titled *Lincoln on Democracy*, edited by...Mario Cuomo! Conservative defenders of Lincoln must surely cringe when Cuomo writes, "I've always admired Lincoln because he's reassuring *to politicians like me*." (Emphasis added.) Cuomo has even visited and delivered a speech at Gettysburg, describing Lincoln's presidency as a crucial turning point in the evolution of democracy. He also cited Lincoln's remark that government exists to do what people cannot do for themselves or cannot do as well themselves as justification for Cuomo's vision of big government.

The significance of the Cuomo project is this: Having captured the issue of equality from the Republican Party through the electoral success of the New Deal and the intellectual success of Progressivism, the Democratic party is now trying to capture Lincoln away from the Republicans as well. This comes at a propitious time for Democrats, for Republicans seem poised at last to mount a limited challenge to

Democratic vulnerability over the meaning of equality, particularly on the issue of affirmative action and civil rights.

Cuomo's rhetoric on Lincoln is reminiscent of the politician Cuomo most obviously wishes to emulate—not Lincoln, but Franklin Roosevelt. Before he became president, FDR said, "I think it is time for us Democrats to claim Lincoln as one of our own." Later, FDR stepped up his attack. "Does anyone maintain that the Republican party from 1868 to 1938 (with the possible exception of a few years under Theodore Roosevelt) was the party of Abraham Lincoln?" Like Cuomo, FDR cited Lincoln's passage about government doing what the people cannot do for themselves as justification for New Deal measures. Despite Republican protests, FDR was so successful that by the 1940 campaign Republican nominee Wendell Willkie pleaded for an armistice in the partisan fight over Lincoln's legacy: "It will do us no good to draw these historical illusions [sic]."

So far today the only Republican to pick up Cuomo's thrown gauntlet is HUD Secretary Jack Kemp, but even he hasn't built his case on a principled understanding of equality, without which any Republican rhetoric against affirmative action will be vulnerable to charges that it is merely the low politics of racial resentment. Kemp instead adapts Lincoln for the purpose of advancing the "new paradigm" theme of "empowerment"—the same term used by the radical multiculturalists on the campuses.

It is astonishing that no Republican has used Lincoln's many statements that clearly run against the redistributionist ethic at the heart of modem liberalism. In his letter to the Democratic Republican Workingmen's Association of New York, for example, Lincoln wrote, in words that could instantly correct Cuomo's moral indignation about wealth, that "Property is the fruit of labor—property is desirable—it is a positive good in the world. That some should be rich, shows that others may become rich, and hence is just encouragement to industry and enterprise. Let not him who is houseless pull down the house of another; but let him labor diligently and build one for himself, thus by example assuring that his own shall be safe from violence when built."

One of the small ironies of the Cuomo collection is that it includes Lincoln's letter to his stepbrother John D. Johnston, in which Lincoln refused Johnston's request for charity. Lincoln instead offered to match dollar for dollar for one year what Johnston earned by working. But Johnston didn't wish to work. Clearly, Lincoln recognized that unlimited charity will corrupt the character of the recipient, and he would likely be aghast at today's welfare state, which offers a legal "entitlement" to charity.

For the most part, people on the right have abandoned Lincoln to the left. But in doing so we have given up solid ground on which to base a principled argument from the American tradition about the meaning and proper application of equality and, by extension, for limiting the expansion of government power. This requires making a case for Lincoln's understanding of politics. The case for Lincoln requires not only recovering the natural-rights understanding of equality, but also understanding how these principles relate to the questions of states' rights, majority rule, and the rule of law.

It is important to understand why Lincoln thought the argument for secession was an "ingenious sophism" that threatened the very basis of free government. Some libertarians today defend a right of secession in principle as a means of checking the power of centralized government. For instance, Nobel laureate James Buchanan delivered a paper at last year's Mont Pelerin Society meeting arguing that a right of secession is essential in any scheme of European union. Buchanan lamented that the Civil War foreclosed this possibility in America.

But while the right to break a compact might help fight one evil—centralized government—it opens the door to another evil—majoritarianism. Secession is a two-way street. If it is right that the people of South Carolina may secede without the consent of the other states, then it is equally right for a majority of other states to "secede from" (in effect, to expel) South Carolina without the consent of South Carolina. Indeed, many Northern abolitionists in the 1840s and 1850s wanted the North to expel the South from the Union on the grounds that the slave states violated the constitutional mandate that each state have a republican form of government. What would defenders of secession say if, today, even a supermajority of states wanted to secede from California, on the grounds that California had become disproportionately powerful within the federal government (52 members of the House, sucking up more federal money than the state puts in, etc.)?

Lincoln's view, in short, can be taken as an adaptation of Jefferson's remark that for majorities to be rightful, they must be reasonable. In other words, there must be an antecedent purpose to the legislative authority of the people, and that purpose can only be understood within the context of the doctrines of equality and natural rights. An unqualified majoritarianism will lead to the erosion of liberty. The question of states' rights cannot be disconnected from the substantive question of what the states intend to use their authority for.

22

This is where slavery must be confronted squarely. It was acknowledged at the time of the Founding, even by nearly all Southerners, that slavery in a regime of liberty was a jarring anomaly. When the Missouri question of 1820 first revealed the future conflict in its full severity, Thomas Jefferson—a slave owner—wrote: "This momentous question, like a firebell in the night, awakened and filled me with terror. I considered it at once the death knell of the Union." When the next step came in 1832—South Carolina's nullification doctrine— James Madison wrote in dismay that the country was losing sight of the Founders' understanding of the principles of the nation's fundamental compact and denied that his and Jefferson's Virginia and Kentucky Resolutions of 1798 were a valid precedent for asserting that a *single* state could nullify the actions of the national government.

Slavery having been swept under the rug in the interest of compromise during the writing of the Constitution, it was becoming clear that it would be more difficult to eradicate than the Founders had hoped. Indeed, Lincoln understood that under the Constitution it was difficult to see "how [slavery] could be at once eradicated, without producing a greater evil, even to the cause of human liberty itself." Far from being contemptuous of states' rights, Lincoln frequently acknowledged that because slave property was protected by the Constitution, the federal government couldn't rightly touch it in the states where it existed. He parted company with the abolitionists and argued that Congress was obligated to pass, and the states were obligated to enforce, a fugitive slave law.

The postwar Southern line that the Civil War was about states' rights cannot really square with Lincoln's stated views about the relation of the federal government to the states. Lincoln's position was that slavery could only be lawfully abolished in a gradual way, by prohibiting its spread to the territories and new states (as had been done in the Ohio valley by the Northwest Ordinance of 1787—passed under the old Articles of Confederation), and by convincing the South to accept a program of *compensated* emancipation over several decades. Lincoln had no illusions that freed slaves would be easily assimilated into American society, which is why he favored a program of repatriation of freed slaves to Central America or Africa.

The most significant factor in the equation wasn't states' rights or nullification or the doctrine of concurrent majorities. Rather, it was the gradual abandonment of the view that slavery was a great evil that should somehow be ended someday. Southern public opinion had hardened to the point where Lincoln's moderate policy was impossible. In Lincoln's

23

view, the real cause of the Civil War was the spread of the opinion that slavery was a positive good and that there should be no legal limit to its extension. The "peculiar institution" had shed its embarrassing peculiarity.

Recall Alexander Stephens's "cornerstone" speech, which stated that the Southern constitution would be based on the "great truth" of inequality and the rightness of slavery. Stephens's speech was merely the culmination of the writings of proslavery apologists such as George Fitzhugh and John C. Calhoun, who argued that the Declaration's phrase "all men are created equal" really meant "all white men are created equal." Lincoln replied that if such was the case, then each of us would be rightly enslaved by the first person we met with fairer skin. (Or if intelligence were the operative principle, then by the first person we met who was smarter.) At the same time the South came to this view, many Northern leaders, such as Lincoln's great rival Stephen Douglas, became neutral about slavery and its further extension. Douglas was the perfect majoritarian, advancing "popular sovereignty" as the highest principle of democracy and caring not whether the people voted slavery "up or down."

It is in the light of these changes in public opinion that the meaning of Lincoln's famous phrase about "a new birth of freedom" becomes more clear. A people that reinterprets its fundamental charter of freedom to justify an institution (slavery) so obviously inimical to those principles cannot do so without placing at risk all of their other rights. The American Founding was preeminently a theoretical undertaking. Controverting the fundamental principles of liberty to justify slavery undermined the basis of all rights. Thus the Civil War wasn't just about whether the Union would be preserved or slavery abolished, but whether the people would recall and cherish the great principles of the nation's Founding, without which the cause of free government is lost.

Today in many respects public opinion about the principles of free government is in a worse state than it was before the Civil War. The mainstream of political science today teaches that the idea of natural rights is nonsensical. Today's heresy about equality is that rights belong to groups, not to individuals. Hence the hateful doctrine has crept into Supreme Court decisions that policy must be made to serve not individuals but members of "discrete and insular minorities," as the Court first put it in the *Carolene Products* case in 1938. This equality is incompatible with liberty.

The modern principles of administration by bureaucracy have trampled on the older principles of the separation of powers. Modern

24

bureaucratic government increasingly resembles slavery in that it governs us without our consent. Bureaucracies are designed to be largely sealed off from public opinion and are only remotely accountable to the ordinary political process. Elections don't change things very much. Bureaucratic policy and personnel carry on even if a strident ex-actor is elected president by a landslide.

Reversing this trend may require a struggle greater than the Civil War—not in terms of blood and bullets, but in terms of the change in public opinion that is necessary to bring reform about. Politics in a democracy necessarily involves teaching the people. That is why Jefferson and Madison labored so seriously over the civic education curriculum when they founded the University of Virginia. Neither of the major political parties appears willing, let alone able, to make the principled case about equality and limited government.

Reforming our government along the lines designed by the Founders may require a division of the house no less severe than that caused by Lincoln's "house divided" speech. Rather than vilifying Lincoln as the author of centralized government (surely the blame for the centralizing effects of the Civil War must be shared equally by the South), we should study Lincoln as the model of how fundamental political realignments are made by reclaiming and rearticulating the principles of the Founding. For in one sense the poets and sentimentalists are right: The American Revolution and the Civil War are never over. Every time the people forget what they mean, they have to be fought again.

—*Reason*, May 1991

Chapter 4

Still the Brightest Mirror

Tocqueville: A Biography, by André Jardin

The French, who practically invented the superfluous intellectual during the Enlightenment, also gave us Tocqueville, whose *Democracy in America* is still unsurpassed as a mirror on the political intentions of the founding and on political circumstances today. Although far less obscure than Montesquieu, whom Tocqueville took as a model, Tocqueville has remained subject to endless interpretation and revision. Yet, while the articles and books about his thought could fill a modest library, few are the works about the whole of Tocqueville's life.

This is so chiefly because Tocqueville is a difficult person to write about. His letters and papers yield little information about his private life, and his political career, with one brief exception, failed to advance to the point where he played a role in vital political events such that he would have been recorded prominently in the memoirs of his contemporaries. He lives on through the medium of his intellectual output, with only scant material available to suggest events and influences that shaped his "new science of politics."

Still, there is a good deal more to Tocqueville than just his *Democracy in America*, and André Jardin's biography deserves a wide readership among those who would seek a more complete understanding of Tocqueville. From Jardin one learns many details of interest. Tocqueville was a descendant of Malesherbes, the indulgent chief censor of the French government during the heyday of the Enlightenment, and Tocqueville's aristocratic forebears were largely unaffected by the Reign of Terror following the French Revolution. His family, in fact, felt some sympathy for the liberal aims of the Revolution, which perhaps helps explain why Tocqueville's *Old Regime and the French Revolution* sounds not at all like Edmund Burke's frantic *Reflections*—a fact that might give pause to conservatives who hold Tocqueville in high esteem.

Throughout his life Tocqueville was transfixed by what he saw as the inevitable historical transition from aristocratic politics to democratic politics. He was naturally fascinated with America, although he understood that what made the American Revolution unique was the absence of any feudal tradition to overcome.

Tocqueville's visit to America in 1831–32 was part official junket and part political exile. The upheaval in France in 1830 clouded his career prospects—he was at the time a mid-level civil servant. The ideal time was at hand to satisfy his fascination with America, while allowing things to settle down in France. Tocqueville and his traveling companion in America, Gustave de Beaumont, hit upon a professional excuse for the trip: to study the American penal system, which then enjoyed a very low rate of recidivism.

At the time Tocqueville went to America he did not harbor prejudgments in favor of American democracy. Indeed, the events in France had cast him into one of his frequent bouts of melancholy, such that, Jardin tells us, Tocqueville wondered whether America was a model for the future or somehow a scene from the past. In a letter Jardin cites, Tocqueville described his transformation: "I went to America only to clarify my thoughts on these matters. The penitentiary system was an excuse; I used it as a passport that would allow me to go everywhere in the United States. In that country, where I encountered a thousand things I didn't expect, I also found some that were related to the questions I had so often asked myself. I discovered facts that seemed useful to know. I didn't go there with the idea of writing a book at all, but the idea of the book came to me. I said to myself that a man is under the same obligation to offer up his mind in the service of society as he is, in time of war, his body." Voila, as the French would say.

America was not the end of Tocqueville's study of things foreign. He traveled to Algeria and wrote critically about French colonial administration. He also studied the Koran and rendered judgments that might prove dangerous today. "There have been few religions in the world as deadly to men as that of Mohammed….it is the principal cause of the decadence so visible today in the Muslim world." As a way of exploring how a colonial administration of a foreign culture could work, Tocqueville planned a book on the British in India, but he abandoned the project ostensibly because he wished to spare France the embarrassment of unfavorable comparison with England.

Interspersed throughout Jardin's narrative are otherwise inaccessible citations from notebooks and letters that amplify the great Tocquevillian themes about equality, government centralization, and religion. Readers of *Democracy in America* will remember the warning about intrusive government that "chooses to be the sole agent of (the people's) happiness; it provides for their security, foresees and supplies their necessities, facilitates their pleasures, manages their principal concerns, directs their industry, regulates the descent of property, and subdivides their inheritances: what remains, but to spare them all the care of thinking and the trouble of living?"

Circumstances in America were opposite of this at the time of Tocqueville's visit, a fact he recorded during his trip in a note reproduced by Jardin: "One of the happiest consequences of the absence of government...is the development of individual strength that inevitably follows it. Each man learns to think, to act by himself, without counting on the support of an outside force, which however vigilant he supposes it to be, can never answer all his social needs. Man, thus accustomed to seeking his own well-being only through his own efforts, raises himself in his own opinion as he does in the opinion of others; his soul becomes larger and stronger at the same time."

These two statements indicate why we still read Tocqueville closely today, even as other French intellectuals like Diderot and D'Alembert have become mere curiosities. For it is more than his aphoristic prose or his jeremiads about bureaucracy that makes Tocqueville live on. Tocqueville combined a rare understanding of both the new principles of democracy and the mostly ennobling effects democracy would have on the great mass of men, and the subtle corruptions to which democratic politics are susceptible. It is because modern democracy has largely succumbed to these corruptions that Tocqueville's wisdom is a vital means toward recovering our fundamental bearings. Andre Jardin has enhanced this project by enlarging our view of this great man.

—*Reason*, June 1989

Chapter 5

Whose Republicanism Is It?

The Spirit of Modern Republicanism: The Moral Vision of the Founders and the Philosophy of Locke, by Thomas L. Pangle

This is not a book for the general reader. However, Thomas Pangle's *Spirit of Modern Republicanism* is concerned with a scholarly controversy that holds important implications for the public debate about many issues. Pangle aims at nothing less than the fundamental questions: What kind of nation is America supposed to be? What is the nature of individual rights in the American regime? How is the "spirit of commerce" to be understood within the context of the American Founding?

The return to these fundamental questions is today urgent because of the remarkable success of what I call the "post-Progressive" school of historians, who have made it a project to discover a non-Lockean "soul" in the thought of the American founding, so as to controvert the philosophical basis of individual natural rights and free-market commercial society. This debate is vital because today's scholarly opinion can affect tomorrow's public opinion. As Pangle notes, "the turning points in our history and the leaders who have stepped forward in those periods have usually drawn us back to very deep wellsprings of theoretical controversy." Though Pangle is a political theorist, he recognizes clearly that the present historical controversy over the nature of the founding is closely related to "the unfinished argument over the political economy of a liberal democracy ushered in by the New Deal."

A little background is in order. The godfather of the Progressive historians was Charles Beard, whose neo-Marxist *Economic Interpretation of the Constitution* (published in 1913) argued that the authors of the Constitution were not the high-minded, disinterested statesmen we have always envisioned, but that instead they acted with the lowest motive of protecting their own property and fortunes. Though influential for a long time, Beard's narrow thesis did not hold up well under sustained scrutiny, and Beard has become a mere curiosity or period piece, still included on every graduate student's reading list, but enlisting no devotees.

31

But the essence of Beard's attack on the founding has been taken up by a much more subtle and sophisticated group of left-wing historians who, instead of directly attacking the founding as duplicitous, make the case that the Constitution and the thought in *The Federalist* is low and contemptible in its aims. This argument has been built carefully step-by-step, starting with Louis Hartz's *The Liberal Tradition in America* (1955). Hartz argued that the lack of any serious socialist movement in America was in part due to an "irrational" Lockean ardor for individualism. This anti-Lockean strand has been greatly transformed and amplified in recent years by Bernard Bailyn, Garry Wills, and others and finally culminates in Gordon Wood's 1972 book, *The Creation of the American Republic.*

By the time we get to Wood, the argument is much richer than Beard's, or even Hartz's. It is, in short, that the impulse to revolt in 1776 was generated by an ideology derived from classical republicanism, which held as its ideal not the regime of individual rights but rather a moralistic communitarian vision. "Ideally," Wood wrote, "republicanism obliterated the individual." Locke and natural rights have no place in Wood's account. But in 1787, as Wood tells it, the authors of the Constitution pulled a Brinks job on the principles of 1776, by giving sanction to individual rights and the spirit of commerce. The implication is clear: the commercial republic of the Constitution is untrue to the Revolution of 1776; let's rewrite the Constitution and bring in some socialism cloaked in the "true" American tradition. The "Wood thesis" is now widely accepted among American historians.

That is why a book like Pangle's is so necessary. I say a book "like" Pangle's, because *The Spirit of Modern Republicanism* errs too far in the opposite direction of seeing the founding as being *wholly* based on modern political philosophy. Pangle is among the Straussian scholars who see an impenetrable gulf between classical and modern thought. The post-Progressive attempt to claim a neo-classical basis for their attack on the founding neatly skewers the Straussians, who prefer ancient to modern thought and who are therefore not necessarily paying honor when they say, as Pangle does, that the founders were "under the tutelage of modern political philosophy."

The Spirit of Modern Republicanism is divided into three parts. In the first, Pangle summarizes and critiques the post-Progressive view I have limned above. He observes that these historians have a very poor grasp of the classical and Whig texts on which they base their argument—for instance, they completely misunderstand or misinterpret "the radically libertarian character of 'Cato'"—and that the real animus behind the post-Progressive view is a left-wing moral dogmatism.

The third and longest section of the book is devoted to a textual analysis of Locke's teaching. Pangle is intimately familiar with the Lockean corpus, and his exposition is graceful and brilliant. He situates Locke's teaching about property within the difficulties posed by the Christian teaching about dominion and stewardship—a relation seldom understood by those who routinely appropriate Locke's language in defense of property rights. But Pangle admits that the Lockean teaching he presents here goes far beyond the founders' understanding of Locke. Why this abstraction from the historical argument?

This brings a reviewer back to the central part of the book, where Pangle's version of the founders' philosophy appears. Here there is a strange and unfortunate convergence between Pangle and the post-Progressives. After having established in the first part and opening chapters of the second part that the post-Progressive school had misinterpreted the philosophical sources of the founding—that there had in fact been "no break" with the revolution in the writing of the Constitution—Pangle goes on to say that, indeed, the principles of the founding really do "subordinate the high in mankind...to the low," the low being the regime of commerce based on individual rights.

In the end Pangle overstates the case for Locke. The founders were not Straussians and did not necessarily see the same gulf between ancient and modern thought. Because of this methodological straitjacket, Pangle commits some crudities in order to maintain his argument. For instance, there is his dealing with the famous letter in which Jefferson portrays the Declaration of Independence as an "expression of the American mind" resting on the "harmonizing sentiments of the day" as expressed in "the elementary books of public right, (such) as Aristotle, Cicero, Locke, Sidney, etc." Pangle dismisses out of hand Jefferson's suggestion that there can be any harmonious understanding between ancient and modern with the statement that Jefferson and the founders were "unwilling, and perhaps unable, to plumb the depths of the chasm" between ancient and modern thought. In this Pangle violates his own adopted rule of understanding the founders as they understood themselves.

It is possible to maintain *both* the place of Locke—and individual rights—and the classical nobility of the American republic. Certainly the signers of the Declaration who pledged "our lives, our fortunes, and our sacred honor" thought so. Pangle's book gets off to a great start against the left-wing post-Progressives and closes with a scintillating exposition of Locke, but the middle leaves us with "unanswered questions," which, coincidentally (?), is the title of the central chapter of the book.

—*Reason*, April 1989

Chapter 6

The Political Economy of the Death of God

Reaching for Heaven on Earth: The Theological Meaning of Economics, by Robert H. Nelson, Savage, Md.: Rowman & Littlefield, 378 pages, $24.95

Writing several years ago about the crisis in economic thought, Irving Kristol observed that, along with the general decrepitude of social science and moral philosophy, "theology has practically ceased to be a respectable form of intellectual activity." This circumstance, Kristol thought, leaves economists with moral passion nowhere to go.

Robert Nelson has taken up this profound challenge and has produced a treatment of this issue that goes beyond what might be called the Michael Novak Project, i.e., the religious sanctification of market economies. Nelson aims deeper, observing that even though the Enlightenment abandoned the idea of a transcendent God, the biblical view of man and society has remained largely intact. Material forces replaced natural and divine law, faith in Progress replaced faith in Providence, and economists replaced priests. Not just the form but even the substance of economics became theological in character.

Nelson aptly cites Keynes's remark that economic controversies resemble "medieval disputations at their worst." And Nelson has a point in observing that the wars of the 20th century in many ways took on the character of the religious wars of old partly on account of competing visions of political economy. If Nelson's thesis is ultimately judged defective, as I shall argue below, we must still give him his due for recognizing something very important. That economics, which was once considered a subdiscipline of political philosophy, can be regarded now as a theological discipline owes largely to the fact that it is the only humane science left with any intelligible idea of value.

"When studied with any degree of thoroughness," Irving Babbitt wrote way back in 1924, "the economic problem will be found to run into the political problem, the political problem in turn into the philosophical problem, and the philosophical problem itself to be almost indissolubly bound up at last with the religious problem." Babbitt's declension suggests perhaps that economics has achieved theological stature by default, on account of the various crises of the other humane sciences (theology included), and that Nelson is setting out on the right track.

The great virtue of *Reaching for Heaven on Earth* is that it squarely confronts the fact that the intelligible value of economic theology— Progress—is itself now in crisis. We still believe in material progress, of course, but we no longer believe, as "modern economic theology" has taught since the Enlightenment, that material progress is a sufficient basis for a general human progress. The faltering of the idea of progress is the defining characteristic of what everybody today is calling "the postmodern age." Hence, Nelson observes: "The character of the postmodern era may well be defined by the theological answer given to the loss of faith in modern progressivism and its various offshoots."

Rather than anticipate new theoretical breakthroughs, Nelson sees the shape of the postmodern age deriving from another oscillation between the two very old theological frameworks that Nelson understands generically as Romanism and Protestantism. From the Roman tradition we inherited the ideas of reason, law, private property, markets, economic growth, and the modern welfare state. From the Protestant tradition we inherited a distrust of reason and individualism, skepticism about human nature and the prospects for human improvement, and belief in the inherent corruption of human institutions.

Nelson's discourses on which thinkers belong to which tradition are the most intriguing and compelling part of the book. Nelson provocatively challenges the familiar themes of Max Weber and others about the economic and political consequences of Romanism (and especially its derivative, Roman Catholicism) and Protestantism. Even if Protestantism tends mostly to generate disorder, Nelson nevertheless understands the necessity of protest in human affairs. (He even makes the old can't-live-with-it, can't-live-without-it gambit.) So, Nelson writes, "the current age is, in short, a Roman era that is being challenged by a new band of protesters against its theological foundations." With the demise of Marxian socialism, the most substantial protest to the present order comes from radical environmentalism, which supposes nature to be a God, instead of supposing there is a God of nature.

Having labored so exhaustively to establish the bipolar framework of Romanism and Protestantism, Nelson attempts to propel us into the postmodern age by harmonizing Roman order and Protestant pluralism. His constitutional device to accomplish this harmonization is something called "free secession." Nelson subordinates all principles of individual liberty and market economics to the principle of "free secession."

"The Right of free secession might thus supersede economic principles of free markets, free trade, and other past freedoms in providing a founding principle for a postmodern economic order," he writes.

The nation-state, Nelson thinks, is obsolete or even dangerous. Groups of people should be allowed to secede from their existing nations and form their own local political units, based on whatever values they prefer, mediated perhaps by several single-purpose world government agencies (arms control, environment, etc.). It sounds like an ugly crossbreeding between the New World Order and the spontaneous order.

There is no need to refight the American secession crisis of 1861, to which Nelson makes several unfortunate references, to see the defects of this scheme. The defects become apparent by pushing immediately to the reductio ad absurdum: What happens when single individuals decide to secede from everybody else and declare their solitary sovereignty?

Don't laugh. There is an eccentric fellow in West Australia who has declared his ranch a sovereign nation. Prince Hal of Hutt River Province will stamp your passport and exchange currency to spend in his gift shop. The lack of a limiting principle to free secession, or the specter of individual sovereignty it presents, points back immediately to the necessity of individual rights and the limiting principle of government by consent of the governed. In this light, "free secession" is seen not as postmodernism but as a mere devolution of pluralism and individual rights that opens upon Hobbesian vistas.

Regardless of the merits of Nelson's prescriptions, it is not merely churlish to raise the deeper issue of whether Nelson's analysis is truly theological. Although Nelson skillfully insinuates a theological character to economics dating back to antiquity, economics does not really achieve its theological character until transcendent Providence is secularized through the idea of Progress. In other words, "economic theology" only achieves its theological status with the death of God.

But without a serious regard for transcendence, for a higher order beyond this order (including, perhaps, the immortality of the soul), Nelson's "economic theology" only takes on the form rather than the substance of theology. Theology without God is rather like football without the ball.

Why is this important? Although it is not immediately obvious, the rise of the kind of Scientific Progressivism represented by the death of God and "economic theology" presents serious theoretical challenges to individual rights and limited government. The metaphysical or transcendent basis for liberal democracy can be summarized as follows: Because men are not God or gods, unqualified wisdom is unavailable to man, and therefore unqualified power should never be entrusted to human hands.

This is not to say that one must believe in God to believe in the principles of limited government. Rather, it is simply to recognize that the secularization of Providence through Scientific Progress implies that unqualified wisdom—or complete explanation and mastery of human affairs—is possible, and hence that unqualified power can be benevolently exercised. By negating the Socratic skepticism that is the basis of limited government, modern secular theology diminishes the scope of human freedom.

Nelson's admirable attempt to rescue theology from irrelevancy and economics from the emptiness of value-free positivism does nothing to remedy this problem; in fact, it reinforces it. "Economic theology" and other secular progressivisms should abandon their claim to theological status. Nelson and others might be reluctant to do so, for such a step would relegate economics to the subdiscipline where it began.

—*Reason*, June 1992

Chapter 7

The Forgotten Founder

Founding Father: Rediscovering George Washington, by Richard
Brookhiser.

George Washington is the neglected founder. He is either debunked
at the hands of revisionist sophisticates, or sentimentalized through what
might be called the eternal return of cherry-tree iconography. Richard
Brookhiser has produced a valuable and, I predict, enduring contribution
to the literature on Washington that turns a deserved cold hand to the
debunkers while keeping sentimentalism to a minimum. Along the way,
Brookhiser's "rediscovery" of Washington shines a refracting light on the
afflictions of our historical outlook today, and supplies the material for
useful reflection on what is possible from public figures.

Of the two hazards to Washington's reputation, sentimentalism is
probably the worse foe. Brookhiser rightly notes that "The humanizers
have done more damage to Washington than the debunkers." Certainly
Parson Weems's fable of the cherry tree is a bit of noisome bunk that
deserves the contempt of the debunkers. But our generation's recoil from
sentimentalism and filial piety has left Washington "in our textbooks and
in our wallets, but not our hearts." This condition has made Brookhiser's
task–"a moral biography in the tradition of Plutarch," as he describes it–
very tricky indeed. Brookhiser wants to reestablish Washington's
reputation as more than just a subject of antiquarian curiosity. To attempt
such a "moral biography" in an age that prefers Fawn Brodie to Plutarch
requires that the author reacquaint readers with the possibility that the
moral horizon of Washington's time is plausible in our own.

This would seem an especially tough sell to today's so-called
liberals, who dismiss the American Founding as irrelevant to modern
politics. But the more serious objections to Brookhiser's Washington
project may come from the contemporary champions of classical
liberalism (or at least its "public choice" variant), who generalize from
the ample evidence in modern politics that all ambition can be reduced to

calculations of self-interest. Washington appears as either an insincere or simply incredible figure. "The pursuit of power with the capacity and in the desire to use it worthily is among the noblest of human occupations," Winston Churchill wrote in his biography of Marlborough. Today power is so distrusted–with all good reason–that it has become difficult even for the friends of liberty to imagine that a noble and self-limiting ambition for power is even possible. Hence the incredulity over Washington.

Washington was often compared in his day with Cato the Younger, of whom Plutarch had written that "every class of men in Utica could clearly see, with sorrow and admiration, how entirely free was everything that he was doing from any secret motives or any mixture of self-regard." Brookhiser's account is entirely harmonious with this seemingly archaic view. "Washington was worthy of honor," Brookhiser concludes, "because the last thing he had done with power was to resign it....Washington's last service to his country was to stop serving." No term limits were necessary in those days. Washington's self-limiting example sufficed until the coming of the Leviathan state during the New Deal erased not only Washington's example but his principles as well.

Brookhiser's account makes clear, however, that neither Washington nor his 18th-century admirers were oblivious to interest, nor did they seek to draw a veil over interest through classical heroic imagery. Washington himself wrote that "it is a maxim founded on the universal experience of mankind, that no nation is to be trusted farther than it is bound by its interest; and no prudent statesman or politician will venture to depart from it." But for Washington, as for the other Founders, while interest must always be reckoned as a motive force that would tend toward the dissolution of republican government, it was also true that educated men have an interest in the noble possibilities that republican government has to offer, namely, the independence and individual flourishing that democratic self-government alone makes possible.

That is why the constitutional arrangements of our government were crafted to channel self-interest to noble ends. This is an aspect of the thought of the Founders that is badly underappreciated, even by the modern-day friends of the Founding. As James Madison wrote in *The Federalist*: "As there is a degree of depravity in mankind which requires a certain degree of mistrust: So there are other qualities in human nature, which justify a certain portion of esteem and confidence. Republican government presupposes the existence of these qualities in a higher degree than any other form." Washington, as Brookhiser's rediscovery makes clear, was the highest exemplar of those republican qualities.

40

Washington might be dismissed as being the Colin Powell of his day–widely respected for his command of a fortuitous military venture and for the indeterminacy or derivative nature of his political views. On the surface, one can point to a mixed military record. He lost more battles than he won. Brookhiser does a singular service in reviving Washington's credentials as a no-nonsense strategist and commander. The revolutionary army had of necessity to fight a defensive war against the superior forces of the British, anticipating Lord Kitchener's dictum that "One cannot wage war as one ought, but only as one can." But Washington was able to conceive the war in such as way as to change the strategic equation. He did this by confining the British for most of the war to the northeastern theater, between New York and Philadelphia, alternately hitting the British and retiring beyond their reach. "But by fighting an aggressive defense," Brookhiser notes, "he raised the cost of victory for the British to an unacceptable level," and "destroyed whatever strategy the British possessed."

The accounts given by his contemporaries of his manner of command and his strategic sense in battle reminds one of similar accounts of great commanders such as Marlborough or Napoleon. Alexander Hamilton noted that "he directed the whole with the skill of a master craftsman." This and countless other assessments track closely with Churchill's descriptions of his great ancestor, Marlborough, whose presence on the battlefield "diffused a harmony all around him."

Off the battlefield, in the arena of political thought, Washington has always taken a back seat to Jefferson, Madison, and even Hamilton (not to mention the anti-Federalist writers such as Patrick Henry and George Mason). Brookhiser makes clear that this is an unwarranted slight. Brookhiser observes: "Washington's relation to ideas has been underestimated by almost everyone who wrote of him or knew him, and modern higher education has encouraged this neglect....Neither Washington's ideas, nor his belief that right ideas were a necessary attainment of public men, have survived in their original form." Washington wrote no political broadsides or pamphlets like *Common Sense* or *The Federalist*. His political thoughts were set down mostly in letters, and as Brookhiser notes, "Appreciating Washington's spoken and written words takes time and effort."

Brookhiser comes close to repeating the common mistake of supposing that Washington and the other revolutionaries were fighting merely for their "rights as an Englishman," rather than for universal natural rights. But Brookhiser notes quickly that Washington quickly came to conceive of his rights in universal terms. Washington's most

41

ringing expression of this view came in his "Circular to the States," written on the eve of his resignation from command of the army following the conclusion of the treaty of peace with Britain: "The foundation of our empire was not laid in the gloomy age of Ignorance and Superstition, but in an Epocha [sic] when the rights of mankind were better understood and more clearly defined, than at any former period; the researches of the human mind, after social happiness, have been carried to a great extent; the Treasures of knowledge, acquired through a long succession of years, by the labours of Philosophers, Sages, and Legislatures, are laid open for our use...." Here is a confident expression of Enlightenment reason at its highest. But, Washington was quick to warn his fellow citizens that if the nation "should not be completely free and happy, the fault will be intirely [sic] their own"–a recognition that self-government allows no excuses.

Washington also penned one of the best formulations of the idea that is most prominently associated with Jefferson: religious freedom (as opposed to mere toleration). In his letter to the Hebrew Congregation at Newport, Washington again anchors the idea on the firm ground of natural right: "It is now no more that toleration is spoken of as if it were the indulgence of one class of people that another enjoyed the exercise of their inherent natural rights, for, happily, the Government of the United States, which gives to bigotry no faction, to persecution no assistance, requires only that they who live under its protection should demean themselves as good citizens in giving it on all occasions their effectual support." (Brookhiser's book does not contain these passages in their entirety; readers who wish to delve into the fullness of Washington's prose should obtain the Liberty Fund edition of Washington's letters and papers, edited by W.B. Allen.)

Washington's greatest service, in the end, was his tenure as the first president. With more than just an eye toward the precedents he would set as the first occupant of the executive office, Washington was aware that, as he wrote a friend, "We now have a National character to establish." Hence his goal in office was, according to Brookhiser, "to develop an etiquette appropriate to the republican model of government." Washington experienced nearly all of the tensions that we witness today between the legislative and executive branches of government, and had Washington acted differently then, circumstances might be very different today–probably for the worse.

Above all, Brookhiser's book makes a clear case that the goal of Washington's statecraft was to establish that government by the consent of the governed meant that the reasonable decisions of the majority–

decisions that did not trample an individual's natural rights–could not be negated by a willful minority. "If a self-governing people decided legitimately to do a thing," Brookhiser summarizes the issue, "could some people then prevent it from being done?"

The issue presented itself in acute form in the Whiskey Rebellion on the frontier. Washington felt some sympathy with the burdens the whiskey tax imposed on frontiersmen, but he also felt the authority of the republic was in jeopardy if its laws could be willfully flouted. Washington wrote that "if the laws are to be so trampled upon with impunity," and "a minority…is to dictate to the majority, there is an end put at one stroke to republican government." Washington readied a strong show of federal force, but deployed it with restraint, with the Whiskey rebels deciding among themselves to back down from their radical threats.

If Brookhiser avoids the sentimentalism of past encomiums, he nonetheless produces a new sentimentalism borne of today's cultural conservative fixation with fatherhood and family values. "The contemporary failure of fatherhood is perhaps the subtlest barrier to our understanding of Washington, the greatest source of the distance between us and him," Brookhiser writes in the introduction. Hence the chapter on Washington and fatherhood is written too much as a mirror to our own time rather than Washington's. "We are not sure what the fathers of families do," Brookhiser laments, "much less fathers of countries." The childless Washington, Brookhiser concludes, settled on his countrymen as his substitute children. This is taking the metaphor of fatherhood–which alludes to the most fundamental act of politics (founding)–too far. It is doubtless true that in the age of liberal democracy (the "end of history"), the idea of political founding seems remote, but it is a stretch to lump the pathologies of the contemporary family together with the desuetude of the idea of founding. Not to mention that Brookhiser seems to assume that no one in modern America has a decent father–quite a stretch. Conservatives at times get so wrapped up in their rhetoric that they forget that most Americans, and certainly most Americans likely to read this book, do in fact have perfectly decent fathers. And that we may have strong fathers without having 18th-century ones.

This chapter is the only part of the book that seems incongruous, though even here one must assent to Brookhiser's summary judgment that "Washington was the most important man in America, whether he was onstage or off, for twenty-four years; for seventeen of those years, he was front and center. It is a record unmatched in our history, scarcely matched in the histories of modern democracies."

Finally, Brookhiser provides a nice account of the blend of Washington's character, showing us his moral, dramatic, religious, and intellectual influences. He also ably brings out Washington's nasty temper, which sounds as though it could have matched the oft-described "volcanic" temper of the current occupant of the White House. In this passage the reader is again reminded of Churchill's description of the various aspects of Marlborough's character and aims, of which Churchill wrote that "No one of these purposes could be removed without impairing the others, and part of his genius lay in their almost constant harmony." Likewise, Brookhiser notes of Washington's many traits that "Each aspect was necessary, however. Without his physique and the threat of his temper, he would have been inconsiderable; without his ideas, he might have been directionless. If he had lacked any of the three or possessed any to a lesser degree, he could not have been the father of his country."

—*Reason*, March 1996

Chapter 8

The Making of LBJ

The Years of Lyndon Johnson: Master of the Senate, by Robert Caro

All through Lyndon Johnson's political life," Robert Caro writes near the end of this magisterial volume covering Lyndon Johnson's Senate years (1949-1960), "there had been striking evidence not only of compassion but of something that could make compassion meaningful: signs of a most unusual capacity, a very rare gift, for using the powers of government to help the downtrodden and the dispossessed."

There, in one sentence, is both what is wrong with Johnson and what is wrong with Caro's otherwise extraordinary biography, a lifetime project that has now reached its third volume. There is nothing at all "rare" about using the power of government—that is, using other people's money—to ameliorate the sufferings of Americans. It is the epitome of modern liberalism, and is the defining feature of American politics today—so much so that our current president feels it necessary to define himself as a "compassionate conservative," which is hard to distinguish from a low-budget liberal.

Johnson's only "rare gift" was his supreme success at finding new ways to institutionalize the spending of other people's money. Most of that success came during his presidency, which Caro will treat in future installments. Caro's first two volumes, *The Path to Power* and *Means of Ascent*, are highly critical of Johnson, offering juicy details about the many loathsome features of his character and behavior. This volume, too, is frank in its description of LBJ as power-hungry, cruel, bigoted, ruthless, deceitful, vain, grasping, and even "immoral." He urinated in public, raged at and belittled his staff, used racist epithets with abandon, stole elections, and collected prodigious sums of campaign money in cash (how much of it may have ended up in Johnson's own pocket Caro does not speculate).

45

And yet the LBJ who emerges from Caro's pages atones for these sins through his compassion and his skill at making the dysfunctional U.S. Senate work, as Caro supposes the American Founders meant it to work. Despite Johnson's pettiness, power-seeking, and unvarnished ambition, Caro puts him on a plane nearly equal to Lincoln: "He was to be the President who, above all Presidents save Lincoln, codified compassion, the President who wrote mercy and justice into the statute books by which America was governed."

To be sure, Johnson's Senate career presents a spectacle of unparalleled political mastery, worthy of close study. And Caro's exhaustive researches and fine-grained narrative are a marvel of the biographer's art. (His book makes you appreciate the smallness of the most recent Senate majority leaders, Tom Daschle and Trent Lott.) Yet Caro's description of Johnson's Senate years cannot sustain LBJ on such a high plateau. This may not be an accident or inconsistency, however. Caro's approach to LBJ, as many critics have observed, is ambiguous, despite the comparisons to Lincoln (which Caro makes more than once).

Some reviewers (Ronald Steel in *The Atlantic*, for example) argue that Caro has difficulty understanding or accepting political power. There is much to this criticism. His majestic tale of Johnson could be a cautionary tale of the hazards of power—the hazards to one's own soul, and to a nation when too much power is accumulated in the government. The deeper source of Caro's ambiguity is the intellectual problem LBJ poses for liberals. As civil rights leader Roy Wilkins succinctly put it: "With Johnson, you never quite knew if he was out to lift your heart or your wallet." Caro's praise and partial admiration for LBJ owes to Caro's filtering Johnson through a sympathetic liberal lens, portraying LBJ as an agent in the progressive march toward greater "social justice," a phrase that Caro uses frequently in the expository sections of his narrative.

His attempt to redeem Johnson appears to be part of a quiet trend. Reflecting on the ineptitude of the Carter presidency and the fecklessness of the Clinton presidency has led many liberals to begin reappraising Johnson in a more favorable light. His Great Society delivered more landmark social legislation than even FDR's New Deal. The disaster of Vietnam and the unrest in the streets in the 1960s, which together fractured the Democratic Party, eclipsed this record for a long time. Yet the judgment John Kenneth Galbraith offered in 1967 is reasserting itself: "Our gains under the Johnson administration on civil rights outweigh our losses on behalf of Marshall Ky."

That liberals, who distrusted Johnson in the Senate and then hated him in the White House, might come to regard Johnson as their most worthy modern champion is a startling irony. It also presents a huge intellectual problem. Unless it is assumed that "character doesn't matter," a way must be found to lessen Johnson's ugliness. Caro finds it in Johnson's maneuvering in 1957 to break the hitherto invincible Southern filibuster against civil rights legislation.

Johnson arrived in the Senate in 1949 as a full-throated adherent to the Southern cause. He attacked desegregation and civil rights in his 1948 campaign (in statements he suppressed in the 1960s), and his maiden speech in the Senate was titled "We of the South." He immediately fell in with Georgia Senator Richard Russell, the captain of the Southern opposition to all civil rights legislation, and, Caro believes, attended meetings of the Southern Caucus, the regular gathering where Southern Senators would plot strategy. (Johnson also denied this in later years.)

Johnson immediately distinguished himself in the Senate as someone who understood how to accumulate power around him and get things done. Some of these "accomplishments" were dubious at best, such as his Red-baiting attack on Federal Power Commission chairman Leland Olds, providing the model for Joseph McCarthy several years later. Caro records LBJ telling Olds after having engineered the destruction of his career: "Lee, I hope you understand there's nothing personal in this. We're still friends, aren't we? It's only politics, you know."

More significant in Caro's narrative is Johnson's decision to pursue the party leadership post in the Senate, hitherto the graveyard of Senate reputations and careers. Caro's account of Johnson's years as majority leader is superb. No one could read a man—understand his motives, his weaknesses (and therefore how to get his vote)—like Johnson. "If you liked politics," Hubert Humphrey remarked, "it was like sitting at the feet of a giant." Caro's summary judgment is that "Johnson transformed the Senate, pulled a nineteenth-century— indeed, in many respects an eighteenth-century—body into the twentieth century."

Johnson's decision to break with the South and midwife the 1957 Civil Rights Act is portrayed throughout the book as a naked political calculation on Johnson's part. Even with Johnson's already legendary skills at manipulating the Senate, it still seemed like an impossible task. Yet there were many reasons why the political interests fell into line. If LBJ was ever going to have a chance of becoming President, he had to be acceptable to Northern liberals in the Democratic Party—"You got to clean him up on civil rights," in the words of liberal lawyer Joseph Rauh. Southerners were willing to go along because they recognized that Johnson was the only Southerner with a realistic chance to reach the White House, where, Richard Russell assumed, LBJ would protect the interests of the South. Johnson found the lowest common denominator—a weak voting rights bill that Caro himself admits had little effect on black voting registration in Southern states. From this nakedly cynical and self-serving stratagem Caro makes Johnson into "the greatest champion that the liberal senators . . . had had since, almost a century before, there had been a President named Lincoln."

Caro's evaluation of LBJ depends on a historical premise, that because of the filibuster rules the Senate prior to Johnson had ceased to operate as the Founders intended. In fact, Caro writes a synoptic history of the Senate that precedes the main narrative about Johnson, arguing that the Senate had become "a mighty dam standing athwart, and stemming, the tides of social justice. [The Senate] empowered, with an immense power, the forces of conservatism and reaction in America." Caro's "underbook" about the Senate concludes that the long-running Southern filibuster against civil rights was not a geographic anomaly but the essence of the Senate at work.

With this premise, Caro reveals himself to be a relic of Progressivism. LBJ comes to sight in Caro's narrative as a supremely talented man bobbing like a cork on the tides of history. This is the basis for both LBJ's greatness and his shortcomings, as is evident in Caro's ambivalent comments such as "there were times when [LBJ's] interests coincided with America's interests." The repeated comparison to Lincoln is instructive. In Caro's hands LBJ was plainly not imbued with great purpose like Lincoln or even like Franklin or Theodore Roosevelt, nor does he have the even-tempered virtues of Eisenhower or Gerald Ford. Instead, LBJ's success derived from the happy confluence of the tides of history and personal ambition. Abraham Lincoln came to his views about slavery and equality because of a principled understanding of the Constitution and Declaration of Independence. Johnson, by contrast, said that "It's not the job of a politician to go around saying principled things." The Constitution, Johnson remarked, is a series of compromises, and this statement suggests that Johnson had little awareness of or regard for the principles behind those compromises.

Caro's historicist premise makes it impossible to draw meaningful distinctions between Lincoln and LBJ—and will make it impossible, further along in Caro's epic account, for him to distinguish between civil rights law informed by the principles of natural right and civil rights distorted by the ideology of egalitarianism. While Master of the Senate clearly foreshadows LBJ's troubled presidency, it also fills readers with skepticism about how Caro will judge the defects of Johnson's Great Society.

Master of the Senate ends with a vignette that captures the problem with Johnson in a way that Caro probably doesn't fully appreciate. After the election of 1960, which elevated Johnson to the vice presidency, Johnson went to the Senate Democratic Caucus before resigning his seat and attempted to get the consent of his fellow Senators to continue presiding over the caucus and, in effect, still run the Senate. He was startled when his fellow Senators rebuffed this brazen invitation to violate the separation of powers. It is hard to decide whether LBJ's greater failing here was lack of respect for constitutional principle, or his complete misreading of his former colleagues. For someone renowned for his ability to read other men, this failure of perception is stunning.

Caro dwells on this episode only as a marker of how fast Johnson lost his political clout on the way to an unhappy vice presidency. But it anticipates the problem that should be at the center of Caro's forthcoming volumes on Johnson's presidency: how could such an astute politician persist for so many years in misjudging the nature of his most determined political enemy, North Vietnam's Ho Chi Minh? Johnson's White House aide John P. Roche wrote years after LBJ died that he could not make Johnson understand that Ho Chi Minh was a dedicated Leninist. Johnson, Roche recalls, kept asking, "'What does Ho want?' as if Ho were a mayor of Chicago holding out for five new post offices." Such a question could only come from a man for whom politics is merely a nihilistic series of deals, utterly without any principled ground. Although the Vietnam mess is behind us, much of the Johnson legacy in domestic policy, especially the unprincipled civil rights legacy of affirmative action, is still with us. Caro's thorough narrative will be well worth waiting for, but Master of the Senate leaves us with the feeling that he will resolve neither his ambivalence nor our doubts about this giant figure.

—*Claremont Review of Books*, Fall, 2002

Chapter 9

Liberal Elites

[Note: I have considerably revised upward my opinion of Lasch and Revolt of the Elites *since this review appeared almost 30 years ago. Many of Lasch's views that I criticize here have turned out to be a solid guide to leftist elitism and the populist reaction to it in the age of Trump and Brexit. I include it unchanged as a marker of how circumstances and opinions change over time.—SH]*

In Defense of Elitism, by William A. Henry III

The Revolt of the Elites and the Betrayal of Democracy, by Christopher Lasch

The United States, a nation founded by a self-conscious elite, is the most anti-elitist of nations. This is one of the paradoxes that has made the nation thrive. Elitism, however defined, is of course coextensive with all political and social life. The classical understanding of the hierarchy of human excellence, as most notably illuminated in Aristotle's *Nicomachean Ethics*, is what made political life and progress possible.

But the very reference to the classical origins of the idea of human excellence, with its obvious implication of a division between superior and inferior, brings to mind one of the variations on elitism that has long been a pejorative: aristocracy. The common modern meaning of aristocracy suggests the institutionalized elitism of heredity or wealth that tends over time to corrupt both politics and creativity. It is the great innovation of liberal democracy to replace aristocracy with meritocracy; recall Thomas Jefferson's famous correspondence with John Adams about why the United States could dispense with an artificial aristocracy (which Adams desired to have) in favor of a "natural aristocracy" of excellence and virtue.

51

The flaw of democracy, as Tocqueville (an elitist par excellence) foresaw 150 years ago, is that the idea of equal rights—the central premise of democracy—would dissolve over time into an extreme, levelling egalitarianism. "The ills produced by extreme equality," Tocqueville warned, "only become apparent little by little; they gradually insinuate themselves into the body social." Liberty requires effort and sacrifice, while "equality offers its pleasures free." Neither gentle reason nor ferocious remonstrance seems to dissuade someone who has fallen under the egalitarian spell. "It is no use telling them that by this blind surrender to an exclusive passion they are compromising their dearest interests," Tocqueville warned. "They are deaf."

This background is useful in evaluating these two recent offerings on the subject of elites and elitism, which might seem to represent examples of authors miraculously cured of egalitarian deafness. Both William Henry, a senior writer and drama critic for *Time* magazine, and Christopher Lasch, a sociologist, have fashionably "liberal" credentials. Henry's plaintive passage boasting of being a Jesse Helms-hating "registered Democrat" and a card-carrying member of the ACLU brings to mind Phil Ochs's parodic tune, "Love Me I'm a Liberal." Lasch's 1978 book, *The Culture of Narcissism*, was rumored to be Jimmy Carter's favorite book and the inspiration for his notorious "malaise" speech.

Both Henry and Lasch offer up attacks on egalitarianism that sound like something from the pen of the young William F. Buckley Jr. Henry's book, clearly the better of the two, assails "quixotic liberals," "liberal tolerance gone haywire," and agrees that "we have taken the legal notion that all men are created equal to its illogical extreme." He begins and ends his book by announcing that his central theme is that "the wrong side (egalitarianism) has been winning." Lasch is less explicit about egalitarianism, but nonetheless offers that the "cultural diversity" movement (whose motive force is egalitarianism) is "clearly a recipe for universal incompetence."

The best parts of both books could be taken as clear signs that at least among a few honest-minded figures aligned on the left there is growing recognition of the foolishness of egalitarianism, and perhaps a new appreciation for liberty. Henry's book especially offers up many aphoristic attacks on egalitarianism that could have come from a radio talk show host. In some places, Henry throws down the gauntlet with in-your-face prose that is clearly intended to provoke more than persuade. The most widely quoted sentence in the book comes in a passage attacking the egalitarian premises of cultural diversity, where he bluntly notes, "It is scarcely the same thing to put a man on the moon as to put a bone in your nose."

Henry argues that were we truly consistent, "Native Americans""would have to be called "Siberian Americans." He refers to the disabled-rights movement as "crippo liberation." He attacks the central rhetorical message of Democratic Party, Clinton-style politics, as the insinuation that "the gains of the rich are somehow ill-gotten" and behaving "as though all of one's salary belonged to the government in the first place, and it is only Uncle Sam's beneficence that determines how much one should keep." Most significantly, Henry concludes, "The missing element in every phase of American life, from education to culture to the thicket of identity politics, is what used to be called rugged individualism."

Lasch's book is more of a thematic muddle, just like most of his previous books, which political scientist Stephen Holmes once described as "glum mood pieces." But even allowing for the usual quotient of silly postulates the readers have come to expect from Lasch, there are still many arguments in his book to celebrate. Like Henry, Lasch deplores the aggrandizement of "self-esteem," sanitized speech, and the "caring class" that feeds off these therapeutic nostrums. He laments the abolition of shame. He attacks Robert Reich, comparing his brand of interventionist, managerial economics with the mismanagement of the Vietnam War by Robert McNamara's "whiz kids." He criticizes at length the legacy of Horace Mann, blaming this usually revered figure for setting public education on direct course toward the blandness and mediocrity that afflicts it today. Public education, Lasch argues, "has never recovered from the mistakes and misconceptions built into it at the very outset."

The strongest common point of both books is their recognition that preserving racial grievances has become the vital necessity of egalitarianism and the multicultural movement, regardless of whatever real racism there is in society. Henry criticizes the "addictive attachment to past grievances," while Lasch argues that "the thinking classes'…eagerness to drag every conversation back to race is enough in itself to invite the suspicion that their investment in this issue exceeds anything that is justified by the actual state of race relations." Henry and Lasch recognize that the political utility of race baiting by the left, and the policies it justifies, are now causing rather than curing racial divisions.

But while there is much to appreciate in *In Defense of Elitism* and *The Revolt of the Elites*, both books are a bit like the cliché about Chinese food: filling but not really satisfying. In the case of Lasch, this criticism is easy to make out, because of his soft-collectivist communitarianism. For every worthy aphorism, there is a blooper that gives away the game.

Luxury is morally repellent, Lasch argues at one point, and incompatible with democracy. There is some of the old nonsense about the "third way" between open markets and the welfare state that died a much-deserved death in the 1980s. He also waxes romantic about populism, suggesting vaguely that populism could be a noble and uplifting basis on which to renew American political life. But he does not offer any reflections on the usual face of populism, which might be summarized in two words: Ross Perot. Populism is occasionally justly aimed—as in the case of the tax revolt—but more often, as the case of Perot shows, populism is simply the fancy dress name for demagoguery.

At the heart of Lasch's argument about the "revolt" of our elites is the idea that elitism in a democracy is only acceptable if the elites are conscious doers of good works. John Rawls receives only a single mention in the book, but the spirit of his famous argument is pervasive throughout the book: People may cultivate superior talents only if they can be proved to benefit the disadvantaged parts of society.

While it may be reasonable to speak of "reciprocal obligations" as a voluntary matter, an individual ethic that is praiseworthy on its own terms, you get the uneasy feeling reading the communitarian followers of Lasch that they would not hesitate, if they had the power, to try to institutionalize their vision of noblesse oblige.

Lasch doesn't like meritocracy, though he stops short of the common invective that all success is due to luck or sinister calculation. He is really annoyed at the mobility of the elites made possible by modern markets and technology. Whereas old money elites tended to be rooted in some local place, the new elites are rootless cosmopolitans who have more in common with their Asian and European commercial partners than with their American neighbors. The implication is that liberal guilt is a fine thing, and the elitism that Lasch, and to a more limited extent Henry, would obviously approve is the elitism of the Kennedy family: It's OK to make a pile as long as you feel guilty and "give back" other people's money.

Lasch doesn't formulate actual public policies, but he has always made a better Jeremiah than a Moses. The same complaint cannot be made of Henry. Henry not only offers specific criteria for recognizing a superior culture, he also offers the radical suggestion that the number of students who receive a college education be cut nearly in half. His favorite target for the education ax are the "community" colleges, which, he notes, used to be called "junior" colleges. And he argues that tenure for college faculty should be abolished: "Competing for one's job on an on-going basis could introduce a little more healthy elitism into the professorial lifestyle." If acerbic barbs about putting bones in noses don't set off the chattering class, this idea surely will. Henry is surely right, as David Frum has also argued recently, that much of the egalitarian excess of our time derives its energy from the bloated higher-education establishment.

While both books' criticisms about egalitarianism are most welcome, what's missing is a recognition that contemporary liberalism paved the way for our current condition by having no immune system to ward off the tendency toward extremism. It needs to be remembered that it was precisely because of the liberal collaboration with the crusade for the redistribution of income that the subsequent absurdities of radical egalitarianism became possible.

There is little recognition that classical liberal warnings about the poisonous effects of egalitarianism were right and should have been heeded decades ago. Henry only grudgingly admits that "even lifelong liberals of an elitist bent are forced to find common cause with conservatives" on these issues. But it is probably churlish to demand mea culpas, and the long-suffering friends of liberty should perhaps celebrate newfound allies against the relentless levelling current of our time. It is bad form to check the other fellow's dog tags in the foxhole while the battle rages. (Besides, these guys could use some friendly air cover: Since both Henry and Lasch died shortly before their books were released, we can expect the left to dismiss both books as being the products of "dead white American males.")

The real defect in Henry's argument is not simply that it is more of an attack on egalitarianism than it is a defense of elitism, but that his defense of elitism seems to be a defense of elitism for elitism's sake, rather than an argument that elitism can represent a standard of excellence that is good and defensible in itself. The success of Bill Bennett's *Book of Virtues* offers evidence that such a defense would find a wide and eager audience.

Henry's criteria for a superior culture include liberty, respect for science and art, a comfortable middle-class existence, recognition of hierarchy and authority, and a useful basis for perceiving the difference between mediocrity and excellence. But for the real thing, for "elitism with-out tears or guilt," so to speak, readers should go back to Aristotle's *Ethics*.

—*Reason*, April 1995

Chapter 10

Grab a Whip and a Chair

Taming the Prince: The Ambivalence of Modern Executive Power, by
Harvey C. Mansfield, Jr.

Harvey Mansfield's inquiry into the nature of executive power poses
a disturbing challenge for political theory. If Mansfield is right, classical
liberals (along with many others) have some tough thinking to do about
the sufficiency of the rule of law.

Taming the Prince explores the largely ignored territory of the
ambivalence or ambiguity of modern executive power. The executive—
especially the American president—is both subordinate to and
independent of the legislature. Consider the ordinary sense of the
term *executive* as the office that "executes" the laws made by others. On
the surface the executive is said to follow the "will of the people," strictly
as an agent. But the executive is also an independent political power in
his own right, in ways that go beyond the enumerated powers to veto,
command the military, and so forth. Remember, in the presidential oath
the executive promises to execute the *office* of president, not merely the
laws.

Beyond the consideration of the formal and informal aspects of
political executives, Mansfield makes a serious philosophical argument
about executive power: Strong executive power is necessary because the
rule of the law is incomplete or insufficient without it. The implication is
that nonarbitrary politics is inherently impossible. Executive power, says
Mansfield, is "intended to secure the difference between free government
and tyranny by giving the former some of the power and techniques of
the latter." Moreover, this necessity—and the true nature of executive
power—must be concealed. Another way of thinking about this would be
to say that the executive is the point of tension between the theory and
practice of politics.

We should derive little comfort from the fact that the modern
executive has been republicanized and constitutionalized. The American
president "claims the silences of the Constitution" (Richard Pious's

phrase in *The American President)* and so is "above the law," not in the sense of being exempt from it, but in the sense of transcending it. Although libertarian theorists such as F.A. Hayek identify executive administration as the "gap" through which a people's liberty may be driven out, Hayek and others view executive power in the same way as judicial power—as being merely instrumental to the rule of law.

For theorists such as Hayek, legislative power is the keystone to the rule of law and successful politics. For Mansfield, executive power is the keystone to the rule of law and successful politics. In light of Mansfield's powerful argument, libertarians need to confront and "tame" executive power for themselves.

The greater part of *Taming the Prince* is a sweeping survey of the evolution of the idea of executive power, beginning with Aristotle, who had no explicit theory of executive power. Aristotle's political science aims to discover the one "best regime" according to nature, which would promulgate the attainment of human excellence—human excellence being understood as the perfection of the virtues outlined in the *Nicomachean Ethics.* Such a regime might be founded and governed through the "kingship over all" by the man or men of superior excellence and virtue. But Aristotle, unlike Plato in the *Republic,* knows that such a ruler is unlikely ever to be found. Thus, Aristotle concentrates on improving actual regimes, which is to be done through the rule of law and the pursuit of justice.

Mansfield's account perks up when he arrives at Machiavelli. Mansfield is among those political theorists who see Machiavelli as the decisive break in Western political thought. Machiavelli rejects the Aristotelian notion that there can be a best regime according to nature. For Machiavelli, the flaw of classical political science is that it sets its aims too high by seeking to achieve justice and human excellence. Better, Machiavelli teaches, to lower the sights of the regime and abandon the pretense of justice. If there is no best regime according to nature, no objective claim to justice, then politics will always be an imposition and a fraud, and all rule will be tyrannical to a greater or lesser degree.

For Machiavelli, the rule of law cannot attain what it attempts; for a regime to succeed—and Machiavelli wants a regime to succeed grandly—outside assistance is needed, in the form of a strong-willed, unscrupulous prince. The purpose of Machiavelli's executive, says Mansfield, is to remind men of their fear. Machiavelli thought the strong, amoral prince could conquer chance or fortune, which, for Aristotle, was the factor that made the one best regime unlikely to be founded or preserved. Paradoxically, Machiavelli's regime of the strong prince would be much more likely to promote both human excellence and justice, albeit a more modest form of excellence and justice.

The remaining history of the doctrine of executive power consists in "taming" or "domesticating" this ruthless prince so as to make the executive palatable within liberal constitutional regimes, which aim at preserving and enhancing individual liberty. Mansfield traces this taming process at length through Hobbes, Locke, Montesquieu, and *The Federalist*. For Hobbes, Locke, and the social-contract school, individuals are free and equal in the state of nature, but their self-preservation requires government. Recall Hobbes's memorable line that life in the state of nature without government would be "solitary, poor, nasty, brutish, and short."

Locke brings us what might be called the sanitized version of Machiavelli's strong prince in the form of "executive prerogative," which Locke understands as the power to do public good without a rule—a power Locke admits to be arbitrary. Together with Montesquieu and the American Founders, Locke developed the doctrine of the separation of powers, which further "republicanizes" executive power.

Mansfield is an open admirer of strong executives, and he believes only strong executives can direct a nation toward its chosen ends. His models are Roosevelt and Reagan, and although he says an executive must be principled to succeed, Mansfield as a political scientist is neutral as to what those principles should be. In fact, he makes it clear in his conclusion that he views principles as merely instrumental to political success.

Executive power has always been a troubling feature of politics, not just for ordinary liberals such as Arthur Schlesinger, Jr. (*The Imperial Presidency*), but also for true partisans of liberty such as Robert Higgs, whose *Crisis and Leviathan* traces the way activist executives have used periods of crisis both to expand permanently the power of the state and to curtail individual liberty. Machiavelli might well have approved of these aggrandizements of the American state. But if Mansfield is right that executive power is the keystone to politics, then libertarians need to think hard about how to square a regime of individual liberty based on the rule of law with the executive power "to do public good without a rule."

The answer to this may seem disconcerting. Libertarian political theory, especially that of Hayek and Nozick, would appear to be designed within the lowered horizon of post-Machiavellian political philosophy as adapted by Hobbes and Locke, which stresses the protection of individual rights through limited government. But by combining the liberal understanding of limited government with the recent insights into the nature of free markets, libertarian political theory is rather more Aristotelian than anyone has explicitly noticed. It aims for a substantive, nonarbitrary outcome—in a word, justice. Libertarians believe they have the design for the best regime according to nature.

The pure libertarian theory of the self-regulating spontaneous order of free individuals bounded only by a body of law based on natural right and free exchange is, however, inadequate without executive power. So we must tame executive power for libertarian purposes, as Machiavelli would put it. Alas, this probably cannot be done through constitutional means or in theory, but instead requires politics. In other words, only executives who understand the importance of the minimalist state will do. If this seems daunting, remember that Machiavelli would probably say that libertarian political science, like Aristotelian political science, sets its aims too high. To this charge we should cheerfully plead guilty, even as we go about the difficult task of taming our princes with the doctrines of liberty.

—*Reason*, August/September 1990

Chapter 11

Bill and Ron

The Reagan I Knew, by William F. Buckley, Jr.

There are layers of bittersweet melancholia in Bill Buckley's memoir of his 30-year friendship with Ronald Reagan. *The Reagan I Knew* is Buckley's final book; indeed, he was working on the finishing touches the day he died in February. The memory of Reagan, and especially the élan of ascendant conservatism in the 1970s and 1980s that Buckley's memoir rekindles, burns hotter now that conservatives find themselves in the political wilderness again. And there are finally the sentimental qualities of both men–the talent for happiness and friendship along with a leavening of wit and a fitting sense of self-deprecation–that are exceedingly rare among great men in public life today.

The Reagan I Knew is equal parts memoir and a collection of the personal letters that passed between Buckley and both Nancy and Ronald Reagan starting in 1965. In fact the first communiqué came from Nancy, a thank-you note for a Christmas plant Bill had sent. One startling aspect of their friendship is that Buckley seemed to have been as close personally to Nancy as to Ronald, and perhaps closer given Ronald's famous reserve. Had Kitty Kelley seen any of the letters between Buckley and Nancy, she would no doubt have twisted their playful expressions of affection into a tawdry tale in her execrable biography of Nancy. "Longing to see you," Buckley wrote in one typical chatty missive, most of which were concluded with a running joke about meeting Nancy in Casablanca. Nancy could be equally affectionate in her replies: "I thought you had dropped out of my life completely!" she wrote Bill after a ten-month hiatus in contact in 1969. "I won't mention the months and months you've neglected me terribly and the awful effect this can have on a girl." The depth of their affection was not unnoticed by Ronald Reagan; he ended one letter to Bill: "Nancy sends her best (though she used a different word)."

While Buckley's memoir is silent on the Reagans' marriage and the frequently repeated theme of Reagan's supposed personal remoteness, he does lift the curtain on a few intimate details of the Reagans' family life, chiefly the difficulties with their two younger children. Buckley laments the atheism of Ron Reagan and the politics of Patti, even as he displays his typical generosity by celebrating their talents and personalities. (Included are a few letters from Buckley to a teenage Patti, praising her poetry.) Buckley offers a mild reproach of the Reagans' parenting: "The withdrawal, by Ron Jr., of any interest in spiritual life illuminates a study of him as well as of his parents. . . . What efforts were made–if any–to acquaint the boy with the historical and philosophical role of God in history?" The Reagans enlisted Buckley to the role of surrogate parent in one crucial matter: Ron Jr.'s decision to drop out of Yale to pursue a career as a ballet dancer. When the effort at dissuading Ron from his rash decision failed, Ronald Reagan cut off all financial support for his son: "Ronald Reagan was as determined to subject his son to poverty as Ron Jr. was to live in it."

Then there was the "endless matter" of Patti, "an unsilenced and evidently unsilenceable liberal." Throughout the 1980s Patti seemed determined to exploit every opportunity to repudiate her father's politics and embarrass her mother, culminating in an appearance in Playboy. The reader winces when Buckley records a tearful Nancy telling him, "I love my children, but I don't always like them."

The political connection between the two men is the dominant attraction of the book, however, and while Buckley's memoir is spare in its interpretation of Reagan, his retrospective account does contain a few revisions and revelations about his perception of Reagan. Buckley first met him in 1961, before Reagan's political career had begun in earnest, and like many others Buckley initially underestimated his political potential. But not for long. The book includes a long excerpt from Reagan's first appearance on Firing Line in 1967, where Reagan displayed thoughtfulness toward governing and a principled grasp of federalism. At this early moment it was clear to any unbiased observer that Reagan was no lightweight.

Buckley writes at the outset that he views himself as having been a "tutor" to Reagan, and recalls that after Reagan won the 1980 election he considered changing his occupational designation in Who's Who to "ventriloquist." Although Reagan gave Buckley and National Review some credit for his having become a Republican, there are subtle traces in Reagan's letters of his independent, self-taught mind. Buckley surely knew this, and it explains why he resisted the obvious temptation to send

Reagan a constant stream of thoughts during Reagan's Oval Office years. (Buckley had the special address code to get letters directly to the president's desk.) Buckley was content to allow National Review to be the chief vehicle of communication with Reagan on political matters, and only occasionally wrote directly to Reagan about pressing political topics. He recalls some disagreements and anxieties he had about Reagan's course in the Oval Office, but the pattern of how each man dealt with the other had been established by their most significant disagreement, which Buckley records at length: the Panama Canal treaty of 1977.

This clash illustrates several traits of both men. Reagan showed his resolution and imperviousness to criticism even from a close ally, while Buckley showed his gentleness in opposing his favorite politician. Both displayed their playful sides in the aftermath: Before Buckley arrived for a visit, Reagan put up signs in his driveway, Burma-Shave style, reading: "We Built It . . . We Paid For It . . . It's Ours!" For the next decade Buckley ended many of his letters to Reagan with a mock warning against giving away the Erie Canal, alternating with a running jest about being Reagan's ambassador to Afghanistan and directing the anti-Soviet effort there.

Fully appreciating Reagan's independence of mind, Buckley engaged Reagan selectively and with finesse during his presidency. In the early 1970s Buckley had advised Reagan to come out against détente, and recommended that he consult Senator Henry "Scoop" Jackson's staff ("the best pool of young men around"), many of whom would later join Reagan's administration. Yet by 1980 Buckley was a go-between in establishing a détente between Reagan and Henry Kissinger, who had been a major target of Reagan's attack on détente in 1976.

Buckley fretted to and commiserated with Reagan about personnel appointments, about hanging tough with his economic program during the grinding 1981–82 recession, about David Stockman's defection, about China policy, about the ruckus over Reagan's visit to the Bitburg cemetery in West Germany in 1985, and about many other topics. Buckley watered down some criticisms of Reagan that appeared in National Review, and on a few occasions suppressed contemplated criticisms, above all assuring Reagan that "no personal criticism, i.e., questioning your motives, will be published."

In a 1984 letter, Buckley wrote Reagan: "I can't pretend I swing with all your decisions, but with most of them I do most heartily." But in the second term Buckley told him he was increasingly worried that the president "seemed to me and to many conservatives to come perilously close to trusting the Soviet Union." This anxiety crystallized with the signing of the Intermediate-Range Nuclear Forces (INF) treaty in 1987. Buckley joined Kissinger, Richard Nixon, and a large cast of conservatives in opposition to the INF pact. Reagan defended himself stoutly in his private replies to Buckley, leaving Buckley to repair to their friendship and agreeing to disagree. "Damn I wish I could be on your side on that one," Buckley wrote to Reagan in January 1988. "Haven't had a significant difference with you since the Panama Canal."

Recalling this chapter in the Reagan story leads to Buckley's one significant revelation and revision: the doubt that, had the Soviet Union launched a nuclear attack, Reagan would have ordered a retaliation. Buckley reprints the moving speech he gave at National Review's 30th-anniversary gala dinner in 1985, with Reagan present, where he explained that the West's existence depended on our willingness to sacrifice it in an instant if necessary. "Twenty years after saying that, in the presence of the man I was talking about, I changed my mind," Buckley wrote.

Reagan's sincere anti-nuclear pacifism is not a new theme among the writers who have studied him, but it is still amazing to contemplate. That Reagan largely concealed his probable dereliction from the pre-programmed duty of Cold War presidents was of a piece with his personal reserve, and must be closely related to his drive for the end of the Cold War by supremely Machiavellian means. It suggests new dimensions of Reagan's remarkable political character. It would have been good to hear more from Buckley about this tantalizing aspect of the Reagan story, given that the Cold War was the central preoccupation of Buckley's career.

Despite this revision, the conclusion of Buckley's 30th-anniversary meditation holds up as strongly today as it did that night in 1985, and serves as a fitting coda for both of our deceased heroes: "I pray that my son, when he is sixty, and your son, when he is sixty, and the sons and daughters of our guests tonight will live in a world from which the great ugliness that has scarred our century has passed. Enjoying their freedom, they will be grateful that, at the threatened nightfall, the blood of their fathers ran strong."

—*National Review*, December 29, 2008.

Chapter 12

Psychoanalyzing George W. Bush

George W. Bush and the Redemptive Dream, by Dan P. McAdams

The remarkable combination of character, ambition and political skill seen in the men who reach the presidency clearly deserves serious psychological analysis. While ideology and historical circumstance are primary to evaluation, the psychological aspects of, say, Lincoln's depression or Reagan's willful optimism or Franklin Roosevelt's polio should not be overlooked. The hazard of psychoanalyzing presidents, however, is that it can lapse into crude reductionism, overemphasizing sub-rational or irrational causes and thereby trivializing more obvious traits and political ideas. Too often psychological approaches become one-dimensional devices for critics to use as another partisan tool.

George W. Bush is an irresistible subject for such psychological profiling, given his family's political and private history and his embrace as an adult of religious faith, sobriety and responsibility. It is almost impossible not to speculate about how Bush's relationship with his father affected his decisions. His penchant for bestowing nicknames, his certitude, his seeming equanimity under the pressures of the post-9/11 world, and his self-conscious Texas swagger-traits that make him notably different from his father and brother Jeb-all support plausible theories. Bush will be a cottage industry for psychologists for years to come.

Dan P. McAdams, professor of psychology at Northwestern University, offers one of the first comprehensive psychological profiles of Bush in "George W. Bush and the Redemptive Dream." To his credit, McAdams tries not to pre-judge Bush, and he avoids making moral or political judgments about the president's major decisions. McAdams will further disappoint the Bush-haters in his measured rejection of several pop-psych themes, such as that Bush was in thrall to an Oedipal rivalry (though he does think a desire to avenge his father in Iraq was a factor). But in the end, McAdams's framework sinks into a mire of professional jargon that tells us more about contemporary theory than about the former president.

McAdams's thesis is that "a perfect psychological storm of traits" determined Bush's decision to launch the Iraq invasion. "Of course," McAdams allows, "the decision was also informed by many factors that were not themselves psychological. Political, economic, and world-historical factors all played important roles." But these traditional political factors would not have been enough, he thinks, to start the war in the absence of Bush's powerful psychological makeup. Unfortunately, McAdams makes a weak case for downplaying traditional political factors in favor of psychology, and most readers will be left with the impression that he attributes every political decision to psychological factors. To calibrate accurately the role of psychology versus "traditional political factors" in the large decisions of presidents and prime ministers might require the combined insights of Tocqueville and Freud. But in this case, a simple thought experiment may suffice: If you think that John McCain, had he been in the White House then, would also have decided to invade Iraq, you will not find McAdams's analysis persuasive.

The key traits McAdams divines in Bush include some obvious ones, such as his extreme extroversion; the effects of the death of his younger sister in childhood; his transfiguration of Midland, Tex., into a new Eden; and, above all, his narrative of redemption involving his sudden sobriety and conversion to fervent Christian faith. McAdams argues that Bush sought to impose his own redemptive narrative on the entire world through his "freedom agenda" and the war on terrorism.

The book suffers from banality ("Shakespeare was surely right when he said that all the world's a stage and each of us a player") and repetitiveness, especially of the theme that Bush suffers from "low openness to experience." I lost count of the instances of this phrase, but it is the touchstone of McAdams's ultimate denigration of Bush. The phrase is a synonym for Bush's stubbornness, and McAdams understands it in its formal clinical dimensions, which allows him to escape confronting the potential ideological sources of Bush's hardheadedness, or rendering judgment about whether Bush's stubbornness was right or wrong. But is this trait peculiar to Bush? Has there ever been a successful non-stubborn president? To be sure, stubbornness served some presidents poorly (Woodrow Wilson, Jimmy Carter), while it served others well (Harry Truman, Ronald Reagan). Psychological analysis cannot tell us whether stubbornness is an asset or a liability in a president. For that we need to turn to old-fashioned historical and character analysis.

Chapter 13

The Return of the Unabomber

A conservative comedian of my acquaintance (David Deeble) remarked to me recently, "I see *New York Times* editorial writer Ted Kaczynski has passed away." This is a callback to one of the earliest reactions to the Unabomber's famous manifesto, "Industrial Society and Its Future," that led to his capture in 1996. The late Tony Snow of Fox News was the first to notice a number of striking—and embarrassing—similarities between the language of Kaczynski's manifesto and Al Gore's pretentious and cliché-ridden *Earth in the Balance.*

In other words, many arguments of the manifesto were entirely familiar and even conventional, which is why he could easily be confused for the rote cliché writers of monotonous *Times* editorials. Today it could even be written by ChatGPT, which is maybe what drove Kaczynski to his reported suicide in prison. The eminent political scientist James Q. Wilson, who Kaczynski cited in his manifesto, observed in 1998 that "his paper resembles something that a very good graduate student might have written based on his own reading rather than the course assignments. If it is the work of a madman, then the writings of many political philosophers—Jean Jacques Rousseau, Tom Paine, Karl Marx—are scarcely more sane."

But combined with the evidence that Kaczynski had corresponded with—and perhaps attended events of—environmental radicals such as Earth First, the image of the Unabomber as a murderous eco-terrorist stuck, and stuck hard.

A careful reading of his entire 35,000-word manifesto presents a more complicated picture, however, and one that in the end is more disturbing for what is missing from it, and hence the conclusions that should be drawn about him. And far from being a violent outlier, we ought to be concerned that the conditions that helped generate

Kaczynski's homicidal rage are more prevalent today than when Kaczynski formed his dark view of the world in the 1960s and 1970s.

It turns out that not very many people actually read the manifesto completely or carefully when it came out, and certain aspects of it read with prescience in the aftermath of COVID and the rising concerns about artificial intelligence and data privacy. Younger people who weren't alive during the time of Kaczynski's bombings today are coming to the manifesto with fresh eyes and discovering things they like about it. Suddenly there is a new chorus—including some *conservatives*—who speak approvingly of being "Ted-pilled."

It is startling to discover that Kaczynski's strongest ire—aside from his primal hatred of industrial society—is for *the left*. His critique of and contempt for the left and especially the academic left, read in isolation, is one that easily matches any current conservative critic of wokeness and identity politics. Consider these passages from early in the manifesto:

Leftists tend to hate anything that has an image of being strong, good and successful. They hate America, they hate Western civilization, they hate white males, they hate rationality. The reasons that leftists give for hating the West, etc. clearly do not correspond with their real motives. They SAY they hate the West because it is warlike, imperialistic, sexist, ethnocentric and so forth, but where these same faults appear in socialist countries or in primitive cultures, the leftist finds excuses for them, or at best he GRUDGINGLY admits that they exist; whereas he ENTHUSIASTICALLY points out (and often greatly exaggerates) these faults where they appear in Western civilization. Thus it is clear that these faults are not the leftist's real motive for hating America and the West. He hates America and the West because they are strong and successful. . .

Helping black people is not [leftists'] real goal. Instead, race problems serve as an excuse for them to express their own hostility and frustrated need for power. In doing so they actually harm black people, because the activists' hostile attitude toward the white majority tends to intensify race hatred.

If our society had no social problems at all, the leftists would have to INVENT problems in order to provide themselves with an excuse for making a fuss.

Kaczynski goes on for 17 paragraphs in this vein, before returning at the close of his manifesto with another 19 long paragraphs denouncing the left again, calling leftism "a totalitarian force," "a kind of religion," whose thirst for power and domination are "dangerous." The left is only obsessed with gaining and using power.

Kaczynski devotes just a single short paragraph to conservatives, dismissing them as "fools."

They whine about the decay of traditional values, yet they enthusiastically support technological progress and economic growth. Apparently it never occurs to them that you can't make rapid, drastic changes in the technology and economy of a society without causing rapid changes in all other aspects of the society as well, and that such rapid changes inevitably break down traditional values.

Likewise Kaczynski's image as a radical environmentalist becomes fuzzy on closer inspection. He viewed environmental extremists like Earth First as only potential allies—providing they eschewed leftist ideology, which he doubted they could do. He offers a sneering description that likely had people like Al Gore or John Kerry in mind, who he saw as "crypto-leftists," having "some deep lack within him that makes it necessary for him to devote himself to a cause and immerse himself in a collectivity." In another passage he dismisses out of hand the idea that a "Green" party electoral majority could succeed in doing what is necessary.

Why so much time devoted to attacking leftists, including environmentalists, who might seem Kaczynski's natural allies against "the system"? Kaczynski must be understood as a radical revolutionary, but not a *leftist* revolutionary. At first glance he seems like a new-age Trotskyite: "The revolution must be international and world-wide. It cannot be carried out on a nation-by-nation basis." But was never bamboozled by the Frankfurt School's fixation with culture, still less the orthodox Marxist obsession with means of production or economic class conflict, as the drivers of consciousness, history, political change, and power dynamics. He is scornful of "social justice," and is uninterested in racial conflict. His target is not capitalism, but the industrial revolution as a whole.

Kaczynski's preposterous claims that the industrial revolution has been a disaster for humanity, and that "factories should be destroyed, technical books burned, etc," can be refuted by recalling a single *New Yorker* cartoon of two cave men sitting around a fire, with one wondering: "Something's just not right—our air is clean, water is pure, we all get plenty of exercise, everything we eat is organic and free-range, and yet nobody lives past thirty." Whatever social problems and dislocations have occurred because of the industrial revolution, the gains to humanity are so overwhelmingly positive that there is little constituency, beyond nutty but noisy environmentalists, for turning it back.

Unlike environmentalists or small-is-beautiful romanticists, Kaczynski's beef with technology is not with its impacts on the environment, but that modern science and technology are the dominant form of tyrannical rule. His views on technology are neither original nor ill-founded. Several passages were prophetic of the authoritarian "science" we experienced with COVID; he worried about data harvesting of private information, and offered speculations that anticipated the current worries about the advance of artificial intelligence. He had a thorough grasp of the leading critiques of technology, and had even corresponded with Jacques Ellul, the French thinker who wrote one of the earliest critical analyses of the subject back in 1965, *The Technological Society*.

Ellul, however, never became an anti-technology radical. To the contrary, by the 1970s Ellul had become an evangelical Christian, and largely discarded his early fixation on the evil of technology. But Kaczynski became a homicidal fanatic, writing that "In order to get our message [Kaczynski wrote in the voice of the royal "we" throughout the manifesto] to the public with some chance of making a lasting impression, we've had to kill people."

Kaczynski's violent revolutionary ethos generated not by leftism, but nihilism. The almost droll embrace of killing brings to light what is conspicuously missing from his manifesto: any sense of ethics or a ground of morality that would both foreclose violence, or offer a pathway to putting technology in perspective and finding meaning in life, as Ellul's religion did for him. If asked, Koczynski would say any ethical or moral code was impossible in our technocracy because the premises of modern science have proven that there is no objective ground for morality or meaning.

This is the case Alston Chase made in his remarkable 2003 biography of Kaczynski, *A Mind for Murder: The Education of the Unabomber and the Origins of Modern Terrorism*. Chase's thesis in one short sentence: *Kaczinski was made at Harvard*, where he was a student from 1958-1962, immediately after Chase had matriculated there. "The 'Unabomber Manifesto'," Chase wrote, "embodied ideas with which I was familiar.

70

And virtually all of these ideas could be found in the lectures and reading that students encountered at Harvard and other liberal arts colleges during Kaczynski's undergraduate years."

Chase notes that Kaczynski was raised an atheist by his liberal parents (his father committed suicide), and his brother, a Columbia graduate, was equally disaffected by American society. By the time Chase and Kaczynski arrived at Harvard, "the faculty had lost faith in the idea that morality was rational. . . Although no one noticed, the religion of reason was giving way to something one could call the culture of despair. . . He became a true believer in the scientific method and its philosophy, positivism, which allowed him to think that morality was meaningless. It was there that, by his own admission, his developing alienation bloomed into disillusionment with society."

Beyond the broad issue of technology or the specific issue of climate change, the general point that our universities teach an unremitting dogma of nihilism means that the ground for creating future Kaczynskis is fertile indeed. An acquaintance of mine recently described attending his 45th Harvard reunion, where fellow classmates were all highly prosperous and mostly at the top of their professional fields. And all bitterly disaffected from racist, retrograde America. Kaczynski nailed it when he said leftists suffer from low self-esteem.

Chase, not known as an especially conservative or political writer, concluded his assessment of Kaczynski thus:

The crisis of reason was a loss of faith in what the Declaration of Independence called the 'self-evident' truths that individual rights and the legitimacy of government derived from 'the laws of nature.' By the 1950s, this belief had been undermined in academic circles especially (as we have seen) by the success of science and its companion philosophy, positivism. And this philosophy convinced many—including Kaczynski—that as only empirically verifiable statements are meaningful, moral and political beliefs, such as those expressed in the Declaration, being untestable, are nonrational as well. Government rests, they concluded, not on 'laws of nature' as the founding fathers supposed, but on power alone. By removing ethics from the equation, positivism laid the foundation for radical ideologies—including Kaczynski's—which preached that 'the system' was illegitimate and violent overthrow acceptable.

Finally, even though Kaczynski disdained environmentalists, his overall anti-technology, anti-Western civilization view does illuminate

71

the innermost character of the environmental movement. Most environmentalists are not (yet) homicidal maniacs, but Kaczynski's line of thought does illuminate the actions of Extinction Rebellion and other groups that are blocking highways and defacing artwork and monuments on behalf of the fanatical climate change crusade.

Kaczynski dogmatically embraced the view that technology can offer no solutions to any of our problems, climate or otherwise. This explains the fanatical resistance of climate activists to carbon-free nuclear power, carbon capture, and "geoengineering" proposals to deal with climate change. Conventional climate policy wonks mistakenly think the issue is about carbon emissions, and can't comprehend why leading climate activists have come out hard against hydrogen as an energy source, even though it is the cleanest source imaginable. Leave aside the massive production difficulties that make it impractical for the moment; like other technological answers to the supposed crisis of climate change, leading environmentalists oppose hydrogen power because it won't roll back the industrial revolution. When the climate crusaders utter "de-growth," you should take them at their word. If we don't, it will only be matter of time before the bombing resumes.

—*The Pipeline*, June 25, 2023

Chapter 14

Was Churchill a Zionist?

Churchill and the Jews: A Lifelong Friendship, by Martin Gilbert

Churchill's Promised Land: *Zionism and Statecraft,* by Michael Makovsky

It's inevitable that scholars and authors will plumb every facet of our larger historical figures, a trait made evident by the fact that a book exists with the title *Lincoln and the Coming of the Caterpillar Tractor.* The subject of Winston Churchill and the Jews is not a trivial or peripheral subject, but it is difficult to treat this delicate matter in isolation, as the virtues and defects of these two books demonstrate.

Sir Martin Gilbert, fresh off *Churchill and America,* brings his familiar strict chronological treatment of Churchill's interactions with leading Jews and Zionist issues throughout his long career, and as useful and thorough as Gilbert always is, this approach leaves some important interpretive gaps. It's amusing to know that Churchill received oranges from Israel on his 83rd birthday, but it would be more useful to understand better the factors behind Churchill's frequent distraction and hesitation over Jewish issues.

Michael Makovsky's more analytical volume attempts to fill these gaps by placing what he calls Churchill's "nonlinear" or "erratic" Zionism into the larger context of Churchill's grand statecraft, but his judgment of Churchill shifts as often as Churchill's did, leaving some questions unresolved.

What is undeniable from both books, however, is Churchill's extraordinary philo-Semitism, which represented an important departure from the comfortable anti-Semitism of his political and class peers, and is yet another piece of evidence that Churchill cannot be explained simply as a product of the Victorian age.

Churchill was the ardent friend of leading Jews in Britain and a supporter of Zionism, expressing as early as 1908 his sympathy for a "restoration" of a Jewish homeland in Palestine, and successfully opposing an Aliens Bill brought to the House of Commons in 1904 that would have sharply restricted Jewish immigration into Britain. Later, as colonial secretary in the 1920s, Churchill took steps that enabled 300,000 Jews to emigrate to Palestine over the next decade, providing the nucleus for the future nation of Israel. As prime minister, in 1941, he proclaimed that "I was one of the authors" of Zionist policy. Indeed, among the lengthy catalogue of criticisms of Churchill was that "He was too fond of Jews."

Churchill's interest and sympathy for Jews had philosophical and cultural roots. Both Gilbert and Makovsky highlight Churchill's comment, offered in the fifth volume of his World War II memoirs, that "No two cities have counted more with mankind than -Athens and Jerusalem. Their messages in religion, philosophy, and art have been the main guiding lights of modern faith and culture." This was not merely a casual one-off but a highly unusual reflection coming from an otherwise unreligious man. The essential harmony of reason and revelation implied in this comment was usually found only among Roman Catholics in the mid-20th century.

Churchill understood that Christians owed this tradition to Judaism; as early as 1921, while visiting Jerusalem, he commented, "We owe to the Jews in the Christian revelation a system of ethics which, even if it were entirely separated from the supernatural, would be incomparably the most precious possession of mankind, worth in fact the fruits of all other wisdom and learning put together. On that system and by that faith there has been built out of the wreck of the Roman Empire the whole of our existing civilization."

The story of Moses, including the exodus across the parted Red Sea, Churchill wrote in a remarkable essay in 1931, should be taken literally. Moses was "one of the greatest human beings" who is to be associated with "the most decisive leap forward ever discernible in the human story." The Mosaic establishment of monotheism was "an idea of which all the genius of Greece and the power of Rome were incapable." Like all of Churchill's other historical speculations, this was not mere antiquarianism. He liked to repeat the phrase attributed to Disraeli that "the Lord deals with the nations as the nations dealt with the Jews."

This philosophical dimension, more than his romantic imagination, or views of how Zionism was compatible with his imperialism (as Makovsky sometimes suggests), explains Churchill's fundamental regard for Jews. But as is the case with so many other prominent aspects of Churchill's career, there are a number of inconsistencies and contradictions in his expressed attitudes and policies toward Jews and Zionism to be observed and, if possible, reconciled.

As Makovsky puts it, Churchill was "a Zionist who often abandoned Zionism." Now and then Churchill wobbled. Gilbert devotes several pages to recounting a controversial newspaper article Churchill published in 1920 commenting on the "struggle for the soul of the Jewish people" represented by the clash between Zionism and Bolshevism–the latter being understood as a "conspiratorial" Jewish movement. Both Gilbert and Makovsky note that Churchill was apparently taken in by *The Protocols of the Learned Elders of Zion*, a copy of which Churchill had recently encountered.

Makovsky's account captures in copious detail how Churchill's views of Zionism "were seemingly all over the place. At times he ignored and even scorned Zionism, and at times he vehemently endorsed it." On the surface, Churchill seems susceptible to the criticism that he picked up and set aside his Zionist sympathies to suit his convenience. Churchill strongly opposed the Peel Commission's White Paper of 1939 advocating Palestinian partition, but did nothing subsequently as prime minister to undo the White Paper. He was publicly indifferent to Zionist causes at various points in his career, but often lurched to the other extreme, sometimes making support for Zionism a "litmus test" of political rectitude.

Makovsky's narrative of Churchill's course often feels whipsawed by Churchill's constant course corrections, culminating in perplexing summaries such as this: "He felt the need to distance himself from Zionism partly, and ironically, because it was never more integral to his being." Had Churchill the amateur painter rendered his Zionism on canvas, Makovsky writes, "the final product would resemble the scattered and splattered swirls of Jackson Pollock."

The better artistic analogy for Churchill would be the neo-impressionist Georges Seurat, whose pointillist images only become clear when one steps far enough away from the canvas to take in the whole. Makovsky explains Churchill's inconsistencies chiefly as a function of the clash between his capacious romanticism and his British nationalism: His Zionism frequently had to take a back seat to Britain's national interest (not to mention his own political self-interest). But the clash between sentimentalism and national interest will explain anyone's course, while Churchill's case in this, as in so many areas, remains exceptional.

Missing is a serious treatment of the statesman's prudence, which is the crucial ingredient for evaluating Churchill's many otherwise troubling changes and inconsistencies across all aspects of his career. Churchill understood (though seldom articulated directly) that the cause of Zionism depended upon the health of Western democracy itself, the precariousness of which was the dominant focus of his statecraft from the outset of World War I. He understood that the Balfour Declaration of 1917 was inspired by wartime calculations, not unlike Lincoln's Emancipation Proclamation, and that it would be awkward to fulfill in the short term after the war, which explains his limited public engagement with it.

Gilbert's steady narrative captures this better, noting that Churchill saw the establishment of a Jewish state in Palestine to be one of his prime postwar tasks, but which had to wait until the war against Hitler was won, to the great frustration of David Ben-Gurion and other Zionists. That Churchill could have, or might have, done more on behalf of Jews during the war is not necessarily clear, even in hindsight; and in any event requires placing the issue within the larger context of Churchill's whole statecraft, which is never easy to do. Just as Lincoln often disappointed the Abolitionists (to whom 20th-century Zionists can be compared in some ways) by his measured course toward emancipation, Churchill's essential sympathy and support for Zionist ends can only be understood justly from the standpoint of the prudent statesman, of whom we rightly honor Churchill as the highest modern example. When this is done, it becomes easier to share the sentiment of a Jewish prisoner in a Soviet labor camp during the war, recounted by Gilbert: "We have no bread, but we have Churchill."

—*Weekly Standard*, June 16, 2008

Chapter 15

Beyond the Myth

The Forgotten Man: A New History of the Great Depression, by Amity Shlaes

This new book is the finest history of the Great Depression ever written. Hold on–this is supposed to be a review, not a dust-jacket blurb; but it can't be helped. Although there are several fine revisionist works about the Great Depression and the New Deal, Shlaes's achievement stands out for the devastating effect of its understated prose and for its wide sweep of characters and themes. It deserves to become the preeminent revisionist history for general readers.

The "forgotten man" theme arises from the ideological sleight of hand at the core of the New Deal. The phrase originated with the supposed "Social Darwinist" William Graham Sumner, who had in mind the taxpayer who was the forgotten third party when politicians dreamt up schemes of social improvement that depended on the forgotten man to provide the means. The New Deal turned this on its head through its portrayal of the "forgotten man" as the little guy left behind in the collapse of economic growth. Instead of being the productive citizen best left alone by government, the forgotten man of the New Deal was the lowly citizen whose salvation depended on government.

Most revisionist histories of the Depression depend on subsequent economic insights coupled with hindsight–a problem Shlaes notes early in her narrative: "Neither the standard history [that glorifies FDR and the New Deal] nor the standard rebuttal entirely captures the realities of the period." Shlaes's answer is to begin with a portrait of the 1920s that puts us inside the perspectives of the key figures of the time. "The 1920s was a great decade of true economic gains," she writes, "a period whose strong positive aspects have been obscured by the troubles that followed." Shlaes prompts the thought that the real tragedy of the Great Crash was that Calvin Coolidge had not sought re-election in 1928; he

77

could have spared us the "priggish" (Shlaes's word) personality–and social-engineering mentality–of Herbert Hoover. (Of him, Coolidge shrewdly observed: "That man has offered me unsolicited advice for six years, all of it bad.") Had we followed the course we did in the sharp recession of 1921, when Warren Harding's government let markets correct and adjust, the aftermath of the Great Crash might have been short and mild compared with what happened.

Shlaes rids us of the temptation of thinking that Hoover, had he contrived reelection in 1932, might have avoided the macroeconomic mistakes FDR made. Instead of letting markets correct, Hoover raised taxes, signed the disastrous Smoot-Hawley tariff, and inveighed against short-sellers and other ostensible market manipulators. Shlaes is not the first to observe that Hoover and FDR represented, in political scientist Gordon Lloyd's phrase, "the two faces of liberalism," but she offers rich detail to the comparison. Both men lacked confidence in markets, and Hoover's interventions between the Crash in 1929 and FDR's accession in 1933 paved the way for the New Deal: "From 1929 to 1940, from Hoover to Roosevelt, government intervention helped to make the Depression Great."

Two things propelled FDR's New Deal beyond the depredations that would have come from Hoover's social-engineering mentality: the presence of the intellectuals and political operatives whom Shlaes calls "the pilgrims," and FDR's own intellectual instability combined with his political opportunism. "The pilgrims" refers to the handful of future New Deal intellectuals, Rexford Tugwell being the most prominent among them, who made a junket to the Soviet Union in 1927 that culminated in a six-hour interview with Stalin. Here Shlaes's prose is at its understated best. She does not portray the pilgrims as crypto-Communists bamboozled by Potemkin tours, though an element of that gullibility is inescapably present. Rather she discerns the "dreamy" cast of mind that was soon to create the New Deal's belief in vague, non-Marxist central planning. "The heroes [of the USSR] were not precisely *their* heroes," Shlaes writes. "Still, the meetings had their effect. The travelers were now transformed from obscure analysts of the Soviet Union into bearers of news. . . . The conservatives were having their day, and the planners would get theirs." Giddy with excitement, the pilgrims returned to the U.S. on the steamship *Leviathan*, "and the irony of that name may not have escaped some of them."

With the election of FDR, the pilgrims had their chance. Those conservatives who lately have inclined to some sentimental affection for FDR (this includes Conrad Black and, occasionally, this writer) will be roundly disabused by the damning portrait Shlaes offers. "Roosevelt was not an ideologue or a radical," she judges, but his affinity for experimentation and improvisation yielded inconsistent and destabilizing economic policy at a time when certainty was the most needful thing. FDR's intellectual instability was terrifying in its fullness; fortunately, it was tempered by the rivalries and disagreements within his menagerie of New Dealers, and by the countervailing power of American political institutions (which prevented him from, e.g., packing the Supreme Court).

When presidential candidate Ronald Reagan remarked that "fascism was really the basis of the New Deal," liberals and the media hooted; the *Washington Post* huffed that "several historians of the New Deal period questioned by the *Washington Post* said they had no idea what Reagan was referring to." Thanks to Shlaes's book, journalists in the future will not be able to plead such ignorance: She notes that FDR's first attempt at centralized economic planning, the National Recovery Administration (NRA), owed its inspiration in part to Mussolini's Italian model. The NRA's ineffectuality could be demonstrated in a number of theoretical or technical ways, but Shlaes captures the futility of the enterprise in two magnificent sentences: "In a period of a year, 10,000 pages of law had been created [by the NRA], a figure that one had to compare with the mere 2,735 pages that constituted federal statute law. In twelve months, the NRA had generated more paper than the entire legislative output of the federal government since 1789."

But when the Supreme Court saved FDR from this folly by ruling it unconstitutional, FDR veered farther left, with punitive tax measures that deterred capital formation and investment, and prosecutions of the rich (especially Samuel Insull and Andrew Mellon) that were purely political. The result of these and other ill-conceived measures was a needlessly prolonged Great Depression.

Shlaes offers a new gloss on the old theme of how FDR used the Depression to craft the durable New Deal coalition. Here her narrative sparkles, as she recounts how FDR transformed the failures of his economic policy to his political advantage in the 1936 election. The failure of the New Deal to deliver meaningful economic growth lent paradoxical validity to FDR's class-warfare rhetoric: "Many in the country believed that the United States was actually becoming the society of social classes that Roosevelt now described in his speeches. And they responded accordingly," that is, by re-electing Roosevelt. The secret was purposely dividing people into interest groups, and pandering to enough of them to create a majority.

As the story approaches the end of the 1930s, Shlaes's most interesting subtext comes to the fore: the evolution of FDR's 1940 challenger Wendell Willkie. In the early chapters Willkie is seen as a naïve utility executive with reformist sympathies who thought he could cut deals with FDR, only to be bitterly disappointed when he was ground up along with the rest of the malefactors of great wealth. He couldn't say he wasn't warned. Insull told Willkie in 1934: "Mr. Willkie, when you are older you will know more."

Insull was right. By 1938, by which time the Depression was coming to seem permanent, Willkie had joined the Republican party, and, because of his trenchant criticisms of the New Deal, was emerging as a surprise candidate for the GOP presidential nomination. The GOP had done well in 1938, and, according to Shlaes, "the reputation of the New Deal was continuing to drop": "People were taking in the longer-term consequences of all the experiments." Willkie's themes in the campaign that followed in some ways prefigure Reagan in 1980: "I saw that we must substitute for the philosophy of distributed scarcity the philosophy of unlimited productivity," Willkie said in his kickoff speech; "I stand for the restoration of full production and reemployment by private enterprise in America." Willkie manfully attempted to reclaim the "forgotten man" theme for Republicans: "What that man wanted us to remember was his chance–his right–to take part in our great American adventure." The Gipper could hardly have put it better.

But looming in the background, Shlaes thinks, was the European war, and the Republicans' latent isolationism diluted their appeal. Although Willkie was an internationalist, FDR was a more convincing one. "As leaders and oppositions since have discovered," Shlaes writes, "war trumps everything–economics as well as politics." In the absence of the specter in Europe, Shlaes thinks Willkie might have defeated Roosevelt. Shlaes's judgment about Willkie and the 1940 election is probably correct, but it is the only thinly argued part of *The Forgotten Man*. To complete this account, more needs to be said about the cognitive dissonance that characterizes public opinion toward America's global involvement. (FDR, for example, was quietly consulting pollsters during this time to determine how far he could go with his European policy.)

Shlaes leaves it to the reader to project lessons forward to our own time. The Democratic party lived large on FDR's high-tax, class-warfare playbook for nearly two generations. The Reagan Revolution put some of it into receivership, but the impulse to tax, regulate, and plan the economy remains embedded in contemporary liberalism, with John Edwards, among others, doing his best to revive New Deal-style populism and animus against wealth. We are now so far removed from the economic ruin of the New Deal's ill-considered economic interventionism that resistance to grand central fixes for health care, global warming, or outsourcing may be on the wane. With this prospect in mind, Shlaes's book could be called *The Forgotten Lesson.*

—*National Review*, July 30, 2007

Chapter 16

The Oswald Effect

Camelot and the Cultural Revolution: How the Assassination of John F. Kennedy Shattered American Liberalism, by James Piereson.

Encounter Books, the publisher of this provocative and penetrating new book about John F. Kennedy, could scarcely contrive a more apt confirmation of its thesis about the destructive self-delusion of the left than *Time*'s cover package for the week of July 2 on "What We Can Learn from JFK."

"Americans are still trying to figure out nearly a half a century after his abbreviated presidency who Jack Kennedy really was," David Talbot's jejune thumbsucker tells us.

But whoever he was, we know he was great–or at least would have been great had he lived to fulfill his promise as "a man ahead of his time." Talbot faithfully reiterates the family/party line that "there was a heroic grandeur to John F. Kennedy's Administration," adding the latest thinly based revisionism that JFK had in mind a grand strategy to end the Cold War. In a separate piece Robert Dallek reminds us of the second part of liberalism's coda that Kennedy was committed to progress on civil rights, and the manner in which his murder helped propel the Civil Rights Act to passage has lent verisimilitude to the theme that his death amounted to a "martyrdom" for civil rights.

If we are still trying to "figure out" Kennedy after all these years, it is because, James Piereson's book argues, we so grossly distorted him in the aftermath of his death for a variety of confused and debilitating motives.

None of the eight–eight–articles in *Time*'s JFKfest, including the obligatory pro and con on whether his killing was a conspiracy, mentions the one fact that Piereson finds most salient to probing the political effects of JFK's death: JFK was murdered by an ideological Communist.

"The assassination of a popular president by a Communist should have generated a revulsion against everything associated with left wing doctrines," Piereson writes. "Yet something close to the opposite happened. In the aftermath of the assassination, left wing ideas and revolutionary leaders, Marx, Lenin, Mao, and Castro foremost among them, enjoyed a greater vogue in the United States than at any time in our history." Piereson argues convincingly that it was the reaction to the assassination itself, within the mainstream American establishment as well as among liberal intellectuals, that caused liberalism essentially to suffer a nervous breakdown.

That Kennedy was killed at the hands of a Communist should have had a clear and direct meaning: "President Kennedy was a victim of the Cold War." Everyone had reasons for averting their gaze from this fact. For Lyndon Johnson, it would have carried frightful implications for foreign policy if it turned out that Lee Harvey Oswald had links to Castro or the KGB (which Piereson suggests is remotely possible). Liberals didn't want to dwell on this fact for a mix of other reasons. In the early hours after JFK was shot, we didn't yet know of Oswald's Communist background, and the media jumped to the conclusion that Kennedy's killing must have been the work of right-wing extremists. The day after the assassination, James Reston wrote in the *New York Times* that the assassination was the result of a "streak of violence in the American character" and that "from the beginning to the end of his administration, [Kennedy] was trying to tamp down the violence of extremists from the right."

This "meme," as we would say today, so quickly took hold that it could not be shaken, even after Oswald's noxious background began to come out. Indeed, the notion of collective responsibility would be repeated five years later after Robert Kennedy was murdered by a Communist Arab radical who professed deep hatred for America. Piereson's analysis prompts the thought that the phenomenon of liberal guilt owes it origin to JFK's assassination: "Once having accepted the claim that Kennedy was a victim of the national culture, many found it all too easy to extend the metaphor into other areas of American life, from race and poverty to the treatment of women to the struggle against Communism."

Piereson's discerning eye draws out the debilitating consequence of this: It de-legitimated the great liberal tradition of incremental reform, and robbed liberalism of its optimistic patrimony and belief in progress.

Alongside the idea of the collective guilt of American society, Kennedy's assassination disoriented American liberals in several other ways. "The claim that the far right represented the main threat to progress and democratic order," Piereson writes, "was no longer credible after a Marxist assassinated an American president." In addition, Piereson reminds us of the years prior to JFK's killing, when there was an extensive literature from liberalism's premier intellectuals sneering at the far right's preoccupation with conspiracy. The right's fascination with conspiracy theories, writers like Richard Hofstadter and Daniel Bell thought, was a sign of the unseriousness of conservatism. The obsession with JFK assassination theories–which was done in part to deflect the implications of Oswald's communism–has put the shoe on the other foot: From the Grassy Knoll to Halliburton's role in 9/11, it is now the left that is consumed with conspiracies.

The genius of this book is that Piereson situates his account of the radicalization of liberalism in the 1960s within the long tradition of liberal philosophy going back to the progressive era, and it's worth its price for the second chapter alone, which offers a trenchant synoptic account of the evolution of 20th-century liberalism.

Drawing on the perceptive self-criticism of Lionel Trilling and other mid-century liberal thinkers, Piereson notes that liberalism's rationalist and progressive assumptions were too brittle to survive a tragedy on the scale of Kennedy's assassination. The assassination "seemed to call for some kind of intellectual reconstruction" on the left. Instead, the left lost its mind. As the *Time* package attests, liberalism still has not come to grips with this, preferring instead to recycle the old themes and regurgitate the conspiracy theories for the umpteenth time.

Piereson was an academic political scientist before becoming the longtime executive director of the John M. Olin Foundation in the 1980s. As is well known (especially on the left), Olin's support for conservative scholarship was instrumental to building a counter-establishment over the last generation. The Olin Foundation, in keeping with the wishes of its founder, closed down and distributed all its funds in 2005. Reading *Camelot and the Cultural Revolution*, one might have wished it had closed down sooner to release Piereson to write works such as this.

—*The Weekly Standard*, August 13, 2007

Chapter 17

A Cool Look at the Cold War

The Atlantic and Its Enemies: A History of the Cold War, by Norman Stone

The Cold War is rapidly receding in the rear-view mirror of history, with the current war (if you are a conservative) or "long twilight struggle" (if you are a liberal) against radical Islam having replaced it as the preoccupation of political leaders and intellectuals. The Left isn't as interested in disputing or revising our understanding of the Cold War as it once was. All the basic elements of the Cold War story are now well known; barring the unlikely revelation from a still-secret American or Russian source, there is seemingly not much new to say about the matter.

Given this state of affairs, is there room or need for Norman Stone's new history of the Cold War? The answer is a surprisingly strong yes. Stone, the veteran British journalist and historian, has produced an original interpretative narrative that is idiosyncratic and downright odd in places. (The British edition of the book bears a different and more suggestive subtitle: "A Personal History of the Cold War.") His chronology jumps around, requiring concentration on the part of the reader. He omits a lot of familiar greatest hits: Where are Churchill's "Iron Curtain" speech, Kennan's "long telegram" and containment doctrine, Reagan's "evil empire" speech, the Strategic Defense Initiative, and the climactic stare-down with Gorbachev at Reykjavik? Stone downplays the ideological dimension of the East-West conflict, and does not spend much time noting the Left's sympathy for Communism. The "enemies of the Atlantic" referenced in the title were not so much mendacious as idiotic. Yet it is precisely Stone's departures from the standard political-diplomatic themes that enable him to offer a fresh and provocative perspective on events we might have thought thoroughly familiar.

One of the beguiling charms of Stone's narrative is the way in which his cool, understated prose bursts from the page at piquant moments, especially when describing the defects of political leaders of the 1960s and 1970s.

The Atlantic and Its Enemies is perhaps best described as an economic and cultural history of the Cold War from a Eurocentric perspective. Although he sets up his narrative by suggesting the Cold War ought to be understood as "the War of the British Succession" (which superpower would inherit the worldwide British empire?) and gives his due to the United States ("the United States, in it all, was the great creative force"), his main focus throughout is on Europe and some of the peripheral nations of the developing world, such as Egypt, Turkey, and Chile. Although he is properly respectful of Ronald Reagan, Stone's three leading heroes are Margaret Thatcher, Charles de Gaulle, and Helmut Schmidt.

The focus on Europe is a useful complement to the bipolar approach to the Cold War more familiar to American readers. Stone takes us back to the hard winter of 1946-47, when the economy of Europe was still very weak and tenuous, with near-starvation conditions in Germany. The U.S., this time willing to step up to the challenge of holding Europe together, stepped in with the Marshall Plan, which Stone judges was "enormously successful." Whereas most narratives of the Marshall Plan tend to portray it as merely a giant Keynesian welfare-stimulus program, Stone's narrative gets into the details of how the Marshall Plan was integrated into the larger project of restoring Europe's economic foundations, creating the "European Phoenix" out of the ashes.

Today the "European project" of economic and political integration is taken for granted, even if the euro, first contemplated in the Marshall Plan days, looks a little shaky at the moment. In addition to his fine-grained details of the reconstruction of basic industries, the stabilization of currencies, and the revival of trade between European nations, Stone reminds us that making Germany respectable again was the key to the European project and the creation of the NATO alliance. The success of modern Germany was by no means assured in the late 1940s, and Stone singles out Ludwig Erhard's market liberalization, as well as that of the framers of West Germany's post-war political structure–"wise men of the Philadelphia class," Stone judges. By contrast, East Germany's status, culminating in the Berlin Wall, was a perpetual embarrassment to Communism–"a slow-acting embolism in the entire arterial system of European Communism. In that sense the West had won," even though it took more than a generation to consummate the victory.

Despite the creation of a stable Europe with a durable anti-Soviet alliance in the space of a few years after the war, the Soviets had reason for their surging confidence in the 1950s and 1960s, after Khrushchev succeeded Stalin. "Khrushchev was of just the generation to think that Communism would triumph, worldwide," Stone observes, even if it was hated in most places where it ruled and required tyranny to maintain its hold on power. Soviet high culture seemed richer than Western culture, and the Soviets were rushing to fill the vacuum in the Third World where Western empire was crumbling. For a time the Soviets seemed more technologically dynamic: Sputnik "was the calling card of Communism."

Although the U.S. rose to the challenge of Sputnik, the space race was about the only arena in the 1960s and 1970s where the U.S. bested the Soviet Union. Stone gives a mordant survey of the rot that beset the West in that period, notably the American failure in Vietnam. But as in the early chapters, Stone is at his best in describing the economic rot, as the U.S. let inflation run away and the dollar's stability collapse, with baleful consequences worldwide. Stone blames the hubris of liberal economists: "Economists of the younger generation were convinced that they were legislators for mankind, and even that they had abolished all problems. . . . The essence of the Sixties was the belief that there were easy answers, so long as grumbling old men got out of the way."

One of the beguiling charms of Stone's narrative is the way in which his cool, understated prose bursts from the page at piquant moments, especially when describing the defects of political leaders of the 1960s and 1970s. He dismisses John F. Kennedy as "a hairdresser's Harvard man," and is scarcely more impressed with Lyndon Johnson or Richard Nixon. The unraveling of America (what Paul Johnson elsewhere called "America's suicide attempt") that commenced under Johnson and Nixon left America "at its witches-of-Salem weirdest." The less said about Britain's Edward Heath the better. Stone's most splendidly contemptuous prose is reserved for Jimmy Carter: "Carter's regime symbolized the era. It was desperately well-meaning. It jogged; it held hands everywhere it went with its scrawny wife; it prayed, Baptist-fashion; it banned smoking where it could; it sent bossy women to preach human rights in places where bossy women were regarded as an affront to them." The Carter administration invited mostly contempt because Carter "was rather stupid." (Stone obviously isn't a member of the Nobel Prize committee.)

But even as matters continued to deteriorate in the U.S., both the U.S. and the U.K. were experiencing "tissue regeneration under all of this," culminating in the elections of Thatcher (who "meant business, at last") and Reagan a year later. Stone clearly esteems Thatcher the higher of the two, calling her the most able prime minister since David Lloyd George, with the ability to know "when to be Circe and when to be the nanny from hell." His reading of Reagan is fuzzier. Stone credits Reagan with having correct perception of the political and economic crisis of the moment, and with the insight and determination to challenge the Soviet Union directly, but Stone goes astray in understanding Reagan as "a Nixon with charm." Stone's overall reading of the 1980s is pitch-perfect, rebutting the liberal slogan about a "decade of greed." Although Stone judges that both the "Reagan revolution" and the "Thatcher revolution" were "something of an illusion," as government taxes and spending continued to grow despite the two leaders' intention to reverse this, he concludes that "no two decades could have been more different [than the 1970s and the 1980s]. . . . The Eighties had been a magnificent counter-attack: Just when the enemy thought it had won, its ammunition dump had exploded."

Stone thinks "the most interesting question about 1981 is why it did not foresee 1989," though, throughout, he notes the intellectual inertia of Western Soviet-watchers, himself included. (He makes several mea culpas in this regard.) Stone thinks the Afghan invasion of 1979 was the beginning of the end for the Soviet Union, a bookend of sorts with the British decision in 1947 to quit Greece, which "was the pebble, announcing an avalanche." He is unimpressed with Gorbachev, whom he calls "the last useful idiot," and though "obviously a decent man," not really a revolutionary figure as everyone liked to claim. He thinks even less of Boris Yeltsin, calling him "another of those sinister clowns whom Russian history throws up."

If Stone's narrative eschews some of the rhetorical triumphalism of other Cold War narratives, he nonetheless thinks the end of the Cold War "was an Atlantic hour" and "was quite well managed," making the 1980s "the most interesting, by far, of the post-war decades." Here and there are hints and foreshadowings of the present condition of the Atlantic world, raising the implicit question of whether our current leaders are equal in strength or ideas to those of the Reagan-Thatcher-Schmidt era. There are many other subplots (including a rollicking account of Stone's own brief imprisonment in Czechoslovakia in 1968) and themes, such as the self-inflicted debasement of European higher education, that further distinguish Stone's approach and make *The Atlantic and Its Enemies* a worthy addition to the essential Cold War canon. Add it to your shelf.

—*National Review*, July 22, 2010

Chapter 18

Who's Fascist Now?

Liberal Fascism: The Secret History of the American Left, From Mussolini to the Politics of Meaning, by Jonah Goldberg

Back during his 1976 campaign for president, Ronald Reagan made the offhand comment to *Time* that "Fascism was really the basis for the New Deal." When Reagan finally grasped the Republican nomination in 1980, Democrats gleefully retrieved that remark to use as proof of Reagan's supposed extremism. The media dutifully obliged, pressing Reagan on what he could possibly have meant with such an odd and inflammatory comment.

To the dismay of his campaign managers, Reagan defended the remark: "Anyone who wants to look at the writings of the Brain Trust of the New Deal will find that President Roosevelt's advisers admired the fascist system. . . . They thought that private ownership with government management and control *à la* the Italian system was the way to go, and that has been evident in all their writings." This was, Reagan added, "long before fascism became a dirty word in the lexicon of the liberals." The *Washington Post* was agog: "Several historians of the New Deal period questioned by *The Washington Post* said they had no idea what Reagan was referring to."

With the arrival of Jonah Goldberg's *Liberal Fascism*, neither the media nor self-satisfied liberals will be able to retreat any longer behind such a veil of ignorance. Goldberg has set out to rescue the idea of fascism from the dustbin of cartoonish epithets and restore it as a meaningful category of political thought; and, moreover, to demonstrate that contemporary American liberalism owes its origin and character to some of the same core ideas and principles that gave rise to European fascism in the first half of the 20th century.

His thesis will raise hackles, when it isn't deliberately ignored, for the reason Goldberg rightly identifies: Contemporary liberals are strangely uninterested in the pedigree of their own ideas. (When was the last time you heard a liberal discussing Herbert Croly, or even John Dewey, as a relevant source for contemporary understanding?) Instead, the left will go on deploying "fascism" as a conversation-stopper against conservatives, even though the term ought to be associated overwhelmingly with liberalism.

"In reality," Goldberg argues at the outset, "international fascism drew from the same intellectual wellsprings as American Progressivism," which was the precursor to contemporary American liberalism. And conservatism cannot be understood seriously as an offshoot or cousin of fascism.

Goldberg's analysis comes in two parts. The first task is to clear away the tangled overgrowth of misconceptions about the meaning of fascism itself. The term has long been controversial or vague among political thinkers, and its popular conception understandably colored by its Nazi incarnation. Fascism should be understood as a supercharged nationalistic statism, finding its theoretical wellsprings in Hegelian historicism, Rousseau's protean "general will," Nietzschean will-to-power, Darwinian evolution, and a smattering of the Social Gospel thrown in for good measure–all of which overturned the older liberalism of Locke, the Enlightenment, and the American Founders.

In America this soup came to boil as Deweyite "pragmatism," but despite the calm and practical associations pragmatism conjures, fascism thrives in an atmosphere of constant crisis, which only a bigger, more active state can confront.

As Goldberg makes abundantly clear, fascism is a species of revolutionary socialism, with totalitarian implications. Vicious racism is not an inherent aspect of fascism–though many American progressives, such as Woodrow Wilson, exhibited strong racist streaks–and Nazi fascism should be understood as an aberration peculiar to Germany. Mussolini, rather than Hitler, should be understood as the paradigm of fascism.

"Nazism was the product of German culture, grown out of a German context. The Holocaust could not have occurred in Italy, because Italians are not Germans," writes Goldberg. This qualification is essential to his overall argument, because he is emphatic in avoiding the charge that he is engaging in *reductio ad Hitlerum*; that is, in arguing that liberalism is fascistic, he is not trying to suggest liberals are crypto-Nazis. Nonetheless, his survey of the origin and meaning of fascism cannot get around the ways in which the Nazis appropriated and transformed fascist thought to their own uses, and as such, the extreme cases of Hitler and

Mussolini make it difficult to grasp the non-extreme case of American fascism.

Goldberg's delineation of American fascism is the second part of his analysis and the bulk of the book. He identifies three fascist episodes in modern American history: the Progressive Era (and especially World War I); the New Deal; and the 1960s.

Most historical narratives portray World War I as the end of Progressivism; Goldberg rightly sees it as its apotheosis, with its propaganda efforts, its embrace of the purifying effects of militarism, and its ruthless crushing of dissent. Wilson openly argued for redefining the American constitutional order in Hegelian and Darwinian terms, and celebrated the expansion of state power necessary to direct human progress and guide people to "mature" freedom.

Wilson and other progressives disparaged "individualism" and the market economy, and advocated ever more powerful government social and economic planning. It is here we learn that Goldberg is not the first to use the category of "liberal fascism." H.G. Wells used the term approvingly in 1932. He also (remember the date) said that progressives should seek to become "enlightened Nazis."

The New Deal, as Ronald Reagan had the imagination to perceive and the courage to declare, was America's second fascist episode. Goldberg's copious and detailed research demonstrates beyond doubt that the New Dealers themselves understood their project as wholly congruent with what they saw approvingly in Italy and Germany. Waldo Frank declared in 1934 that Roosevelt's National Recovery Administration "is the beginning of American Fascism" and the Nazis expressed their admiration and enthusiasm for FDR's program. (Hitler, in particular, praised American eugenicists.) The *New York Times* reported in 1933: "There is at least one official voice in Europe that expresses understanding of the method and motives of President Roosevelt. This voice is that of Germany, as represented by Chancellor Adolf Hitler."

America's third fascist episode was the 1960s, and especially the rise of the New Left, whose philosophy and tactics bore distinct echoes of the Hitler Youth. Goldberg cites the liberal scholar Irving Louis Horowitz, who recognized that sixties radicalism was "a fanatic attempt to impose a new social order upon the world" and, forthrightly, called it fascism of the left. Moreover, the fascist impulses of the 1960s have not yet run their course. The liberal enthusiasm for regimenting society on behalf of our own good (smoking bans, healthy eating mantras, etc.) or "for the children" (especially Hillary Clinton's style of thought in *It Takes a*

Village) represent the still-vibrant residue of the last wave of fascist enthusiasm.

"The edifice of contemporary liberalism," Goldberg argues, "stands on a foundation of assumptions and ideas integral to the larger fascist moment. Contemporary liberals, who may be the kindest and most racially tolerant people in the world, nonetheless choose to live in a house of distinctly fascist architecture."

This reference to the purported "niceness" and sincere good intent of modern liberalism raises a number of problems for which *Liberal Fascism*, despite all its splendid research and analysis, begs some important questions that, on the surface, the author does not appear to resolve.

Are we supposed to understand liberalism as a hateful and destructive thing, as we do fascism? While deploring fascism and its influence on liberalism, Goldberg draws back from the implications of equating liberal fascism with communism as a species of malignant revolutionary socialism. "Fascism was a human response to a rapidly unfolding series of technological, theological, and social revolutions," he writes. "Those revolutions are still playing themselves out"–and not just on the left. Goldberg rightly scorns some of the same tendencies he sees in certain quarters on the right, such as Pat Buchanan's nationalism and George W. Bush's compassionate conservatism. We're all fascists now, he writes in his last chapter.

Perhaps Goldberg has rehabilitated fascism a bit too much, in hopes of blunting the visceral and unreflective, but inevitable, liberal rejection of his unwelcome parallels. Goldberg goes out of his way to offer exoneration to liberals by reference to their good intentions. On the one hand, he makes clear the totalitarian temptation of liberal fascism: Hillary Clinton's "politics of meaning" speech, for example, "is in many respects the most thoroughly totalitarian conception of politics offered by a leading American political figure in the last half century." But he is quick to add that "Hillary is no Führer, and her notion of 'the common good' doesn't involve racial purity or concentration camps. . . . When I say that Hillary Clinton's ideas in general are fascist, I must again be clear that they are not evil."

This effort at balance and reasonableness may, in part, be designed to set him and the book's inflammatory title apart from the sensational, sales-oriented polemics of other conservative bestsellers of recent years. From the standpoint of the prose alone, it is notable that the wit and snark that enliven Goldberg's newspaper columns and blog posts are conspicuously missing from this sober volume. But in larger measure he has tried to diminish fascism as a mindless epithet so that readers will think harder about the deep general tendencies, both historical and philosophical, that gave rise to the phenomenon in any of its forms.

Goldberg thinks that the extreme kinds of fascism that took root in Europe never caught on in America because of an antigovernment, or antistatist, strain deeply embedded in the American character. Americans don't like to be bossed around, and would never tolerate Canadian-style health care rationing, for example. But this turns out to be the key issue of the whole book, and he unfolds it with such subtlety that casual readers will miss his treatment. Liberal fascism is not about to slam totalitarianism down on America in some *Kristallnacht*-style convulsion. But liberalism, "the organized pursuit of the desirable," *is* committed to an ever-expanding state, without any limits in principle.

The core liberal promise of delivering security and human fulfillment through state action may erode the antistatist American character with the grim effect-iveness of the drip-drip-drip of water torture, and slowly succeed in "rewriting the habits of our hearts," eventually creating "some vast North American Belgium."

"If there is ever a fascist takeover in America," Goldberg believes, "it will not come in the form of storm troopers kicking down doors but with lawyers and social workers saying, 'I'm from the government and I'm here to help!"

—*Weekly Standard*, January 2008

Chapter 19

The Right Stuff

The Conservatives: Ideas and Personalities Throughout American History,
by Patrick Allitt

Patrick Allitt has succeeded admirably in his objective of producing a compact survey of American conservative thought that will be useful to students and general readers. *The Conservatives* features excellent succinct summaries of key conservative thinkers, going back to the Founding era, ably conveying along the way the inconsistencies and internal divisions on the right. If *The Conservatives* is in some way unsatisfying, it is not Allitt's fault; the different strains of conservative thought are difficult or impossible to reconcile. The dynamic tension among conservatives is the secret of the right's success, but is hard to capture in a chronological narrative, and remains baffling to observers on the left.

The virtue of Allitt's book is its focus on American conservatism, which is distinct from European conservatism even as it draws upon European sources. Traditionalist conservatives of the Russell Kirk variety have always tried to implant Old World, Burkean-style conservatism on these shores, but it fits as insecurely as a bowler hat on a sprinter for the simple reason Allitt grasps near the middle of his account: "American conservatism has always had a paradoxical element, entailing a defense of a revolutionary achievement."

The American Revolution has been a stumbling block for some conservatives, who either deny its revolutionary character, or try to portray it as being in essential continuity with British or European political thought. (Hence Kirk's dislike of the Declaration of Independence, for example.) James Madison and Thomas Jefferson, both rightly considered 18th-century liberals, emerge in Allitt's account as "conservative innovators"–only in America would such a phrase not be considered an oxymoron–and *The Federalist*, according to Allitt, should be considered "the new nation's first conservative classic."

The inconsistency and internal divisions among American conservatives derive, Allitt thinks, from a general antitheoretical approach to the world; conservatism is more "an attitude to social and political change that . . . puts more faith in the lessons of history than in the abstractions of political philosophy." But this is another paradox: At some point, deference to history becomes an abstraction. Although Allitt discerns a suspicion of democracy and equality, and constant worry about the fragility of civil society, as recurrent themes across the broad spectrum of conservatives, his narrative offers many exceptions and contradictions of even these lowest common denominators. The social and political split between the North and South, culminating in the Civil War, is obviously the largest stumbling block to a coherent or consistent account of American conservatism. Allitt offers good accounts of the divergent streams of antebellum Northern and Southern conservatism, both suspicious of populism and skeptical of democracy. Allitt subtly conveys the intellectual and political problems of Southern conservatism, as well as the overweening elitism of some strands of Northern conservatism. There is no escaping, however, that the Civil War was "an encounter of two incompatible conservatisms."

While Allitt strives to present an unbiased or objective view of the conservative landscape, he does not shrink from making some judgment calls that will not command universal assent. He offers a long account of why "Lincoln deserves a place in the American conservative pantheon" because, in preserving the Union, Lincoln succeeded "in this most basic of all conservative tasks" while acknowledging that many conservatives (mostly southerners) then and now vehemently reject Lincoln's company.

Many more conservatives will rightly disagree with Allitt's inclusion of Theodore Roosevelt in the conservative pantheon, merely on account of his elitism, opposition to radicals, utopians, and pacifists, and his belief in the value of human struggle. T.R.'s large and admirable personality should not distract us from his anti-conservative and often demagogic progressivism that manifested itself in a cavalier attitude toward the Constitution and saw the transformation of the presidency and the birth of the modern administrative state.

With this much latitude, why not include Franklin D. Roosevelt as a conservative for having preserved capitalism?

Certain other judgments Allitt offers raise problems. "The most lasting and conservative achievement of the Federalists–one from which we still benefit today–was their role in creating a strong independent judiciary," he writes, adding that "judicial review, in effect, means judicial supremacy." Most conservatives disagree with the last part of that judgment, and have conflicting views about the first part. And do all or most conservatives agree with Tocqueville's judgment that (as Allitt

98

summarizes it) "the spread of democracy had discouraged the pursuit of statesmanship"? An adequate treatment of this difficulty is beyond the scope of this book, but it is the kind of detail that brings us back around to the complexity of attempting a broad survey of American conservatism.

Allitt gives a good account of interwar conservatism in the 20th century–figures such as Irving Babbitt, Paul Elmer More, and Albert Jay Nock–though without offering new insights into why this era of conservatism seemed so anemic. The lack of significant contemporaneous intellectual opposition to progressivism and its New Deal successor is one of the important mysteries of American history, and a crucial defect of American conservative thought.

Like most recent surveys of the right, Allitt's narrative really gets hopping in the postwar years, with the emergence of free-market intellectuals such as Hayek, von Mises, and Friedman, and the sensational arrival of William F. Buckley Jr. and *National Review*. Allitt also gives a nod to a few important conservative activists and activist organizations such as Phyllis Schlafly and the Young Americans for Freedom, and notes the centrality of the *Roe* v. *Wade* decision to the shape of modern American politics.

Of course, any narrative account of the contemporary conservative scene runs up against the problem of becoming like a Russian novel, with too many characters and subplots to keep straight. Allitt does as good a job as can be done in a book of this scope, giving generally fair and adequate treatments of the paleocons, neocons, libertarians, and the religious right.

There are some curious omissions, however: Leo Strauss and his circle get barely a mention (with the sole exception of Allan Bloom), while George Will gets two pages. While *The Public Interest* and *Triumph* receive worthy discussion, along with libertarian figures such as Ayn Rand and Murray Rothbard, there is no mention of *Reason*, the preeminent libertarian publication for many years. Possibly these and other figures and themes worthy of inclusion ended up on the cutting room floor for reasons of length, but it leaves the account less than fully complete.

Not until the very last page does Allitt confront the central issue of American conservatism: Is it, as Louis Hartz's famous thesis in *The Liberal Tradition in America* implied, merely a branch of liberalism, or something distinct and antithetical to liberalism? Allitt suggests the latter, writing that "it would be perverse [today] to voice an argument like Hartz's." But this question gets at the very heart of the fractiousness of the right, and it is by no means clear that even the main currents of conservatism represent a fundamental rejection of (or alternative to) liberalism rightly understood.

Allitt shouldn't be faulted too much for punting on this issue, or giving it perfunctory treatment. The fault lines between pro-market classical liberals and champions of community, tradition, and authority mimic, in some ways, the clash between reason and revelation that was such an important part of the story of Europe for nearly two millennia. This story now plays out in America in a new form, mostly on the right, and is just as hard to resolve or synthesize as it was at the time of Thomas Aquinas.

Patrick Allitt's inclusive history is a solid and worthy contribution to the growing literature about conservatism, but it will still leave many observers scratching their heads trying to make sense of this many-sided force in our political and intellectual life.

—*Weekly Standard*, August 2009

Chapter 20

The Churchill Test

Churchill, by Paul Johnson

Paul Johnson, who typically produces large books about large subjects (*Modern Times, A History of the American People, A History of the Jews*), has produced a very small book about a large topic: Winston Churchill. Fans of Johnson and Churchill might wish that he had written more, yet Johnson's succinct treatment still manages to introduce some little-known facts and unusual insights into the great man while offering a useful literary model for short-form biography.

Almost unnoticed, Johnson's book divides into equal halves. The first half is a brisk but not wholly conventional narrative of Churchill's life and political career up to 1940, when he became prime minister. Then Johnson's approach changes, like a composer switching from minor to major key: Instead of continuing with a pocket narrative of Churchill and the events of World War II, Johnson adopts a thematic approach, listing the 10 key "factors and virtues" that made Churchill a successful wartime leader. Many of Johnson's 10 factors are familiar—Churchill's oratory, grasp of strategy (especially airpower), relentless energy, and knack for priorities—but in Johnson's handling they add up to more than the sum of the parts.

"These ten points," Johnson concludes, "are essential to answering the question: Did Churchill save Britain? The answer must be yes. No one else could have done it."

Though Johnson is plainly a Churchill admirer, he is not without strong and occasionally harsh criticism of Churchill's character and judgments. Johnson says that Churchill was by nature "adventurous and reckless," sometimes with a "childish toy soldier mentality," and that he had "a pernicious habit" of violating departmental boundaries and speaking out of turn in cabinet. Johnson does not shrink from labeling several Churchill actions as "huge mistakes," sometimes even "foolish" or "grotesque."

These criticisms are important to note because Churchill is a peculiar provocation for many conventional thinkers, as the reaction to Johnson's treatment of Churchill makes evident. Writing in the *Washington Post*, James Mann acknowledges that Churchill "ranks as one of the 20th century's greatest wartime leaders" but still sniffs that Johnson presents "a cartoon version" of Churchill, and that Johnson wants to "explain . . . away" all of Churchill's mistakes and blunders (which is manifestly untrue, even in a hasty reading). Mann says "the match of author and subject here is a hagiography made in heaven." In the *New Republic*, Isaac Chotiner uses Johnson's book as an occasion to decry "right-wing Churchill worship" verging on "a rather sickly Anglophilia." Neither of these judgments can be derived from Johnson's text.

There is more going on here than a critical disagreement with Johnson's approach to Churchill, or even a mere dislike of Johnson's Tory leanings. Mann and Chotiner are hardly alone among center-left writers in disdaining Churchill and decrying the fondness conservatives display for him. Both Christopher Hitchens and Michael Lind have written disparagingly of the "cult of Churchill" on the right, with Lind going further to designate Churchill as the patron saint of neoconservatives, which is tantamount to saying that Churchill should be regarded as something of a devil.

This lazy disdain for Churchill reveals yet another facet of the decaying liberal mind, for Churchill ought to be as much of a hero of liberals as he is for conservatives. He was an enthusiast of Progressivism and the New Deal, and an early architect of the British welfare state. In American politics Churchill preferred Democrats to Republicans, got on well with Truman but badly with Eisenhower—indeed, he confided to several people that he preferred a Stevenson victory over Ike in 1952. (Lind's complaint against Churchill as a neocon icon is based partly on seeing it as another Straussian/Republican plot, apparently unaware that Leo Strauss was also a Stevenson supporter.)

Churchill's political philosophy, Johnson notes, was somewhat opaque; late in life Churchill told a Labour MP, "I've always been a liberal." Johnson notes that Churchill "found the center attractive," and Churchill's dislike of partisanship, manifested in his multiple party switches, makes him the ideal prototype for today's fetishists of post-partisanship. There's seldom been a better example of ending "gridlock" in government. Far from sending Churchill's bust back to London from the Oval Office, Barack Obama should have added another layer of polish and adapted the legacy to himself.

To be sure, Churchill has had significant liberal admirers: Isaiah Berlin and Arthur M. Schlesinger Jr. come to mind. John F. Kennedy was one, and was greatly disappointed that he could not lure him to the White House during Churchill's final visit to the United States in 1961. And there are a few contemporary liberals (Chris Matthews, Sen. Dick Durbin) who count themselves as Churchill fans. The most popular biography was written by William Manchester, an old school liberal, while Johnson thinks Roy Jenkins, a longtime Labour party leader, wrote the best one-volume biography (in which Jenkins says he changed his mind about Churchill in the course of his writing, coming to regard Churchill as "the greatest human being ever to occupy 10 Downing Street").

For the most part, however, liberals are happy—eager in fact—to cede Churchill as a conservative property, and beyond outliers such as Manchester and Jenkins, one looks in vain for a liberal writer treating Churchill well or at length. The left's hostility, or boredom, about Churchill has several sources, a few of them narrowly substantive (old complaints about imperialism) but mostly derived from the twin scourges of modern liberalism: egalitarianism and nihilism. No amount of liberal acts from Churchill can counterbalance his inegalitarian sentiments—and his example of human excellence. When liberals decry Churchill "hero worship" by the right, it isn't the worship that arrests them but the hero part. What rankles the critics of Paul Johnson's biography is its plain recognition of Churchill's greatness, and the "joy" (Johnson's term) of writing his life. Seeing the churlish response to Johnson's brief biography recalls the judgment of the British historian Geoffrey Elton:

When I meet a historian who cannot think that there have been great men, great men moreover in politics, I feel myself in the presence of a bad historian. And there are times when I incline to judge all historians by their opinion of Winston Churchill—whether they can see that, no matter how much better the details, often damaging, of the man and his career become known, he still remains, quite simply, a great man.

—*Weekly Standard*, May 2010

Chapter 21

Crescendo in C

The Last Lion: Winston Spencer Churchill: Defender of the Realm, 1940-1965, by Paul Reid and William Manchester

This magisterial three–volume biography of Winston Churchill, begun by William Manchester nearly 30 years ago, has at last reached completion, though the path to its finale took a circuitous trip through the wilderness, reminiscent of Churchill himself. *The Last Lion* is doubtless the most popular Churchill biography, its lyrical adulation for the subject comparable to Carl Sandburg's six-volume Lincoln biography.

A literary approach to a political figure is distinctly out of fashion in our revisionist and egalitarian age. Manchester's transparently heroic rendering of Churchill is today rejected by everyone except . . . readers. For a decade after the publication of the second volume, which took the story up to Churchill's arrival at 10 Downing Street in May 1940, readers were demanding to know when the third and final volume would appear with the abiding interest of youngsters awaiting the next Harry Potter installment. Rumors began to circulate that Manchester was having difficulty, that he was scaling back the third volume to cover just the war years, or that he was, most implausibly of all, suffering writer's block.

He took a strange detour in 1993 with a middling-sized book about the Middle Ages and early Renaissance, *A World Lit Only by Fire*, whose appalling factual errors and haphazard organization caused it to be poorly received. Then came the news in the late 1990s that, due to poor health—Manchester suffered a series of strokes—he would be unable to write the third volume. Perhaps a collaborator would be selected to complete the project; but despite a series of rumors and false starts, no successor was chosen until shortly before Manchester died in 2004, when Little, Brown announced that Manchester had at last settled on a writer to complete the last volume: Paul Reid.

No one had ever heard of Reid, a former feature writer for the *Palm Beach Post* who had taken up journalism as a second career in his late forties. He knew little about Churchill, and had never written a book before. Thus, the third and final volume is in some sense two stories: the continuation of the Churchill narrative, and the suspense drama of how it would turn out under another hand. Could a novice biographer possibly emulate Manchester's gripping but sometimes overwrought prose ("Churchill's feeling for the English tongue was sensual, almost erotic") and satisfy demanding Churchillians at the same time?

In hindsight, whatever faults and foibles Manchester may have had, his choice of Reid appears inspired. Coming to Churchill with fresh eyes, Reid has produced a volume about the climax of Churchill's career which ably captures the fullness of the story but with many departures from Manchester's style and assessment of Churchill. Reid's narrative of Churchill during and after World War II is straightforward, well written, and compelling; above all, it surmounts what would have been the likely problems of the third volume had Manchester lived to write it himself.

It turns out that Manchester did, indeed, suffer writer's block after he arrived with Churchill at Number 10, and for a simple reason: The Churchill story becomes much more difficult to tell starting in 1940, because he is now in charge of the scene rather than a prophet in the wilderness. The cast of characters enlarges, the decisions are numerous and difficult to evaluate, even now—though a legion of revisionists are on hand today to point out Churchill's shortcomings and blunders.

It is easy to see how the last third of Churchill's life was harder for Manchester to fit into the purely heroic mode of the first two volumes. The strongest aspect of those volumes—his vivid recapturing of the social and political context surrounding Churchill—was either unnecessary or inappropriate for the last volume. The "overtures" of the first two volumes—the first describing Victorian England, the second the fever swamp of Depression-era Britain—could not find their symmetrical match for the third volume. Manchester's talent as the biographical equivalent of a landscape painter became a disability when the canvas required portraiture. His muse deserted him.

Even Churchill's unabashed champions—of whom I am one—sometimes find Manchester's treatment out of proportion, or incommensurate with his true greatness. Manchester thought him the greatest Englishman since King Arthur (or since Disraeli, he says in the second volume)—an odd comparison since Arthur is partly a mythical figure while Churchill is a real one. Not satisfied with King Arthur, Manchester also compared Churchill to King David and Leonardo da

Vinci, while adding the infelicitous judgment that "he had the temperament of a robber baron."

Manchester rightly offered that "an American is struck by the facility with which so many British intellectuals slight the man who saved their country." Yet he comes close to doing much the same thing with the unconscious way he embraces an essentially historicist approach to Churchill himself. Manchester's most questionable assessment is that Churchill is to be explained and understood as a figure emanating from the "parochial grandeur" of the Victorian era, that his greatness in the struggle against Hitler is due precisely to his being wedded to obsolete, even reactionary values. In fact, without Hitler to summon "enormous stores of long-suppressed vitality within him," it is not clear Manchester would have found Churchill interesting or admirable. In many other respects, Manchester sides with the current conventional wisdom that Churchill was an unthinking racist, imperialist, and anti-Communist.

Churchill's Victorian roots are what make Churchill, for Manchester, the *last* lion, whose like we can't expect to see on the world stage again. But it is an all-too-easy trope: Peter Canellos called Senator Edward Kennedy the *Last Lion* in his 2010 biography. Moreover, the suggestion that Churchill is some kind of remnant of a bygone age does readers a disservice. To be sure, Churchill had his own doubts about the possibilities of heroic virtue and high statesmanship in the 20th century. But for all of Manchester's fulsome admiration for Churchill and his magnificence in describing Churchill's life, his premise is wrong. Roy Jenkins has said that explaining Churchill as a product of Victorian aristocracy is "unconvincing. . . . Churchill was far too many faceted, idiosyncratic and unpredictable a character to allow himself to be imprisoned by the circumstances of his birth." And another biographer, John Lukacs, adds: "Contrary to most accepted views we ought to consider that [Churchill] was not some kind of admirable remnant of a more heroic past. He was not The Last Lion. He was something else."

The "something else" at the root of Churchill's greatness in 1940 derived not from his being a *Victorian* man, but from his being, in a larger sense, an *ancient* man—the kind of "great-souled man" contemplated by Aristotle, among other classical authors. Manchester doesn't go back far enough in explaining Churchill, and deprives readers of reflecting on the eternal nature of courage, greatness of soul, and practical judgment that are the summa of statesmanship in any age.

Paul Reid's summary judgment in this third volume is more sound: "He may have been born a Victorian," writes Reid, "but he had turned himself into a Classical man. He did not live in the past; the past lived on in him." This is just one, though the most important, of Reid's departures from Manchester's Churchill. And while Reid has produced a more restrained and disciplined narrative, it is nonetheless stirring reading because of the subject matter. Reid's contribution is worthy of a place among the best Churchill books. Despite the subtle confusions and runaway grandiosity of Manchester's first two volumes, they remain resplendent reads—so long as readers remember not to take the "last" part of the title literally.

As Reid reminds us, Churchill said that the British people had "the lion heart." Churchill himself only supplied "the roar." So long as the British, or any, people still have a lion heart, there will be statesmen capable of giving a suitable roar.

—*Weekly Standard*, March 2013

Chapter 22

Giant Tennis Shoes

The World of the John Birch Society: Conspiracy, Conservatism, and the Cold War, by D.J. Mulloy

Populism, that ever-lurking and always problematic phenomenon in American politics, is especially galling to liberals when it breaks from the right, as it has done during the last few years in the form of the Tea Party. Conservative populism disorients and frightens liberals (almost as much as the Republican establishment does), such that liberals find it necessary to make out conservative populism to be "extremist" and to magnify its potential threat to democracy.

Fifty years ago, the liberal bugbear was the John Birch Society, which D. J. Mulloy, who teaches history at Wilfrid Laurier University in Canada, thinks is the trailblazer and blueprint for today's Tea Party. His book doesn't really bear the weight of this argument, which was probably added for the purpose of lending it some kind of contemporary relevance. Despite some superficial parallels (*Eisenhower is a Communist! Obama is a Muslim! Impeach Earl Warren! Impeach Obama!*), the differences are more important, starting with the fact that today's diffuse Tea Party is largely a spontaneous populist movement without clear leaders, while the John Birch Society was a focused and more hierarchical organization that owed its origin and staying power to the peculiar genius and drive of its founder, Robert Welch.

The John Birch Society is a worthy topic on its own, and while the society has made appearances in many histories of the 1960s and the Cold War era, Mulloy's is the first in-depth scholarly history concentrating on the Birch Society by itself.

The John Birch Society could be said to have formed out of the ashes of Joseph McCarthy's self-immolation, when Robert Welch, a person of considerable talent and brilliance who enjoyed a successful business career in candymaking (we owe Sugar Daddies and Junior Mints to his company), seized upon the story of John Birch, an American soldier who was killed in August 1945 by Chinese Communists—making him, supposedly, the first American casualty of the Cold War.

In 1958, Welch, a Republican who had unsuccessfully sought office in Massachusetts earlier in the decade, recruited a small circle of his business associates to found the John Birch Society. Some of Welch's business contacts were men of prominence and consequence, such as Fred Koch, patriarch of today's Koch brothers, and William Grede, former president of the National Association of Manufacturers. The "national council" of Welch's new group was no assembly of fringe yahoos.

Nonetheless, the early Birch Society did combine two traits that marked it out for the fringe: its bent for the kind of sweeping conspiracy theorizing that explained *everything*, and what today we might call "viral marketing." Welch's central idea was that it was "not possible to lose so much ground, so rapidly, to an enemy so inferior, by chance or stupidity." There had to have been collaboration from inside our own government, a deliberate slow-motion surrender—nay, "treason" itself.

The earliest version of Welch's schemata was a longish "letter"— eventually growing to 60,000 words in later iterations—informally titled "The Politician." Privately but widely circulated by Welch, it contained the extraordinary charge that President Dwight D. Eisenhower was a "dedicated, conscious agent" of the Communist conspiracy to overthrow the United States. And not just Ike, but everyone around him was in on the game, including Secretary of State John Foster Dulles and his brother, CIA director Allen Dulles. It was turtles all the way down, if you know the old apocryphal line attributed to Bertrand Russell. It was also preposterous.

But it was brilliant marketing. As Mulloy writes, "Certainly no one could accuse [Welch] of lacking ambition." Although circulated "confidentially," the message of "The Politician" caught on. Especially with liberals. While membership of the Birch Society never exceeded more than 100,000 people at its peak, liberals in the early 1960s were certain they were seeing the second coming of McCarthyism. Journalists jumped to attention, making sure they wouldn't miss sounding the alarm.

In a supreme irony, California attorney general Stanley Mosk issued a breathless report about the threat the Birch Society posed to democracy that, he said, was merely his "personal observations," but which was regarded as authoritative since it came from the state's chief law enforcement officer. McCarthy would have been proud. (It was the Mosk report, by the way, that originated the popular phrase that right-wing extremists included a lot of "little old ladies in tennis shoes.") Mulloy writes that the John Birch Society was thought to be "on the verge not only of taking over the Republican Party and propelling a dangerous 'extremist' into the White House, but also of being a threat to the very foundations of American democracy itself, and perhaps even enabling the rise of fascism in the United States."

This kind of reaction from the media and the liberal establishment guaranteed that the Birch Society would prosper. Throughout the next decade, Welch displayed a consistent P. T. Barnum streak, maintaining a fever pitch with periodic "major announcements" of new insights into the latest dimensions and tactics of the Communist conspiracy.

While the deeply conspiratorial paranoia of Birch Society analysis was ultimately its undoing, starting in the late 1960s, some of the political analysis that Welch and others at the Birch Society produced was cogent and sophisticated. Welch was equivocal about the Vietnam war at the outset, thinking the United States was being lured into a trap and making a mistake in bailing out the colonial legacies of France and Great Britain. And while he criticized the Civil Rights Act of 1964, for reasons similar to those of Barry Goldwater, Welch nonetheless argued for desegregation in the South and worked to expunge any expression of racism in the Birch Society. Mulloy notes that the common charge that the Birch Society was anti-Semitic is wrong and that the image of the society as a hotbed of fascism is badly overwrought.

The Birch Society posed significant problems for Republicans and for the nascent conservative movement. Mulloy goes into detail about Welch's interactions with William F. Buckley, who dealt carefully with Welch in part because many of *National Review*'s early financial backers were Birch Society supporters. Buckley cleverly argued that Welch was "an optimist," that the problems of the West were much more serious and deep-seated than what a practical conspiracy could explain. But Russell Kirk had the best riposte: "Eisenhower's not a Communist—he's a golfer."

Buckley would later take a harder public line against the Birch Society, a move that cost *National Review* readers and supporters, but which also began the slow marginalization of the society. (Welch struck back years later, charging that Buckley's effete "ivory-tower" conservatism was useless and that if Buckley had not existed, Moscow would have invented him.) The society's marginalization was not accomplished, however, before its prominence complicated Barry Goldwater's 1964 presidential campaign and, to a lesser extent, Ronald

Reagan's first campaign for governor of California in 1966. Despite being urged by Buckley and other conservatives to repudiate the Birch Society, Goldwater thought he could not afford to alienate the group and its sympathizers.

While the Birch Society's stylings were an albatross for Republicans, let me suggest something Mulloy doesn't entertain: Liberals *loved* the John Birch Society—almost as much as Moscow must have loved it. Liberals secretly enjoy being terrified of right-wing-extremist threats for much the same reason so many moviegoers thrill to horror/slasher movies: They like the *frisson* of having strident opponents whom they don't think they have to take seriously, especially if they can project the fringe as representing the mainstream of their political opposition.

Mulloy's generally straight and unbiased account of the Birch Society falls into this familiar rubric on either end of the main body of his narrative. He thinks the John Birch Society, rather than being mostly a sideshow, "played an essential role in the revitalization of conservatism both as a political philosophy and as a vehicle for the attainment of practical political power in the United States." Does anyone still revere or study Robert Welch as an icon or thinker comparable to James Burnham, Russell Kirk, or William Buckley? Is it really plausible that the conservative movement would not have made the progress it did without the Birch Society? The Tea Party, Mulloy thinks, represents "a revival of sorts" for the John Birch Society, which misses the distinction that the Birch Society depended almost entirely on the leadership of Robert Welch and elected very few people to public office, while the Tea Party, which has no figure remotely comparable to Welch, has succeeded in winning a number of significant races (as well as committing a number of blunders).

Like many histories of conservatism written by nonconservatives, *The World of the John Birch Society* treats the ideas of conservatism lightly or not at all. For all of the interesting detail in this narrative, Mulloy's strained interpretive conclusion will leave many readers puzzled about how the conservative movement actually thrived and prospered in the aftermath of the Birch Society's shooting star.

—*Weekly Standard*, September 2014

Chapter 23

Leading Hearts

The American Presidency: An Intellectual History, by Forrest McDonald

Certain Trumpets: The Call of Leaders, by Garry Wills

The troubled public mind is increasingly fixed on the idea of "leadership." The decline of religious and other mediating institutions has consequently magnified the political dimension of leadership well beyond its reasonable limits, especially for the person and office of the American president. The apotheosis—and nadir—of this phenomenon was reached in the campaign of 1992, in the form of the Ross Perot movement, and especially in the three-way debate in Richmond that resembled a *Donahue* show. This was the episode where President George Bush was stymied by a young questioner who wondered whether Bush could empathize with his "needs."

Having replaced a patrician president with one who says he "feels our pain," we are now watching this self-styled empathic chief executive get hoist by his own petard. But Bill Clinton is merely an egregious example of the now-typical practice in American politics of inflating the people's expectations about the capabilities of political leadership. This trend has been unfolding for many years, and could yet prove to be the undoing of the presidency regardless of the occupant. Such is one of the sober conclusions suggested by Forrest McDonald's magisterial intellectual history of the presidency.

McDonald's book should be regarded as the third in a trilogy of indispensable books about executive power, the other two being Harvey Mansfield's *Taming the Prince* (1990) and Jeffrey Tulis's overlooked 1987 masterpiece, *The Rhetorical Presidency*. Where Mansfield argued that executive power paradoxically secures free government by adopting some characteristics of tyranny, Tulis traced the way changes in presidential rhetorical practice over the decades have corrupted our constitutional order.

For his part, McDonald, long regarded as at least a libertarian fellow traveler, thinks that "the presidency has been responsible for less harm and more good, in the nation and in the world, than perhaps any other secular institution in the world." But McDonald's researches leave him "not sanguine" about the future of the presidency and our republic, and he "does not see how anyone who lived through the 1992 presidential election could be."

McDonald, professor of history at the University of Alabama, is the ideal person to shed light on the irony that prompted him to write this book in the first place: the ideological split over "whether the enormous growth of the responsibilities vested in the American presidency has been necessary, practical, or desirable." In recent decades, ideological perspectives on this question have reversed. During the New Deal and after, big government liberals strongly favored the aggrandizement of executive power, while conservatives deplored it and favored congressional and judicial power. Then, with Johnson and Nixon, liberals discovered the "imperial presidency," while even more recently conservatives have come to champion executive power against the excesses of the "imperial Congress." (Terry Eastland's 1992 *Energy in the Executive* is the pre-eminent example of this.)

McDonald is a historian, not a political scientist, so he eschews writing a brief for either side. But his intellectual history of the presidency sheds light on many aspects of government power that both sides argue incessantly about, from the struggle to direct foreign policy to the battle to control the budget and the bureaucracy. For example, McDonald explains how inter-branch conflicts over foreign policy and the withholding of information from Congress under the doctrine of "executive privilege" began with the presidency of George Washington.

Although McDonald avoids explicitly taking sides in the executive-versus-legislative branch contest, he nonetheless displays a subtle partisanship on the larger question of the proper size and scope of government. Government today, he recognizes and deplores, has become "a huge, amorphous blob, like a creature out of science fiction." The White House has itself become bureaucratized along with the rest of government, to the point that neither the president nor the Congress truly "govern" as that idea was understood by the Framers.

McDonald does not take up the various suggestions for institutional reform of the presidency, such as cabinet government under a quasi-parliamentary system (which was popular with some reformers, such as

Lloyd Cutler, in the 1980s). As McDonald sees it, the central problem with the presidency—and government as a whole—is that popular expectations of government have come to exceed its capacity to meet those expectations. Leadership in the cause of expanding government was easy back when statist objectives were arguably within the capacity of government to deliver. Today, Congress increasingly enacts, and the executive tendentiously administers, unenforceable or profligate laws. Attempts at reform usually make matters worse; McDonald has an excellent discussion of the 1974 Budget Act and how it has made fiscal policy even more irresponsible and uncontrollable. Unfortunately, there is only a brief account of Nixon's attempt to gain mastery of the bureaucracy in 1973, which was quickly aborted by Watergate but which may have been the last serious chance for a president to assert control of our administrative state.

McDonald limits himself to history and does not take on the awesome question of what *kind* of leadership is necessary to reduce people's expectations and shrink the state. Garry Wills is obviously not the person to answer this great question, but he usually has some interesting things to say, even when he is flat wrong or up to mischief (which is most of the time). In *Certain Trumpets: The Call of Leaders*, Wills attempts to get at the thing in itself by examining leaders and "antitypes" across a wide spectrum of vocations and callings. Wills glosses over and dismisses the two most popular notions of leadership— the Periclean "great man" school and the Dale Carnegie "winning personality" school—in favor of a more serviceable three-part understanding. Leaders, says Wills, cannot lead without *followers* and a *goal* to aim for. Goals with some kind of *moral dimension*, he adds, provide the clearest and most compelling possibilities for leadership.

This understanding might seem simple or simple-minded, yet it is fitting for a time when many invocations of the need for "leadership" come off as clichéd precisely because the idea of leadership has been cut loose from clear ends to serve. Leadership has been made into a disembodied virtue not dissimilar to the vacuous meanings of the words *caring, concern,* or *commitment* as they are used in contemporary discourse. A concrete example that Wills himself would not trumpet is the reason why the president has been known for 50 years as the "leader of the free world." The free world followed the United States because we had fairly clear goals and a reasonably consistent policy. But under the direction of Bill Clinton, Warren Christopher, and Strobe Talbott, "American leadership" is fast becoming an oxymoron.

Some of the predictable people (for Wills) show up in his pantheon: Lincoln, FDR, George Washington, Napoleon, Pope John XXIII, Martin Luther King Jr. But among Wills's "certain trumpets" are a fair number of fluegelhorns, thin reeds, and kazoos. For instance, Andrew Young as a diplomatic leader? As with most of Wills's efforts, there are some acute judgments and observations scattered widely through the pages of the book. *Certain Trumpets* is best in its criticisms of the leadership qualities (or lack thereof) of several "antitypes," especially Clark Kerr, General George MacClellan ("MacClellan, in effect, spent his whole war dressing up for a battle he never attended."), GM's Roger Smith, and even Madonna. His analysis of Adlai Stevenson's defects might well apply to Jack Kemp: "Stevenson felt that the way to implement his noble ideas was to present them as a thoughtful idealist and wait for the world to flock to him."

But some of Wills's comparisons misfire and reveal his fondness for statism. Nancy Reagan and her "Just Say No" crusade are held up to ridicule next to Eleanor Roosevelt and *her* brand of do-goodism. Regardless of how one regards the war on drugs, at least Nancy Reagan's slogan appealed to a virtue—self-restraint—that is much in need at the moment, while Eleanor Roosevelt, were she on the scene today, would strike most people as a sanctimonious busybody. A more just comparison, because the circumstances and time frame are more equal, might be Nancy Reagan and Hillary Clinton; in such a contest, it is not clear that Nancy Reagan's style of leadership would come out on the short end. And here and there, Wills verges on a blooper: His comparison of King David to Fidel Castro seems a bit infelicitous, even before the latest round of the "refugee regatta" commenced.

Still, Wills does provide a helpful clue about our times, although he would not acknowledge it as such. He asserts that what we have today is not a shortage of leaders or would-be leaders, but rather a shortage of followers. "We do not lack leaders," he writes. "Various trumpets are always being sounded. Take your pick. We lack sufficient followers." If true, this is good news, because it suggests that individualism may be ascendant. People who are less eager to jump in line behind some "leader" just might be inclined to take responsibility for thinking and doing for themselves.

Perhaps this is the reason for the ambivalence about public attitudes toward contemporary presidents that McDonald notes. We say we want strong, activist presidents, but we also *distrust* strong, activist presidents. If Wills is right that followers are a thinning herd, the "leadership void" we hear bemoaned might well be regarded as society's equivalent of "gridlock" on Capitol Hill. Gridlock, after all, as REASON readers and other anti-statists know, is a *good* thing because it prevents the government from piling stupidity on top of idiocy. All in all, stuffing a mute in the leadership trumpet may not be such a bad idea. Bill Clinton should try it with his saxophone, and learn by analogy.

—*Reason*, January 1995

Chapter 24

Reversing Discrimination

Equality Transformed: A Quarter-Century of Affirmative Action, by Herman Belz

Civil Rights Under Reagan, by Robert Detlefsen

Racial Preference and Racial Justice: The New Affirmative Action Controversy, edited by Russel Nieli

Reflections of an Affirmative Action Baby, by Stephen L. Carter

Amidst all the bright prospects that Alexis de Tocqueville beheld in *Democracy in America*, he could see that race—especially the destiny of the black race—would prove to be the great stumbling block of American democracy. The racial question was "the most formidable evil threatening the future of the United States." Not only did Tocqueville doubt that blacks and whites would ever live on a footing of equality anywhere in the world; he also thought "that the matter will be still harder in the United States than anywhere else." The law can be changed, but more difficult to change are the mores of the people.

The goal of a harmonious pluralism rooted in the American proposition about natural right—the "self-evident truth" that "all men are created equal"—is in a sense unnatural. It is an attribute of human social behavior that different kinds of people prefer their own. The preference for one's own, combined with the fear of others and the inherent competition for scarce economic resources, provides the natural basis for racial, ethnic, and religious rivalries. A regime dedicated to individual liberty will likely find incongruous the task of getting the races to mingle voluntarily, notwithstanding a central commitment to equal rights.

America, more than any other regime, takes seriously the idea of the law as teacher. The Civil Rights Act of 1964 can be viewed both as the culmination and the reinforcement of the deepening influence of the principle of equal rights. The act reflected the progress of America and was intended as the crucial stepping-stone for further substantial progress

119

in achieving America's goal of a colorblind society. Our brightest statesmen have held no illusions about how fast and how far this goal might be realized. Recall Lincoln, who spoke of the "deepening influence" the principle of equal rights would have on America over time, even though it would be "never perfectly attained."

Conservatives and libertarians disagree vigorously about whether the Civil Rights Act is consistent with the principles of limited government. (Can government rightly seek to regulate—or forbid—private discrimination?) But most believe, as Herman Belz argues in *Equality Transformed*, that the Civil Rights Act was consistent with the principles of individual natural rights and equality before the law. The well-known problem, which Belz painstakingly recounts, is that the judiciary has inverted the plain meaning of the Civil Rights Act and imposed race-conscious preferential policies.

Harvey Mansfield observes in his contribution to *Racial Preference and Racial Justice* that it may be possible to impose perfect justice, but that people may not be in a mood to live together when you are finished. Mansfield is merely echoing Tocqueville, who wrote that "some despot...might perhaps force the races to mingle." The judiciary has arguably become Tocqueville's despot, imposing policies that lack the political legitimacy of those that have been generated through the deliberation of the legislative process.

It is not so much that civil rights law has tried to push people too far, too fast, as it is that affirmative action has advanced in a clandestine and underhanded way toward a redistributive goal that a majority of Americans reject. Preferential treatment obviates the language in the Civil Rights Act expressly forbidding quotas and preferential treatment. (Justice Antonin Scalia remarks in one of his dissents that the Civil Rights Act is written with "a clarity which, had it not proven so unavailing, one might well recommend as a model of statutory draftsmanship.") This lack of political legitimacy has contributed mightily to making affirmative action the most explosive issue in American politics today, and has, if recent opinion polls are a reliable guide, actually undermined the moral authority of the civil rights movement.

The controversy over affirmative action has rendered the inherently difficult topic of race even more difficult. Stephen Carter, a professor of law at Yale, notes in his *Reflections of an Affirmative Action Baby* that not only is it hard to hold an honest conversation about affirmative action, it is even hard to hold an honest conversation about the reasons why it is hard to talk about affirmative action.

120

Because affirmative action lacks political legitimacy, its supporters have an interest in avoiding a straightforward debate about it. In part this must be because they know that preferential policies are inconsistent with the American principles of equality before the law, and that a vigorous debate would expose this contradiction. Hence the defense of affirmative action, as Carter observes, has "slipped its moorings," shifting from an argument about corrective justice and equality to an argument about "diversity." Affirmative action is necessary, the new argument runs, to provide representation for the "points of view" of excluded groups. This makes it easier to level the charge of racism, and all the other new "isms" of the moment, from the plausible sexism to the implausible "ageism." What? You oppose affirmative action? You must be a racist or sexist, for to oppose affirmative action is to oppose "diversity."

This development Carter views with great alarm, since its premise is that skin color determines, or should determine, what views a person of each given color and ethnicity should have. This view not only reinforces stereotypes; it requires stereotypes. Blacks who do not toe the "party line," as Shelby Steele has put it, are branded as "traitors" by civil-rights leaders, because their true diversity of views calls into question the premise behind the "diversity" brigade. (Steele, a professor of literature at San Jose State University, was among the first black liberals to dissent on affirmative action, in his 1990 book *The Content of Our Character*.)

Carter is taken aback, for instance, by NAACP Executive Director Benjamin Hooks's reference to Glenn Loury's views as "treasonous," and he devotes a great deal of time discussing Clarence Thomas and his nomination to the U.S. Court of Appeals for the D.C. Circuit. (The book was published before Thomas was named to replace Supreme Court Justice Thurgood Marshall.) Carter notes that Thomas's "principal sin" was combining black skin with conservative views. For black groups to have opposed Thomas for the Court of Appeals, Carter argues, "would have been reverse discrimination with a vengeance."

The self-censorship of the affirmative-action debate swings both ways, however. Opponents of affirmative action also tend to avoid straightforward discussion of the issue. There are several reasons for this. They are, of course, afraid of being called racist.

But more significant is that a basic trend of modern American politics—interest-group liberalism—offers easy encouragement to avoid dealing with the issue on a fundamental level. Modern American politics has practically ceased to debate any issue on the level of fundamental principle, preferring instead the comfortable give-and-take servicing of constituency-group demands.

Hence, even many conservative Republicans would rather strike some kind of deal on civil rights than engage in a candid debate that would reveal the deep and serious divisions within American society over the principles of equality of opportunity versus equality of result. (One of the virtues of Belz's book is its account of how the Nixon administration actively expanded the use of quotas and preferential treatment, hoping for political advantage among blacks, even as Nixon gave speeches condemning quotas.)

It is not a coincidence that supporters of affirmative action would turn to the diversity argument. It represents, in a profound sense, the *reductio ad absurdum* of interest-group liberalism. When government organizes itself to minister to discrete special-interest groups (farmers, retirees, defense contractors, exporters, and so forth), we should not be surprised when "discrete and insular minorities" (the designation repeatedly used by the judiciary starting with the *Carolene Products* case in 1938) step up to the table for their share of the pie. But interest-group liberalism is especially ill-suited to the politics of race because it legitimizes exactly the kind of racial spoils system that the American principle of equal individual rights stands against.

To be sure, some political systems try to solve racial and ethnic problems by taking explicit account of race and ethnicity, dividing political power according to some proportional formula. But woe unto the nation—Lebanon and Yugoslavia today, India, perhaps, tomorrow— where this balance comes apart. Some cultures are open to the possibility of assimilation. The American experiment—the "melting pot"—rests on a higher principle. As with the principle of religious liberty (which is above and distinct from mere religious *toleration*), the American solution to the problem of race and ethnicity transcends mere assimilation by pointing to universal principles of individual rights which all men are bound to respect.

Affirmative action and the diversity argument, then, represent a repudiation of the American principle of equality. And in the end that repudiation will be as harmful to minorities as to society as a whole. Belz concludes that "the struggle to define American equality will determine whether the United States will remain a free society." A debate of this kind must be joined at a fundamental level. Opponents of affirmative action will succeed in a positive reform—instead of merely exploiting racial resentment in the manner of Jesse Helms's notorious television commercial about a white losing a job on account of a minority quota— only by reclaiming the moral high ground on the basis of equal individual rights. A principled rhetoric of equality would not only put an end to

122

preferential policies that treat equal people unequally but would also rescue civil rights from its present course of becoming an explicit racial spoils system.

The Reagan administration attempted with only mixed success to move in this direction, and this attempt is well narrated in Robert Detlefsen's *Civil Rights Under Reagan*. That attempt, of course, faced strong political opposition. But Detlefsen also describes how big business—a supposed bastion of Republican sentiment—vigorously resisted the administration's efforts to eliminate affirmative action.

Big business has learned to live with quotas, and feared, with justification, that the elimination of government-mandated quotas would expose employers to disparate-impact liability on the one hand, or reverse-discrimination liability on the other. But there is another, even lower rationale for this craven position: Affirmative action is anticompetitive. Smaller firms have more difficulty complying with federal affirmative-action requirements.

These difficulties aside, both Detlefsen and Belz make clear that a real deficiency of the Reagan administration's approach to civil rights was its failure to articulate clearly and forcefully the principle of equality and individual rights. The administration failed as well to articulate a positive vision of how a genuine regime of equal rights and economic liberties (the true basis of equal opportunity) would benefit minorities—a failure that was strongly criticized by among others, Clarence Thomas.

Belz, Detlefsen, and the authors on both sides of the question collected by Nieli do a thorough job of exposing the political and legal morass affirmative action has become. The debate will ultimately be settled in the political and legal arena. But political and legal analysis is not fully sufficient for thinking about the issue. There is a social and cultural dimension that must be treated as well.

Carter's very thoughtful *Reflections of an Affirmative Action Baby* adds this much needed perspective. Carter opens this forthright and personal book by declaring that he got into law school because he is black. Although he supports affirmative action, he is clearly aware, from his own experience, that it attaches a stigma to its beneficiaries. As a policy matter, affirmative action targeted at would-be professionals in the black middle-class benefits those least in need of help. Carter senses a shakeout is coming, with the end of affirmative action near—an end he would seem to welcome.

Otherwise, Carter sees the strong possibility that civil rights will lose the moral high ground as a result of the pernicious "diversity" gambit. The erosion of standards in the name of diversity will hurt all minorities in the end. He agrees with the critics who believe racism is an overused and often irresponsible term, analogous to the use of communism as a term of opprobrium in the 1950s.

In the end, Carter agrees with Shelby Steele that racism is a receding force in America, still present, but "no longer the all-encompassing force it once was, and it no longer holds the entire black race in desperate thrall." Carter knows he is likely to be labeled a "black conservative," a label he considers the ultimate stigma, indistinguishable from the lunatic fringe. He goes to great lengths to establish his liberal bona fides—he favors higher taxes and opposes the death penalty—but he senses that his protests will be to little avail.

At other points, his honest open-mindedness gets the best of him. He says perhaps we should try school choice, and he embraces the libertarian view that, at least in the professions, market forces will over time punish the willfully discriminating employer. Equally important, Carter takes seriously the views of black conservatives such Thomas Sowell, Glenn Loury, and especially Clarence Thomas, and he devotes no amount of effort offering advice to conservatives and Republicans on how to treat civil-rights issues more effectively. His most important point is that blacks hold their destiny in their own hands and must commit themselves to achieve any standard, thereby becoming "simply too good to ignore."

Carter stakes out a much needed moderate position between those who would exploit affirmative action politically by inflaming racial resentment and those in the civil-rights establishment who wish to maintain the political utility of racism by expanding its definition to justify huge new remedial claims. It may be, as Carter writes and Tocqueville thought, that "the minefield of racial politics is far too difficult to negotiate." But we have come a long way from Tocqueville's fear that the legacy of slavery could only issue in open racial warfare. Lincoln spoke of "the better angels of our nature." The issue of race relations and civil rights will require a full measure of "the better angels of our nature" if we are to continue on our way toward a colorblind society.

—*Reason*, December 1991

Chapter 25

Power to the People—Again

Populism and Elitism: Politics in the Age of Equality, by Jeffrey Bell

Jeff Bell is probably dying to write the sequel to this book.

Within days of its official release in May, our jaunty vice president launched *l'affaire* Murphy Brown and his attack on Hollywood and media "elites." And Bell's book is a virtual subtext to the Ross Perot phenomenon—the rise of which Bell anticipates in one passage. If being able to say "I told you so" is truly among life's most sublime pleasures, Bell should be sporting a big grin right now.

Abstracted from these fortuitous events, however, this is an odd book. It is reminiscent of John Adams's observation that the Declaration of Independence "contains nothing that wasn't hackneyed two years before" in the Continental Congress. *Populism and Elitism* advances the usual take on liberal elitism, "values" politics, the 1960s, and the causes of the constipated Republican realignment. Bell even includes a retail version of Francis Fukuyama's "end of history" thesis.

Political sophisticates would be hasty, however, to dismiss *Populism and Elitism* for being either obvious or pedantic. A close reading of the key passages reveals a layering of subtlety and careful distinctions. Bell suggests that the real division between populism and elitism is not so much ideological class conflict but temperament: Populists have confidence in the people's capacity to set social and political standards and make important decisions about how to run their lives, while elitists believe the people are incompetent to do so and wish to define the parameters of social and political life themselves. The elite, in other words, desire to be a de facto National Bureau of Standards and Practices. Hence, elitists exist across the political spectrum.

The most powerful elites—in entertainment, in the media, in higher education—are of course liberal or statist. This provides the overlay for the Quayle project. Bell devotes much of this book to explaining why the liberal elites have not been chastened by the poundings their values have taken in recent national elections.

Bell's book is important because his intended audience—the Republican leadership elite (one might call it the Busheoisie)—doesn't have the first clue about most of his key themes. For a party and an administration of ambition without purpose, Bell provides a useful reality check.

The fundamental fact of our time, for Bell, is that our political culture is still working out the divisions generated by the upheavals of the '60s. It is a mistake, Bell's argument implies, to suppose that the Democratic Party and its liberal elites face an irremediable crisis on account of recent drubbings in national elections and are therefore destined to follow the recent path of the British Labour Party, which plans to cut its special-interest ties to labor unions and disavow explicit socialism. Bell provides a useful reminder that the end of radical socialism does not entail the end of egalitarianism or the politics of equal result. But this battle will be fought not on the old familiar ground of economic policy but in the fever swamps of "values." In this arena, the liberal elites are endlessly resilient.

It is astonishing that the party that won the last national election through an appeal to "values" does not have a better grasp of this. Although Republicans are adept at running on "values," they fully appreciate neither Bell's insight into the divide between elitism and populism nor the opportunity open to them were they to capitalize rightly on populism.

This isn't to suggest that Bell buys into the simple "us vs. them" theme that Republicans seem to think they can exploit forever at four-year intervals. Bell understands that the liberal elites may succeed in undermining conservative populist sentiment over time through the relentless crusade to establish—*wait for it*—"moral relativism" as the preeminent principle in American society.

Although there is little new to say about the worn-out subject (Bell makes the obligatory nod toward Allan Bloom in his analysis), Bell sharpens the issue by pointing out how value relativism relates to the liberals' cherished goal of egalitarianism; if all "values" are equal, it follows eventually that politics must make people equal as well. Not justice, but relativism, requires leveling. Call it socialism with a Heideggerian face.

The confluence of Bell's book and Quayle's Murphy Brown argument provides an opening to one of the hot new trends among intellectuals on the right: "cultural conservatism." But Bell's careful analysis of populism and elitism in the age of moral relativism implies that the "cultural conservatism" of the Quayle project is not in the end a winning strategy. Although cultural conservatives can rightly cheer what

126

might be viewed as an attempt at "Charles Murray for the masses," it isn't clear that the war over cultural "values" is best fought in the arena of public policy. This is the liberal elite's home field, and home-field advantage usually wins.

To be ultimately successful, a genuine strategy to exploit a (perhaps only temporary) gulf between populist and elitist "values" must seek to diminish the public and political sphere for the liberal elites' values. This means shrinking the state. In other words, whether a single mother ought or ought not to have a child should not be a national political issue.

The relentless politicization of every aspect of private life reveals itself to be a form of low-grade totalitarianism. Washington cannot counteract Hollywood. To attempt to do so, Quayle-style, without shrinking the state is most likely to aggravate the problem. The Quayle project has not yet challenged the fundamental statism of our era, which sees every social problem as a political problem that requires the attention and action of Washington.

Washington could, had it the will, remove the public-policy incentives for low-income women to emulate TV characters. Such a policy would not simply cut programs but would also remind citizens that they are citizens, with responsibilities as well as rights. Not simply government, but the sufficiency of the private sphere is the deeper issue. Refusing to aggrandize the political illusion would give a whole new meaning to the old Reaganite slogan, "Just say no."

—*Reason*, October 1992

Ill-Liberalism

The Anatomy of Antiliberalism, by Stephen Holmes

Political Liberalism, by John Rawls

Liberalism bears a heavy stigma in the popular mind today. It suffices merely to invoke *liberal*—with leaden emphasis on the first syllable—to produce the image of woolly-headed political incompetence embodied in Michael Dukakis or George McGovern. It is significant that the chief political aim of Bill Clinton is to avoid being perceived as a "liberal."

This is a great disservice to the grand tradition of liberalism rightly understood (or "classical liberalism"), the tradition of individual liberty, contract, and limited government. What people typically mean today when they use *liberal* derisively is better understood as *statist.* The statist impulse in Western liberal democracies derives from at least two problems. Statism can be seen as the internal degradation of liberalism through egalitarianism; the equal protection of individual rights gives way to the desire to ensure the equal *enjoyment* of rights through expanded state power. Statism can also be seen as the weak, inarticulate, concessionary response of liberal regimes to Marxist-based moralism.

Liberalism in the older sense of the term deserves a defense and rehabilitation. Libertarianism may be said to be the project of defending and rescuing liberalism from its modern statist impulses, and it is arguably the only such project on the scene with any vigor. It is unfortunate, therefore, that Stephen Holmes mars his otherwise helpful *Anatomy of Antiliberalism* with a few stray animadversions on libertarianism. These could be safely overlooked, except that these disparagements (one of which appears on the last page) might suggest to the discerning reader that would-be defenders of liberalism have a blind spot for statism, which paves the way for the projects of radical antiliberals.

It would be mistaken, though, to suggest that Holmes has written an unworthy book. To the contrary, Holmes's book is most useful in sharpening the question: What are we defending liberalism from? While libertarians focus on the visible and advancing edge of ideological statism (much of which derives from the internal corruption of liberalism), Holmes has chosen to focus on an antiliberal strain typically neglected by libertarians. His target is the intellectual antiliberalism that has as its unifying theme what might be called Non-Marxist Pre-Modernism. This kind of antiliberalism is the province of neither the left nor the right, but instead thrives nicely at both extremes. Even though non-Marxist antiliberalism is found at both ends of the spectrum, there are common threads running through both varieties.

Holmes examines six key figures and 10 fallacies of antiliberal thought. His figures are Joseph de Maistre, Carl Schmitt, and Leo Strauss on the right, and Alasdair MacIntyre, Christopher Lasch, and Roberto Unger on the left. Holmes draws a distinction between "hard" antiliberals on the right and "soft" antiliberals on the left.

Hard antiliberals reject liberalism in favor of a higher individualism within some kind of aristocratic regime. Hard antiliberals scorn both equality and the supposed unmanly softness of a peaceful liberal society. Holmes notes the incongruity of this depiction of the inherent weakness of liberal society with the fact of the British Empire's flourishing under liberal parliamentary democracy. (The triumph of liberal democracies in two world wars against theoretically stronger antiliberal regimes can also be adduced as evidence that the antiliberal portrait of the character of liberal society is overdrawn, and the examples of Lincoln and Churchill show that liberal democracies can produce vigorous leadership when necessary.)

Soft antiliberals reject liberalism, though not democracy or equality, in favor of a vaguely defined communitarianism. Their prescription for the best regime is less specific than that of the hard antiliberals. Their sentimental attacks on the way liberalism erodes warm and fuzzy community life is usually followed up with a suggestion no bolder than tightening the pornography laws a bit.

Holmes does not mince words in discussing his targets, and he finds slightly contemptible the intellectual Manicheanism of antiliberal scholarship. He charges Strauss, for instance, with "bookworm heroism" for suggesting that the "crisis of the West" will be resolved through close readings of ancient texts. MacIntyre, Holmes writes, "uses the Greek polis as a large paddle for spanking modern man." And Lasch's books are summed up as glum mood pieces.

Holmes has chosen serious targets, rather than the easily dismissed reactionary conservatives who disparage Enlightenment rationality *in toto* and seek after "a better guide than reason." Although one may quarrel about whether Holmes has been entirely fair in his spirited treatments of each thinker, he has done a valuable service in taking up a group whose influence (with the exception of de Maistre) is increasing. Holmes's close reading strips away the familiar sound bites from most of these thinkers and reveals glaring defects in their arguments. The soft antiliberals in particular, Holmes persuasively argues, are guilty of schizophrenic self-contradiction, always shrinking back from any serious proposal to overturn liberalism or liberal institutions. "A high-pitched jeremiad fizzles into a tiptoed retreat," he writes.

The most helpful part of the book is the second half, where Holmes dissects and refutes 10 fallacies common to antiliberal thought. Chesterton remarked that heresy is not outright untruth but rather a small part of truth gone mad. Most of the antiliberal fallacies Holmes identifies are aspects of liberal thought driven to an unreasonable extreme. Liberalism, according to these fallacies, is: hostile to "community," responsible for the "atomization" of the individual, indifferent to the public good, and corrosive of authority. It sacrifices the public realm to privacy, places excessive reliance on the anthropology of "economic man," establishes a theory of rights that leads to selfishness, generates moral skepticism, and places excessive reliance on reason.

Most of these fallacies, Holmes argues, arise partly because antiliberals tend to be bad historians of liberal thought, removing liberalism and liberal ideas from their proper context. Hence, each of these fallacies tends to be manifested in Holmes's 10th and most encompassing fallacy, "antonym substitution." This is a form of intellectual bait-and-switch in which antiliberals contrast an old liberal principle with a modern problem or imperative that the principle was not originally proposed in relation to. Property rights, for example, are held up as a badge of selfishness as opposed to the idea of charity, thus wrenching property from its context as a liberal bulwark against destitution and arbitrary power. This acute analysis reveals the brutal truth that even Holmes is too reserved to speak plainly: Much antiliberal criticism is aimed at straw men and is animated by a nostalgia for a moral-spiritual-communitarian society that never was.

Holmes reserves his most superb scorn for the communitarians. "Communitarians invest this word [*community*] with redemptive

131

significance," Holmes writes. "When we hear it, all our critical faculties are meant to fall asleep. In the vocabulary of these antiliberals, 'community' is used as an anesthetic, and amnesiac, and aphrodisiac." But Holmes thinks that in addition to being theoretically weak, communitarianism is not politically dangerous—a debatable conclusion. Compulsory national service, to take a leading communitarian idea on the scene today, may not be the leading edge of jackbooted fascism, but any nation that can contemplate such a policy in the absence of some argument from necessity is clearly confused about its liberal principles.

Holmes's critique also leaves little room for acknowledging some of the points about which antiliberals are right (though usually for the wrong reasons). Alasdair MacIntyre is surely right about the disarray of contemporary moral discourse. Holmes makes a short but able defense of liberalism against the charge that it is responsible for the moral skepticism of our time, but the reader is left with the sense that Holmes may doubt the seriousness of the issue beyond the bounds of liberalism's relation to it.

And his relentless scorn for the communitarians also causes him to miss a couple of opportunities. The real enemy of inertial or traditional community structures is not liberalism per se but affluence. And it is far from certain that affluent commercial society experiences fewer genuine expressions of communal life than pre-liberal societies. Social policy, especially welfare and Social Security, has weakened some communal and familial bonds. But it is also probably true that, *compared to pre-liberal society,* there are today far more vital expressions of spontaneous community as well as individual charity. This practical or empirical concern may seem inappropriate for Holmes's intellectual analysis, but it is probably necessary. The vague longing for "community" that expresses itself in various romanticisms is a genuine aspect of human nature that is both politically significant and not susceptible to rational containment alone.

Finally, it ought to be noted that the liberalism and antiliberalism portrayed in this book both seem to overlook that fact that America is not simply a liberal regime; it was also founded to be a *republican* regime. The founding era's liberal republicans thought that self-government depended on the moral character of its citizens and also thought that Enlightenment rationality and liberalism were compatible with republicanism and a moderate concern for individual virtue. Contemporary liberalism has forgotten this, and that is part of the reason for its decay into statism and for the opening on the left to the ahistorical nostrums of "civic republicanism."

132

To the extent that very modern thought has discarded the classical view of human nature, as Strauss and MacIntyre argue, both liberalism and republicanism are undermined. To suggest that modern liberalism may have a blind spot about this is not to grant license for brigades of communitarian virtuecrats. It should suggest, however, that one of the things most needful for rehabilitating liberalism is a candid reaffirmation of human nature, which is under withering attack from feminism, deconstructionism, and other fashionable ideologies.

Indeed, it is the collapse of the intellectual consensus about the first principles of liberalism—a general consensus that serves as a practical substitute for unanimous consent to the original social contract—under the assault of radical ideology that constitutes the "crisis" of liberalism. John Rawls's *Political Liberalism* aims to develop a least common denominator above which liberalism and liberal institutions may flourish. But *Political Liberalism* turns out to be mostly a restatement of or series of footnotes to Rawls's 1971 blockbuster, *A Theory of Justice.*

Readers of that earlier work will recall Rawls's two principles of justice: First, each person has an equal claim to certain basic rights—an arrangement we would all choose in an "original position" (supposedly equivalent to the "state of nature" of old liberals) behind a "veil of ignorance" that prevents any knowledge of our particular circumstances or interests; and second, inequalities are only just if they benefit the least advantaged members of society. There have been countless critiques of Rawls from all quarters, which need not be rehearsed in the context of his present revisions.

Instead, a good starting point for thinking about this book is the often remarked upon abstraction of Rawls's style and approach. This may not stem purely from his academic orientation. In fact, Rawls's ginger and indirect approach to critical views contrasts sharply with fellow academic Holmes's spirited and at times slashing style. On close reading it appears that Rawls is chiefly concerned with the antiliberalism of the radical left, but he is also worried about giving offense to this vocal segment of our intellectual elites. (In the introduction, Rawls seeks to reassure these potential critics that although this book doesn't cover it, "the alleged difficulties in discussing problems of gender and the family can be overcome.")

This interpretation becomes more plausible when one considers that Rawls's famous second principle rests upon an a priori acceptance of egalitarianism. His tiny rampart against leveling is inadequate to the passions of the day. When removed from abstraction and juxtaposed against the context of current political life, Rawls's project is seen as trying to moderate, accommodate, or appease radical egalitarianism.

Rawls means to be a friend of liberalism against the extremes of antiliberal thought, but the hard left is not likely to accept his appeasement. The aim of defending and reviving liberalism is better sustained through a book such as Thomas Pangle's *The Ennobling of Democracy: The Challenge of the Post-Modern Age,* which directly confronts radical ideology and seeks to make classical liberalism and republicanism into viable modern alternatives. (Likewise, a nice companion volume to Holmes is Paul Rahe's massive *Republics Ancient and Modern,* which, while situating America as a liberal republican regime midway between ancient and modern, makes the case that the ancient "communities" that some antiliberals pine for weren't so hotsy-totsy after all.)

The end of the Cold War, Holmes points out, has not necessarily left the world in the hands of liberals, Francis Fukuyama notwithstanding. Ideological antiliberalism of the kind Holmes tracks is important to recognize, but much more immediately troubling is the kind of weak Rawlsian liberalism that plays into the hands of statists and antiliberals alike. To paraphrase the old cliché, with liberals like that, who needs antiliberals?

—*Reason,* February 1994.

Chapter 27

Passion over Prudence

Citizens: A Chronicle of the French Revolution, by Simon Schama, New York: Knopf, 948 pages, $29.95

"The first heavy casualties of the French Revolution were rabbits."

Detail and interpretations of this kind fill nearly every page of Simon Schama's magnificent "chronicle" of the French Revolution. In this case, Schama finds significant the widespread rural disregard of the laws protecting wildlife when, in the hungry spring of 1789, a plague of rabbits threatened to devour what was left of a meager harvest. Huge mobs of farmers and laborers roamed the fields, pummeling every form of life encountered. Soon these same mobs would be waylaying grain shipments, leading to disruptions and unrest in Paris. The rest, as the cliche goes...

Citizens ought to be the final book on the subject of the French Revolution. But you know it won't be. The French Revolution will always be a big deal because it raises in pure form many of the classic political questions: How should representation be determined? What is the relationship between violence and legitimacy? Is the good man the same as the good citizen? To what extent can or should government work to mold the virtue of its citizens? Is totalitarianism just an updated form of ancient tyranny, or is it something new?

The French Revolution also raises great historical questions. Cause and effect, always problematic for historians, are even more elusive for the French Revolution. The most basic themes remain controversial. Was it, as R.R. Palmer and many other historians have argued, "the great turning point of modem civilization," the crucible of modernity, and, as Jules Michelet had it, the heir of the Christian epoch? Or was it in fact chiefly antimodern at its core? For intellectual history, the place of Enlightenment philosophy has always been hard to fix. One school of thought, spawned by Burke and De Maistre, has the Revolution as a natural product of the Enlightenment, thereby setting the stage to deplore both, while the Marxist-inspired historians explain events not as the result of ideas at all, but of those hoary impersonal forces.

For Americans and democrats everywhere, the comparative question remains lively: Next to the French Revolution, the American Revolution pales, giving rise to a predominantly liberal school of thought that argues that the American Revolution was not revolutionary at all but should be regarded as a mere War of Independence. (The next step in the argument, of course, is that America needs a genuine egalitarian revolution.) And because of the similar phrasing of Jefferson's Declaration of Independence and the French Declaration of the Rights of Man and Citizen, many American conservatives argue that our Declaration is "tainted" by French influence and therefore not to be regarded as a vital part of the American tradition and certainly not to be accorded any theoretical authority.

There is finally the enormous popular legacy of the French Revolution. It is the standard by which other upheavals are measured. And this historical controversy over its nature has huge popular overtones, as was made evident by the furor that followed Prime Minister Margaret Thatcher's denigration of the Revolution's significance. The French Revolution stands among the handful of historical moments fraught with contemporary importance.

So the historical debate has converged with the political debate. Indeed, it can be said that modern conservatism was generated out of the French Revolution, with Burke's *Reflections on the Revolution in France* being the chief scripture right down to the present day. The Burkean critique is in one respect not necessarily helpful: Its ideological analysis provides ironic sanction to the liberal view that the French Revolution was a modernizing force and to the Marxist view that the Revolution was an important milestone on the Inevitable Course of History, in which bourgeois capitalism displaced relic feudalism. Many historians argue that it was neither of these, and they have to overcome Burke as well as the liberals and the Marxists.

Citizens addresses itself to all of these controversies, in a narrative form that provides interpretations as events unfold before the reader. Schama deliberately chooses the narrative form, because in recent historical inquiries "the causes of the French Revolution were depersonalized, cut loose from the speech and conduct of Great Men and instead located deep within the structure of the society that preceded it....Scientific—or at least sociological—history had arrived and with it, the demotion of chronicle to anecdotal unimportance." It is Schama's

136

purpose to revive this style and yet still offer the reader broad conclusive themes.

Citizens comes down squarely on the side of the recent revisionists, such as François Furet, who see the French Revolution generally as a catastrophe proceeding from rather unremarkable political causes. Although a great many factors combined to give the Revolution its character, the principal cause of the crisis of 1789 was the fiscal insolvency of the French government. Early on, Schama disputes the histories that stress institutional and social forces at the expense of politics. In fact, Schama writes, Tocqueville was right when he argued that the obsession with reform prior to 1789 contributed mightily to the growing disarray.

Many are the historians who hold that the French Revolution was the direct outcome of the Enlightenment, which was carried on nowhere more vigorously than in the *salons* of Paris. Schama yields some ground to this view. "Rousseau's works dealing with personal virtue and the morality of social relations sharpened distaste for the status quo and defined a new allegiance," Schama writes. But the obscurity of Rousseau's political philosophy made its precise application—as well as precise evaluation by historians—difficult. Schama identifies Rousseau's rhetorical style as his most important bequest: "What he invented was not a road map to revolution, but the idiom in which its discontents would be voiced and its goals articulated." Later on Schama describes the rhetoric of the Parisian Jacobin clubs as "Rousseau with a hoarse voice."

The main reason for Schama's restraint about the place of the Enlightenment in the catalogue of causes is his equal appreciation for the other intellectual currents and images. Even as radicals invoked the General Will and other Rousseauian ideas, there was equally prominent in the revolutionary consciousness a strong element of classical Roman republicanism. Just as the Americans adopted the Latin slogan "*Novus Ordo Seclorum*"—A New Order for the Ages—Mirabeau made popular the slogan "*Novus Rerum Nascitur Ordo*"—A New Order of Things Is Born. "Their France would be a Rome reborn," Schama observes. In both speech and popular art, the Revolution as Horatian spectacle is common.

And finally, notes Schama in his epilogue, "it was perhaps Romanticism with its addiction to the Absolute and the Ideal; its fondness for the vertiginous and macabre; its concept of political energy as, above all, electrical; its obsession with the heart; its preference for passion over reason, for virtue over peace, that supplied a crucial ingredient in the mentality of the revolutionary elite: its association of liberty with wildness."

Citizens illuminates many of the basic political questions the Revolution faced. Schama's narrative is especially useful for political scientists interested in comparing the French and American solutions to basic problems such as representation, voting privileges, separation of powers, good citizenship and patriotism, and so forth. Abandoning the historical precedent for the composition of the Estates-General was, according to Schama, the first great turning point of the Revolution. The debate over how to compose the general assembly raised the theoretical question that often dogged the American Founding: What is representation, and how is it provided for? (That there is no satisfactory practical answer is evident from James Madison's remark in *The Federalist* that one "should not dwell overlong" on this question.) The large electorate in the regional assemblies generated, Schama writes, "the most numerous experiment in political representation attempted anywhere in the world." But later in the Revolution, landholding and taxpaying qualifications disenfranchised large sections of the population, resulting in "a *narrower* electorate at the levels where it really counted."

The Revolution also failed to solve the problem of dividing legislative and executive power. It is precisely this issue where Rousseau's notion of the General Will, with its implication of unitary power, did the most disservice to French political thinking. By invoking Rousseau, the revolutionaries turned away from their most valuable intellectual patrimony: Montesquieu and the doctrine of the separation of powers. (It is worth noting that Montesquieu—not Locke—was the most frequently cited European thinker in American political writing of the Founding era.)

And then there is the question first raised in classical Greece: the relationship between citizenship, morality, and patriotism. The one indisputable transformation of the Revolution, according to Schama, was "the creation of the juridical entity of the citizen." But the free citizen and his natural rights were quickly subsumed by what Schama rightly calls "The Dictatorship of Virtue," an all-consuming patriotism that saw all dissent as not just unpatriotic, but unvirtuous. Here again Rousseau's doctrine that government was a form of educational trust, responsible for the moral regeneration of the people, was given active form.

One might posit a general lesson: Where there is undue veneration of the *patrie*, paternalism will not be far behind. The economic dimension of the French Revolution is perhaps the most ironic. Schama points out that, although there was widespread rural poverty, France in the 1780s was prospering and increasingly capitalistic. The economic damage inflicted by the Revolution took decades to repair. The rural poor never benefited from the confiscation of church property, and the inflation and price controls that followed the introduction of paper money were worse than the state bankruptcy that triggered the whole mess.

A segment of the radicals wanted it this way. As Schama tells it, "They wanted paternalism rather than economic liberalism, the regulation of prices rather than free markets." Most surprisingly, Robespierre made it a staple of Jacobinism that the rights of property were not absolute, and Schama concludes, "their [the Jacobins'] war was a war against commercial capitalism."

The truth about the economic interests in the Revolution belies the class-based analysis. Schama frequently breaks off from his steady and careful narrative to deliver much-deserved whacks at historians who have misrepresented this and other aspects of the Revolution. In most instances these demurrers are done politely and without mentioning specific historians by name, but Schama erupts with vituperation when considering the historiography of one issue: The Terror. Schama rejects outright the common view that the French Revolution had two distinct phases, an early "liberal" period lasting until 1791, and then The Terror. To the contrary, "The Terror was merely 1789 with a higher body count. From the first year it was apparent that violence was not just an unfortunate side effect from which enlightened Patriots could selectively avert their eyes; it was the Revolution's source of collective energy." Schama returns to this theme often, and at one point singles out historian Pierre Caron, censuring him for "intellectual cowardice and moral self-delusion." Caron's downplaying of the violence against the rebellious province of Vendée, Schama writes, amounts to "the scholarly normalization of evil."

Schama has received some criticism for breaking off his narrative with the execution of Robespierre in 1794, but this criticism fails to appreciate how Schama's purposes are completed by this point. "What occurred between 1789 and 1793," Schama writes at the last, "was an unprecedented explosion of politics—in speech, print, image and even music—that broke all the barriers that had traditionally circumscribed it." And although Schama is moved by the grandeur of the spectacle, he clearly sees that the logic of utopian revolution is to devour the very people it seeks to free. The difficulty of returning the revolutionary genie to the bottle of state power (Schama's phrase) reminds once again that prudence is the highest political principle of the statesman.

Here the comparison with America tells. In 1791, Thomas Jefferson (who departed from his ambassadorship in Paris in September 1789) wrote to a friend: "I still hope the French Revolution will issue happily. I

139

feel that the permanence of our own leans in some degree on that, and that a failure there would be a powerful argument to prove that there must be a failure here." Jefferson should have known better. What Jefferson the idealist failed to discern was the absence of any prudence and moderation in France that would have led to establishing the principle of limited government. What Americans understood was that only *limited* government can provide for the equal rights of free men; what the French should have learned (it's not clear whether they have) is that unlimited ideals combined with unlimited government must quickly obliterate those ideals. Compare the rhetoric in the French assemblies with the rhetoric in American assemblies. Even though our Declaration of Independence sounds like their Declaration of the Rights of Man and Citizen, the similarity ends there.

—*Reason*, December 1989

Chapter 28

Bridge to Nowhere

The Invisible Bridge: The Fall of Nixon and the Rise of Reagan, by Rick Perlstein

Rick Perlstein, a contributing writer at the *Nation* magazine who was once the chief national correspondent for the *Village Voice,* probably did not expect conservatives to enthuse over his debut book, *Before the Storm: Barry Goldwater and the Unmaking of the American Consensus* (2001). In fact, William Kristol praised it in the *New York Times Book Review,* saying Perlstein told the Goldwater story with "journalistic flair" and "justice," while George F. Will called it "the best book yet" on the Goldwater phenomenon. By 2008, however, Will wrote for the *Times* that Perlstein's second book, *Nixonland: The Rise of a President and the Fracturing of America,* was replete with "jejune incongruities," "adolescent language," and factual weaknesses.

Little surprise, then, that the *Times Book Review* did not assign a conservative to review Perlstein's latest sequel, *The Invisible Bridge: The Fall of Nixon and the Rise of Reagan.* The assignment went instead to the paper's former theater critic and op-ed columnist, Frank Rich. Selecting that writer, whose hatred of conservatism dominated his reviews as well as his columns, had the intended effect: Perlstein's chronicle of the middle three years of the 1970s is, Rich opined, "a Rosetta stone for reading America and its politics today."

Like both Rich and the *Times,* Perlstein never doubts his liberal presuppositions and the resulting contempt for conservatives. It would be a mistake to evaluate *The Invisible Bridge* merely by its partisan purposes or its disputable details and interpretations, however. Partisan histories play a useful role. Perlstein, an able narrative stylist, deserves some credit for reviving the kind of spirited partisan history that defined Arthur M. Schlesinger, Jr.'s career.

There's nothing flat about any of Perlstein's books, which cannot be said of the many other contemporary liberal historians who disguise their ideological leanings through deliberate blandness.

* * *

More important is what Perlstein's ambitious, multi-volume project represents. Many liberals have made peace with conservatism, and with Ronald Reagan in particular, giving him a measure of serious respect. Perlstein wants to resume the war.

Consider Richard Reeves, the liberal journalist who summarily dismissed Reagan before, during, and immediately after his presidency. Yet in the mid-1990s Reeves began to change his mind, writing,

> *I was no fan of Ronald Reagan, but I think I know a leader when I see one, even if I do not want to follow where he is leading.... He was a man of conservative principle and he damned near destroyed American liberalism.... Reagan...was larger than he seemed, indeed larger than life, even if our historians do not quite get it yet.*

By 2005 Reeves would publish a mostly favorable account in *President Reagan: The Triumph of Imagination.* John Patrick Diggins, a neighbor, friend, and ideological soulmate of Arthur Schlesinger made the case in *Ronald Reagan: Fate, Freedom, and the Making of History* (2007) that Reagan deserves to be considered among the greatest American presidents alongside Washington, Lincoln, and Franklin Roosevelt. And Princeton's Sean Wilentz, while remaining generally critical (he thought Reagan deserved impeachment over Iran-Contra), nonetheless acknowledges his accomplishments: "His success in helping finally to end the cold war is one of the greatest achievements by any president of the United States—and arguably the greatest single presidential achievement since 1945."

There have been a few attempts from the Left to cut Reagan down to size, such as Will Bunch's *Tear Down This Myth: How the Reagan Legacy Has Distorted Our Politics and Haunts Our Future* (2009) and William Kleinknecht's *The Man Who Sold the World: Ronald Reagan and the Betrayal of Main Street America* (2009). These and similar efforts attack Reagan's record with wonky arguments about wealth distribution, social policy, civil rights law, and other campus concerns. But neither book caused so much as a ripple in political-literary circles.

The most recent liberal argument, used to gain leverage against Barack Obama's conservative tormentors, is that "Reagan was not a Reaganite!" Rather, he was a crypto-moderate who would be unacceptable to theTea Party and too conciliatory to win the Republican nomination if he were on the scene today. To believe this you'd have to believe that both John McCain and Mitt Romney were more conservative *and* more politically skillful than Reagan, and that the Tea Party faithful who lionize Reagan don't understand him nearly as well as the hosts at MSNBC.

* * *

The Left is rightly concerned about the Reagan legacy. If the Republican Party, or a future presidential standard-bearer, could figure out how to emulate the Reagan formula—rather than just invoke Reagan's name—liberals would find themselves in deep trouble again. *The Invisible Bridge*'s stridency reflects Perlstein's wish for a Left as assertive and confident as the post-Goldwater Right. Obama was supposed to be the Left's Reagan, after all. Though his policy agenda has tried to move the country in a liberal direction as decisively as Reagan moved it rightward, his presidency hasn't catalyzed a *political* change as pronounced as the one Reagan triggered. (At least Reaganomics, unlike Obamacare, was popular.) Above all, Democrats haven't been able to shed vestiges of Reaganism (like hostility to tax increases) that permanently hamper the leftist cause, a point implicit in Perlstein's preface. His book is well timed: the Left's growing anger toward both parties may well erupt in the 2016 campaign in ways not seen since 1968.

Perlstein aims to revive liberals' categorical anathema on Reagan. Dismissing him as an "amiable dunce" won't do, nor will the policy wonk's statistical scorn. Instead, Perlstein depicts a complex and cunning Reagan: a calculating fabulist whose political intention and effect were malign. Rather than correcting or mitigating Nixon's malicious divisions in public opinion, Perlstein's Reagan intentionally deepened them. Perlstein seeks to reclaim Reagan's earlier reputation as a controversial figure, calling him a "divider," not a "uniter." Unlike Nixon's resentments against the establishment, which arose from his character (explored in *Nixonland*), Reagan's resentments were against reality itself, arising from the heroic fantasy world that he began to develop in his youth. Reagan was "an athlete of the imagination" and also "an athlete of denial"—indeed, an Olympian gold medalist of denial.

* * *

Reagan's greatest offense, Perlstein thinks, was to make it unnecessary, and then impossible, for Americans to come to terms with the meaning of their country's weakened, demoralized condition after Vietnam and Watergate. America might have pondered its manifold sins at home and abroad in order to fashion "a new definition of patriotism" from the abundant material made available during the upheaval of the 1960s. *The Invisible Bridge* offers few particulars about this new patriotism, however—extolling it as "a perfect passion for the rule of law, of the fairest possible proceduralism, a longing for political innocence" clarifies nothing— nor does Perlstein describe the process of national introspection that would have forged it. The reader is left to infer that Reagan prevented America from becoming the kind of country Noam Chomsky and Howard Zinn could finally be proud of. In any case, Reagan's romantic optimism and standard-issue American heroism foreclosed all such possibilities: "Then along came Ronald Reagan, encouraging citizens to think like children, waiting for a man on horseback to rescue them: a tragedy."

Worse, Reagan's one-dimensional American patriotism has polluted the Democratic Party as well as the Republican. (Perlstein's stream-of-consciousness meanderings draw upon an endless inventory of phrases, but he never types the words "American exceptionalism," though it's what he's really denouncing.) He laments, for example, that exceptionalism of the sort voiced by Reagan turned up at the 2012 Democratic National Convention: keynoter Julian Castro, Michelle Obama, and her husband all affirmed that the United States is "the greatest nation on earth." This "cult of official optimism," Perlstein thinks, amounts to "hubris." It is the chief reason Americans find it impossible to overcome our "paralyzing" polarization, in order to address climate change, competition from China, stagnant economic growth, and other aspects of "the national apocalypse that may yet come." (Strangely, Perlstein leaves health care off his list of polarized, unsolvable problems. Maybe he thinks it's all but fixed.)

The Invisible Bridge is really just an oblique version of the current liberal conceit that everything would be fine if conservatives would stop being so stupid, stubborn, and vicious, and admit that liberals have been right all along about pretty much everything. To work from that smug premise to the conclusion that conservatism's fundamental problem is hubris betrays a startling lack of self-awareness by liberals. Perlstein's belief that one man can cause this hubris all by himself is even more bizarre. It is tempting to conclude from Perlstein that Reagan was in fact greater than conservatives imagine. Sam Tanenhaus has argued that Perlstein's narrative implies contempt not just for Nixon and Reagan but for the majority of Americans who sided with them. "For Perlstein," he wrote in the *Atlantic*, "the mere fact of a President Nixon is explicable only as pathology." The only exceptionalism that impresses Perlstein is Americans' exceptional ignorance or weakness for the demagogic rage of the Right. Ultimately, *The Invisible Bridge* is an argument less against Ronald Reagan than against the American character that Reagan exemplified and fortified with his rhetoric and statecraft. While Perlstein blames conservatives for this state of affairs, he'd surely be as disenchanted with Franklin Roosevelt's America if he'd been a contemporary.

* * *

It is easy to lose sight of Perlstein's central argument in the tsunami of details that inundates the reader from the first pages. Indeed, his book doesn't really build an argument for his thesis; he intends that you will acquire it by reverse osmosis. An ocean of details exhausts and distracts the reader, evidence of a relentless malice that dissolves all subtlety. Do we really need five pages about the meat boycott of the spring of 1973? We do when you can make a minor tie-in to the fact that Governor Reagan invested in a cattle-related tax shelter, and as a child wrote his first surviving letter about the tastiness of meat. And let's not forget that America's fondness for red meat can be used as a metaphor for our supposed bloodthirstiness. (The effect of Nixon's wage-and-price-control regime in disrupting the meat market goes unmentioned; as does its role in the energy crisis, which begins during this same time period; as do the deeper policy aspects of many episodes that obsess Perlstein.) He returns often to the meat boycott story like a bird returning to carrion on the road, though chiefly for comic purposes. Nixon's consumer advisor made the foolish suggestion that "liver, kidney, brains, and heart can be made into gourmet meals with seasoning, imagination, and more

145

cooking time." Eminently mockable, no question—but Perlstein's book is full of these vignettes as setups for his punch lines. They're the equivalent of what standup comedians call "runners": images or gags that you repeat as an anchor for the set piece.

The author isn't just playing for laughs, though. Like *The Daily Show*'s jests, Perlstein's serve to highlight American hypocrisy, venality, corruption, and imbecility, all the more offensive to liberal sensibilities for being wrapped in pretensions of exceptionalism. (Perlstein is especially annoyed with Reagan's repeated quotation of Pope Pius XII: "Into the hands of America God has placed an afflicted mankind.") What other kind of country could fall for someone like Reagan?

Unfortunately, Perlstein is less talented than Jon Stewart at being derisive without coming across as bitter and mean. The laughs disappear completely in his treatment of the POWs returning from North Vietnam, rendering incredible his pose as a social historian merely outlining our era's polarization. *The Invisible Bridge* opens with a long deconstruction—worthy of Chomsky—of "Operation Homecoming," the national celebration of the American POWs' return from North Vietnam. Though often relying on the words of others to criticize the prisoners and the publicizing of their return, Perlstein makes clear his sympathy for the idea that they were war criminals, not heroes, whose treatment by the North Vietnamese amounted to nothing more than the same kind of "enhanced interrogation" the U.S. practiced at Guantanamo Bay. Of Jane Fonda's denial that POWs were tortured and her advice that they should be regarded as "professional killers" who were "hypocrites and liars," Perlstein says in his own voice that "plenty of ordinary Americans thought what she said made sense." It's highly doubtful, however, that even a majority of the historically small minority of Americans who voted for George McGovern in November 1972 agreed with "Hanoi Jane's" attack.

* * *

See what I did there? Lay down a track of critical quotations and circumstances, and then append my own sarcasm and snark. It's Perlstein's favorite literary device. Of Reagan's youthful desire to make the football squad despite his skinniness, he writes: "A good thing he was scrawny, or he would never have acquired the character it took to be strong." Or of the famous episode of an early-teen

146

Reagan dragging his intoxicated, unconscious father out of the snow: "A good thing his father was passed out drunk, or else Ronald Reagan would not have had the opportunity to come of age." Perlstein is coy about whether he is merely contesting the authenticity of Reagan's self-understanding. In the context of this and his previous books, Perlstein's real argument is against the American archetype of the self-made man. It's as if he wishes to scream at Reagan, *You didn't build that!*

Perlstein's predominant method of cutting Reagan down to size is to flag Reagan's factual mistakes and prevarications. One of the easiest tricks of polemical writing is to array a politician's petty contradictions and logical shortcuts into a brief against him. The larger and more colorful a politician, the easier this method becomes. FDR and John F. Kennedy are easy marks, LBJ is the mother lode, and Perlstein takes note of Jimmy Carter's self-serving prevarications and exaggerations. This is not a new mode of Reagan criticism, though Perlstein's tendentious use of Reagan's slips has the effect of making the earlier treatments by Robert Dallek and Garry Wills— liberals who were equally hostile to Reagan in, respectively, *Ronald Reagan: The Politics of Symbolism* (1984) and *Reagan's America: Innocents at Home* (1986)—seem temperate and judicious by comparison.

Reagan's frequent misstatements of facts and idiosyncratic rendering of circumstances is hardly unique among politicians. Sometimes it catches up with them, as it did with Al Gore in the 2000 campaign. And sometimes it doesn't: Bill Clinton claimed to recollect local black churches being burned in his childhood, though a check of the record revealed none had been torched where he grew up. The discovery didn't hurt Clinton because churches really were burned in the South, and the larger political and social truth counted for more than pedantic accuracy. Americans tend not to care much about perfect factual accuracy if they think you are correct about the underlying issue.

* * *

In addition to never crediting Reagan for the many times when his facts and analysis of an issue *were* correct, Perlstein seldom looks beyond a mistake to ask if Reagan wasn't onto something serious. Perlstein never discusses Reagan's long-running theme of the 1970s: many prominent aspects of contemporary American government—the

147

administrative state—are constitutionally dubious. (Perlstein's unseriousness about this subject is best seen when he mangles some basic separation-of-powers issues in his account of Watergate.) Instead, he serially picks on Reagan's gaffes. For example, he scoffs at Reagan's criticism of the Food and Drug Administration because he had his facts completely wrong about a particular tuberculosis drug, ignoring entirely the substance of the long-running controversy about the character of the FDA bureaucracy and the consequences of its regulatory rulings.

That Perlstein perceives little or no ground for reasonable criticism of the administrative state can be seen in an August comment on his Facebook page: "Not quite ready to forgive Cass Sunstein for his work advancing the deregulatory work Reagan launched." Even Sunstein, the Obama Administration's "regulatory czar," doesn't pass muster. Or consider a Perlstein article in the *Nation* this year, in which he responded to a query: "Who on the right does the best job of covering politics or the economy or anything else, for that matter, in a thoughtful, fair and accurate way?" Perlstein wrote that no one does, since conservatism offers nothing better than the "hustlers, haters, hacks, and conspiratorial lunatics at Fox News." For someone who sneers at Nixon and Reagan for dividing the country and demonizing political opponents, Perlstein either doesn't realize that he does this constantly in his own writing, or exempts himself and his allies out of the belief that rules are for other people.

Perlstein's obliviousness to the deeper substantive dimensions of the political divides taking shape between 1960 and 1980 can be seen in his treatment of economic issues. He notes in the briefest possible way that Keynesian economics stopped working in the 1970s, but evinces no interest in examining why this happened, and offers no account of the critiques and alternatives people of any persuasion put forward. For all his copious research in popular and original source material, there is no evidence that Perlstein spent any time considering serious academic literature (not even Cass Sunstein, apparently) about the major political issues he discusses. Nor is there any acknowledgment that liberalism experienced some bad innings in the 1960s and 1970s, or that some of its difficulties resulted from attacks by the New Left as well as by the Right.

* * *

Perlstein has achieved the extraordinary feat of producing a book that is both richly detailed and completely superficial. *The Invisible Bridge* ends abruptly with Reagan's hardly "impromptu" speech on the last night of the 1976 Republican National Convention, and the widespread assumption that it marked the end of his political career. Perlstein promises a sequel, presumably taking us through the 1980 election and reviving the head-scratching question leaders in both parties asked in the aftermath: "How the hell did this guy get elected?"

Most Americans of all political vantage points have long since stopped asking that question. Perlstein wants to revive it, along with the withering hatred and contempt for Reagan that was its premise. For this we should, in a way, be grateful. Rick Perlstein's contempt for his subject represents a clear rejection of Barack Obama's conceit that the discord between Red and Blue America is all a misunderstanding that can be resolved through good sense and good will. Perlstein is unlikely to persist and offer a similar large-scale account of Reagan's presidency. Though posturing as the Gibbon of our age, he more closely resembles Theodore White—adept at telling the horse-race story of a political campaign, but hopelessly out of his depth when it comes to seriously assessing an actual presidency.

The Invisible Bridge takes its title from a comment Nikita Khrushchev made to Nixon: "If people believe there's an imaginary river out there, you don't tell them there's no river there. You build an imaginary bridge over the imaginary river." Perlstein doesn't need to explain his interpretation of this: American exceptionalism is an imaginary thing, bolstered in its dying innings by a man given wholly to imaginary politics. But because of this book's superficiality about political life, liberals who thrill to it may find that a more recent metaphor is a better fit: a bridge to nowhere.

—*Claremont Review of Books*, Fall 2014

Chapter 29

No Perls of Wisdom

Reaganland, by Rick Perlstein

The first thing a reader will learn from the final installment of Rick Perlstein's epic four-volume narrative on the rise of the right from 1964 to 1980 is that Simon & Schuster, one of the world's premier trade imprints, apparently no longer employs copy editors, fact-checkers, or proofreaders. *Reaganland*, coming in at more than 1,000 pages, is riddled with so many typos, misspellings, factual errors, repetitions, and overindulgences of the author's sarcasm that it distracts from the worthy content of the narrative, which is uneven in any case.

North Carolina's Senator Sam Ervin is transmuted into Sam Erving. The book says the GOP hadn't controlled the House of Representatives since the Hoover administration when it did so in 1947–48 and 1953–54. It says that New York had 21 electoral votes in 1976 when it had 41. It misidentifies ABC News anchor Frank Reynolds by placing him at NBC, where he never worked. It claims that the Liberty Fund was a creation of Charles Koch; it wasn't. It says George H.W. Bush beat Ronald Reagan in the 1980 Oregon primary 58.3 percent to 54 percent, which would be a neat trick of overvoting. Beyond these embarrassments are the gross misstatements and mischaracterizations of many particulars, from the 1965 Moynihan Report on the black family to the landmark *Buckley v. Valeo* Supreme Court decision in 1976. This is merely a sample of what could be a very long list.

What to make of this sloppiness in a doorstop of a book whose effect is based on being a granular account of details typically omitted from most contemporary histories? One clue comes from the fact that Perlstein has announced that his grand project of chronicling the right starting with Barry Goldwater has come to an end with this volume, at Ronald Reagan's inauguration, just when the story of the right reaches a key inflection point. At 51, Perlstein is relatively young; why stop here?

151

The pervasive errors taken together with many of the peculiarities of the narrative lead one to wonder whether both Perlstein and Simon & Schuster have simply lost heart for the enterprise. The four-volume arc of Perlstein's project to chronicle the rise of the right (whose second and third 800-page volumes, *Nixonland* and *The Invisible Bridge,* take us from 1964 to 1976) could be a case study in the decline of liberal historical writing.

The first book in his series, *Before the Storm: Barry Goldwater and the Unmaking of the American Consensus,* came in at a comparatively compact 671 pages and was well received, even by conservatives. The friendly reception they gave *Before the Storm* seemed to have unnerved Perlstein, whose own political commitments skew far to the left. Writing a book that conservatives liked was a mistake he would not make again. He knows that a narrative history is supposed to eschew open partisanship, but his attempts at taking down the right by indirection are betrayed by his peculiar obsessions and inability to resist gratuitous snark. By the end of *Reaganland*, most readers, and not just conservatives, will pine for the elegance of Arthur Schlesinger Jr.'s narratives, whose partisanship was at least rooted in a capaciousness unknown to Perlstein.

Perlstein's main target is Reagan, though he understands that Reagan can't be understood in isolation from the disabilities of liberalism that emerged in the 1960s and grew critical under Jimmy Carter, and the gathering strength of the right as the 1970s progressed. Three strands provide Perlstein with his villains. They include the "boardroom Jacobins" of the business community who organized to oppose government regulation and mismanagement of the economy; the neoconservatives who emerged out of the 1960s left, and the aborning religious right. The latter is Perlstein's dominant obsession, with the narrative returning again and again to long accounts of key figures, organizational formation, crucial meetings, and the strange (to Perlstein) political and cultural fixations of religious folk.

There is nothing novel about liberal disdain for the religious right and its once-prominent leaders—Jerry Falwell, Howard Phillips, Anita Bryant, Phyllis Schlafly, Paul Weyrich, Bob Jones, and many other key activists who are largely forgotten. Yet Perlstein seems to think it a revelation that the entry of the religious right into electoral politics depended on "organizing discontent," as though Saul Alinsky never existed or Henry Adams hadn't described politics as "the systematic organization of hatreds"—or that religiously minded Americans had anything to be discontented about in the 1970s. These passages bring out Perlstein's penchant for ventriloquist journalism, as he delights in quoting unflattering descriptions of his villains culled from contemporary news archives. Paul Weyrich, according to a reporter he quotes, had the mien of "a formal, slightly constipated owl." Perlstein borrows another reporter's description of Howard Phillips as "a man who always looks as if he could use a trip to the cleaners." This method may not leave latent fingerprints, but the DNA of the technique is abundant.

Now to the "boardroom Jacobins." The argument is familiar: Business began moving in a determined way to capture the government in order to capture a greater share of wealth. Here again we are offered little data or any kind of baseline to judge what changes were afoot. Perlstein prefers character sketches and dramatic scenes with heroes and antiheroes. Hence we are offered an idiosyncratic choice of a counter-hero to the mostly nameless boardroom Jacobins: the largely forgotten Michael Pertschuk, Jimmy Carter's choice as chairman of the Federal Trade Commission. In Perlstein's telling, the crusading Pertschuk, a protégé of Ralph Nader's, was the tragic victim of the boardroom Jacobins, as his valiant attempts to protect American consumers from predatory capitalism came undone by the growing anti-regulatory attack.

Perlstein almost stumbles across an important story with his passing remarks that the FTC was "a notoriously toothless regulatory body," a "onetime backwater" that "sparked to life under President Nixon." The real question is why this agency, formed with a broad mandate to regulate "unfair competition" under Woodrow Wilson, would suddenly "spark to life" under Nixon after decades as a backwater. Perlstein echoes the standard liberal history that the FTC had been neutered by pro-business Republicans back in the 1920s, but the fact that it never achieved real importance during the New Deal or after World War II ought to suggest that the old narrative is inaccurate. Perlstein shows no awareness of the regulatory revolution—the use of federal mandates to impose new practices on private industry—that really accelerated in the late 1960s and triggered the response he reviles so much. And he is incurious about an important fact he reports—that many congressional Democrats, never mind Republicans, were not happy with Pertschuk's quixotic crusades. Instead we get a Manichean melodrama missing only the business lobbyists twirling their handlebar mustaches in the shadows of smoke-filled committee hearings.

His handling of other aspects of the economic controversies of the time show this similar pattern of near misses and skewed perceptions. The book gives a lot of attention to the political concern over inflation but offers few data points and even less clarity about this dominant problem of the late 1970s. Perlstein is not a fan of Paul Volcker, the person Jimmy Carter belatedly picked to run the Federal Reserve Board to get serious about inflation. And no wonder. In his acknowledgments, Perlstein records that "important sources [for Volcker and the Federal Reserve] include Mark Blyth, the late William Greider, Edward McClelland, the late Judith Stein, and Matt Stoller"—all leftist ideologues. His sole source for background on Milton Friedman is Soren Brandes, an obscure European. It was too much trouble, apparently, to read Friedman himself. This leads to monumental howlers such as this one: "As Ronald Reagan put it in 1975, [inflation] hits 'those hardest who can least afford it.' But this is not so. Inflation taxes investors: If a bond matures when inflation is high, the bondholder's profit is diminished."

The same is true about the sourcing he cites on supply-side economics: "Jonathan Chait, Robert Kuttner, and Molly Michaelmore"; and for neoconservatism, "Sidney Blumenthal and Peter Steinfels." This is a little like saying your primary source for information on Nancy Pelosi is Sean Hannity. And it's only one aspect of the missed opportunity this book represents. A new or revisionist history that reckoned with the travails of late New Deal liberalism in its dying throes under Jimmy Carter could contribute insight into our present moment. But Perlstein displays little curiosity or discernment about, for example, Carter's terrible relations with congressional Democrats, arguably the worst any president has ever had with his own party. Carter enjoyed large majorities in both houses of Congress, but Democrats struggled to pass any significant legislation, and most of Carter's initiatives, such as his energy bill, were ground to dust before passing without much enthusiasm. Other Carter proposals, for tax and welfare reform and health care, got nowhere. Observers then and now attributed it to Carter's stubbornness and parochial arrogance, but this is to miss deeper changes sweeping over Democrats in the 1970s. What did pass with considerable Democratic support was a large capital-gains tax cut, the first milestone in the supply-side revolution, while the executive branch launched several significant initiatives to deregulate large

154

sectors of the economy in transportation, energy, and finance. Perlstein barely notices this surprising part of the story.

Reaganland's trail lays down a lot of bread crumbs Perlstein doesn't follow, including some interesting details about Joe Biden, a "centrist bellwether" who supported the capital-gains tax cut and voted against the watered-down Humphrey-Hawkins Full Employment Act. Humphrey, Biden complained, wasn't "cognizant of the limited, finite ability government has to deal with people's problems." The Joe Biden of 1978, Perlstein reports, actually received the endorsement of Howard Jarvis, the impresario of California's Proposition 13 who put the tax revolt into high gear, for reelection to the Senate. Perlstein no doubt included these forgotten tidbits about Biden because he surely favored Bernie Sanders in 2020. All great fun, but Perlstein and other contemporary historians continue to concentrate on the growing strength of conservatism in the 1970s while they still miss the simmering civil war inside the Democratic Party that was a key element of the era. Biden resisted the Democrats' own Jacobins, such as the radical insurgent congressional delegation elected in 1974, and that resistance played an interesting role in his success in 2020.

IF PERLSTEIN'S narrative fails to come to grips with the agony of 1970s liberalism or make a serious case that the rise of the right set up the country for supposed disaster upon Reagan's ultimate electoral victory, the fault lies in Perlstein's tacit premise that the country was already pretty rotten. He betrays this premise in the strange fixation with serial killers that appears throughout the book. Ted Bundy, as a former young Republican (albeit a Rockefeller Republican), is an easy target for partisan asides, but John Wayne Gacy, David ("Son of Sam") Berkowitz, and Kenneth Bianchi (L.A.'s "Hillside Strangler") also get mentions. Perlstein says Bianchi proved that "a psychopath could be living next door to you, too" and manages to transform Gacy, who buried his teen victims under the floorboards of his suburban Chicago house, into "one more parable about all the rot hiding underneath of the floorboards of a nation that liked to think of itself as innocent." At another point, Perlstein asks: "Just how sick was Norman Rockwell's nation, that it kept raising up monsters like these?"

Then there are Perlstein's occasional references to pop culture, which are equally uneven and bizarre. *Star Wars*, we're told, "was not a Jimmy Carter sort of film. . . . *Star Wars* was a Ronald Reagan kind of film." Maybe so, though this will come as news to the decidedly left-leaning George Lucas, who conceived the movie partly as a parable of the Viet Cong against the United States. For Perlstein, *Star Wars* merely ratified the rightward—yes, rightward—direction of Hollywood, coming on top of the "vaguely reactionary" *Taxi Driver* and the "disappointing" best picture of 1976, *Rocky*. His long and disapproving retelling of the plot of *The Deer Hunter* culminates with a quotation from movie maven Peter Biskind that *Deer Hunter* director Michael Cimino was "our first home-grown fascist director."

For all of the painstaking detail Perlstein dug up for this fine-grained narrative, there are many key events he describes in rushed or inadequate fashion, such as the failed Iran hostage-rescue mission in 1980 or key episodes from the final weeks of the Carter–Reagan election showdown. Other major issues, such as arms-control diplomacy with the Soviet Union, are treated perfunctorily at best. *Reaganland*, in the end, is more a visit to Perlstein's ultimately uninteresting brain than it is a fulfilling return to America in the 1970s.

—*Commentary*, November 2020

Chapter 30

Standing Pat

Daniel Patrick Moynihan: A Portrait in Letters of an American Visionary, edited by Steven R. Weisman

In 2000, shortly before he left the Senate, Daniel Patrick Moynihan gave a speech fully displaying the paradoxes that defined his career. Soaring prescription drug prices were a hot issue at the time. Incoming President George W. Bush's eventual solution was Medicare Part D, a costly new entitlement that had the dubious distinction of being wholly unfunded. Moynihan urged a different approach: price controls. But, he added, "when we do that, we'd better hope the Swiss pharmaceutical industry keeps working," because the shrunken profits of American pharmaceutical companies would constrict their ability to innovate. There, distilled in consecutive sentences, was the Moynihan contradiction—the confidence in using government to solve social problems, alongside the clear-eyed recognition that the limitations and unintended consequences of government intervention cannot be wished away.

Moynihan seemed to be in the middle of every major political controversy for 40 years. As a result, this new collection of his letters, memoranda, and diary entries, ably edited and annotated by former *New York Times* reporter Steven Weisman, illuminates not only Moynihan's thought and character, but the age he lived in.

Few analysts were more prescient; the harder questions about Moynihan's legacy are to what extent he made a difference, and whether the differences he did make were for the better or worse. Moynihan predicted back in 1965 that the increase of illegitimacy and single-mother households would bring social disaster for black communities. He told Richard Nixon in 1969 that women's rights would be the emerging issue of the 1970s. Moynihan and Ronald

157

Reagan were the only two public officials who predicted in the early 1980s that the Soviet Union was on the verge of collapse. "The defining event of the decade," the senator wrote in 1980, "might well be the breakup of the Soviet Union."

Moynihan didn't get everything right. In 1964 he brought Ralph Nader to Washington—a mistake that had the unintended consequence of preventing an Al Gore presidency 37 years later. Moynihan thought Watergate would destroy conservatism. Above all, he was spectacularly wrong in predicting that the 1996 welfare reform act would result in millions of destitute families and children living on the street. "Thus ends the progressive era," he declared in a note to himself. If only.

Because Moynihan wrote and spoke with an insider's discernment and clarity about the defects of liberalism, conservatives often liked him. Although he compiled a near-perfect liberal voting record during his 24 years in the Senate, liberals often did not like him. His candor about the severity of social pathologies and the limited ability of public policy to ameliorate them was a greater affront than conservatives' opposition. Like devout adherents of other faiths, modern liberals believe apostates are worse than infidels.

In 1989 Moynihan defended his consistency in a letter to Louis Henkin of Columbia University: "I had never represented myself as anything other than a liberal Democrat. Accordingly, my votes didn't take any explaining. What would have taken explaining was to have started voting differently." (In one of his older letters—from 1963—Moynihan says "I believe in quotas and lots of other un-American devices.") He went on to explain why so many on the Left made him a pariah:

Those of us who began writing about these [social policy] matters in the 1960's were fully in agreement with all that liberalism was attempting. But we began to worry as to whether we would bring it off. This kind of critique was much too often greeted as a renunciation of goals rather than an inquiry as to means.

As a White House advisor writing to President Nixon in 1969, however, Moynihan expressed deep misgivings about what liberalism was attempting: "The fact is that the more one knows about welfare the more horrible it becomes: but not because of cheating, rather because the system destroys those who receive it, and corrupts those who dispense it." He made a similar point 20 years later in a letter to a liberal Democrat, Governor Mario Cuomo of New York: "There are simply limits to what can be achieved by large hierarchical government organizations." Yet Moynihan seldom seemed to mark out those limits in his legislating. How to make sense of this cognitive dissonance, which looks like political fecklessness?

* * *

The simplest explanation is that Moynihan, who was elected to the Senate in 1976 after narrowly defeating the far-left congresswoman Bella Abzug in a Democratic primary, had a practical need to vote Left if he wanted to survive as a New York politician. Indeed, in subsequent elections left-wing activists made noises about running a challenger against him. A more generous account is that as an FDR Democrat who identified with the working class, Moynihan was, for all his intellectual independence, a loyal team player when it came time to vote aye or nay.

Both explanations are perfectly reasonable, as Moynihan himself might have put it. But a close reading of his letters suggests other, more discouraging possibilities. As one would expect, Moynihan is more candid in private communications about certain delicate points than he chose to be in his speeches and published articles. In the 1970s, for example, Moynihan wrote publicly, "Liberalism faltered when it turned out it could not cope with truth," and contended the new political culture of the Left "rewarded the articulation of moral purpose more than the achievement of practical good." In his letters he was more accusatory, writing to E.J. Dionne in 1991, "The liberal project began to fail when it began to lie. That was the mid sixties...the rot set in and has continued since."

Moynihan had raw personal reasons for feeling this way. As an assistant secretary of labor, he wrote the famous report in 1965 on the looming crisis of the black family. Both he and the report quickly became the objects of remarkably strident attacks that marked the beginning of political correctness—the willful, often enforced closing of minds to inconvenient topics and perspectives. (The denunciations grew louder four years later when Moynihan's "benign neglect" memo to Nixon was leaked to the press. It argued, quite sensibly, "We may need a period in which Negro progress continues and racial rhetoric fades.") The author of the "Moynihan Report" noted in 1985 that because of the firestorm it occasioned, "a twenty year silence commenced in which almost no one worked on the subject [of race]." In another letter to an old colleague he added, "We have paid a fearful price for what American scholars in those years decided not to learn about."

As important as race was, liberals closed ranks and minds about even bigger questions. By the time Moynihan went to work for Nixon in 1969, he perceived that liberalism was fast decaying into something loathsome and terrifying. In 1970 he wrote to H.R. Haldeman, Nixon's chief of staff:

What we are facing is the onset of nihilism in the United States.... The three most important points are that nihilists are almost entirely drawn from the educated, even upper classes. They are extremely idealistic, seeing themselves as agents of the purest charity. They are violent in the most extreme ways.

As an example Moynihan singled out Bernadine Dohrn, a leader of the anti-war terrorist group, the Weather Underground, who went on to become one of Barack Obama's Hyde Park supporters.

That he wasn't thinking just of the New Left radical fringe was made clear in Moynihan's speculation to Nixon, "Are we then witnessing the ultimate, destructive working out of the telos of liberal thought?" In another note to Nixon he observed: "The elite intelligentsia of the country are turning against the country—in science, in politics, in the foundations of patriotism. How can we not pay for this?"

* * *

Given such clarity about the completeness of the liberal collapse, how is it that Moynihan never seriously considered switching sides, openly joining the conservative opposition? His private writings offer several explanations, starting with his basic conviction that conservatives weren't up to the job. Several letters attest to his belief that the Left was more competent than the Right. "I kept trying to tell people in the [Nixon] administration that a fundamental fact of their dialectical and rhetorical position was that they were permanently outclassed." To Vice President Spiro Agnew, whose fierce rhetoric against liberals he wanted to tone down, Moynihan argued:

It comes to this. You are hopelessly outnumbered.... There are not a half dozen other Republicans who are in any way so disposed and so equipped. You are alone. You have no troops. No one carries on your argument, no one elaborates it, no one initiates comparable and parallel arguments. No journal of any intellectual status is open to your point of view.... My point would be this. You cannot win the

160

argument you are now engaged in. Frankly, the longer you pursue it, I expect the more you will lose.

These firm beliefs about the correlation of political and intellectual forces help explain the single instance in which Moynihan worked to make a Republican administration less, rather than more, cautious and centrist. As ambassador to the United Nations in 1975-76 under President Gerald Ford, Moynihan pointedly said the U.S. should "raise hell" and go into explicit opposition in the General Assembly. And then he raised hell, calling out Turtle Bay's tyrants and kleptocrats just as Agnew called out the "effete corps of impudent snobs" in the intelligentsia. Indeed, Moynihan's splendid speech attacking the risible "Zionism is Racism" resolution ranks next to Lincoln's "House Divided" speech as a career-maker, propelling Moynihan to the Senate a year later.

But that speech might also be seen as an attack against a proxy for the American Left, which Moynihan believed was too powerful to be attacked directly. His reflections about the competence and strength of the Left suggest he was willing to openly oppose its nihilism at the U.N. precisely because in that forum, at least, it was essentially powerless. This raises the troubling possibility, however, that Moynihan lacked the courage of his convictions. It requires little bravery to oppose those who cannot strike back.

He offers evidence for this hypothesis in a remarkable 1973 letter to sociologist Nathan Glazer, ostensibly about the growing Watergate disaster. It quickly turned, however, to Moynihan's extended reflections on his ambivalence about supporting Nixon openly against George McGovern in 1972, despite admitting that he privately supported Nixon's re-election:

What do you call such a person? A Moynihan, I suppose. A term suggestive of moral and political failing. Yet what is it? Two things, somewhat opposed. First, the moral failing of being more concerned with deviations from one's own general position than with positions flatly and openly opposed.

Previously Moynihan had told Nixon that "I know there is an authoritarian Left in this country, and I fear it." Now he seems to admit that this fear is for himself as much as for his country, a suspicion that deepens when Moynihan gets to the second explanation of his admitted failing—that the Left is simply stronger and more competent that the Right, and therefore cannot be successfully resisted. Even though the American people were moving

161

to the Right, "there was a movement of political competence to the left."

We knew this. Over and again Norman [Podhoretz, editor of *Commentary*] would tell me that the administration would someday be ruined by its seeming relentless insistence on incurring the hostility of *men who simply outclassed it.* (Emphasis in the original.)

In other words, Moynihan was unwilling to leave the winning side to join the losing side. He was intimidated. At best, doubting conservatism's ability to resist liberalism effectively, he feared relinquishing the presumptive moral authority of liberalism if he joined the Right.

His perception that the Right was not up to the job of effectively challenging the Left (or even running a serious conservative administration) was accurate in the Nixon years. Moynihan's admonitions could be read as a thoughtful, prudent strategy for navigating through the unprecedented political storms of the day. But the relative strength of the Right was growing fast, in no small part because some disaffected liberals were willing to make a clean break.

Others in his cohort—Podhoretz, for example—became "neoconservatives." Though it clearly fit him, Moynihan hated and resisted that label. His rejection of it points to the most obvious difference between him and those who accepted it: none of them was ever much interested in holding public office. In fact, it's impossible to imagine Irving Kristol or Nathan Glazer enduring Senate life, let alone engaging in the grubby glad-handing of campaigning. Moynihan, by contrast, relished retail politics, and loved being a senator. He was a public man, in the classical sense of the term. Perhaps, then, the judgment that the Left intimidated him is too harsh. A more charitable interpretation of his political career would emphasize the pragmatic maneuvering needed to remain viable within the Democratic Party, in the slim hope of reviving the more sober liberalism that had predated the Great Society. An honorable cause but, alas, a hopeless one.

* * *

Another troubling strand emerges in his private writings: his insecurity, bordering at times on an inferiority complex. In a journal entry from his post as ambassador to India in 1974, he writes:

I have turned down the kindest of offers to join the Committee on Social Thought at [the University of] Chicago, writing [university president Edward] Levi that while [Edward] Shils and [Saul] Bellow and [William] Kruskal don't know this, I am not their equal. Were I to settle among them they would find out, and while they would never in the least way suggest that they had come to realize this, I would know they had and that would make it a waste for everyone. I have had singular difficulties in these matters.

The "singular difficulties" probably involve his travails in obtaining a tenured faculty position at Harvard; several passages in Weisman's collection suggest it was a close affair. The vain and surely ineffectual protests against what he considered slanders, such as his alleged fondness for strong drink and his oft-expressed anxiety about impecuniousness, all seem to be of a piece, even after discounting for false modesty. As one reads his least guarded writings, Moynihan's insecurity comes into sharper focus, and looms large as a factor in his political choices.

This insecurity brings to mind Charles Peguy's harsh aphorism, "It will never be known what acts of cowardice have been motivated by the fear of looking insufficiently progressive." Unhappily, this seems to explain quite a lot about Moynihan. Ultimately, he was not up to the job of successfully opposing what was worst and most dangerous in liberalism.

Added to a body of published work that was already formidable, these newly available writings offer evidence lifting the Moynihan story toward tragedy—for both him and the nation. He was a member of a very small club: politicians good enough at politics that they would be remembered if they had done nothing else, while good enough at something else that they would be remembered if they had never been in politics. Thus, we miss him. The pity is that had Pat Moynihan chosen or been constituted differently, we might miss him even more.

—*Claremont Review of Books*, Winter/Spring, 2010

164

Chapter 31

Sensibility as Soulcraft

The Conservative Sensibility, by George F. Will

As George Will nears his 80th birthday, he has produced *The Conservative Sensibility*, the summa of his long career in opinion journalism. Unlike his periodic collections of topical columns, this big book is written to last for many seasons to come. (The name "Trump" does not appear once.) A close look at the sweep of Will's career reveals subtle changes in his political outlook, reflecting the maturation of his own views but also of American conservatism. An impressive achievement, *The Conservative Sensibility* deserves to take its place with such classics as Friedrich Hayek's *The Road to Serfdom* (1944) and Richard Weaver's *Ideas Have Consequences* (1948).

In 1981, on the occasion of his 40th birthday, Will whimsically remarked that "I have been eagerly anticipating my 'mid-life crisis,' that moment when the middle-aged male does something peculiar." It was not forthcoming, and he quickly admitted that "my mid-life crisis is that I am not having a mid-life crisis." But arguably he did have a slow-moving midlife *intellectual* crisis: *The Conservative Sensibility* shows him working it out at last. Will's midlife intellectual crisis, and its resolution, mirrors the midlife crisis of post-Reagan conservatism, which is still working itself out even as it recalibrates its meaning in relation to Donald Trump's presidency.

* * *

Will also delivered the Godkin Lectures at Harvard University in 1981, the basis for his slender book *Statecraft as Soulcraft: What Government Does* (1983). It was, he self-deprecatingly wrote later, "read by dozens," but some of those dozens found it "peculiar" in just the way a midlife crisis might manifest itself. In those days, Will described himself as a "Tory," because "I trace the pedigree of my philosophy to Burke, Newman, Disraeli, and others who were more skeptical, even pessimistic, about the modern world than most people are who today call themselves conservatives." (His collection of columns published the previous year was titled, *The Pursuit of Virtue and Other Tory Notions*.) Though Will's erudition encompassed American thinkers and writers, he chose three British thinkers as his inspirations.

The Conservative Sensibility repudiates the main argument of *Statecraft as Soulcraft*. Will now believes that he was "quite wrong" to think "that the American nation was 'ill-founded' because too little attention was given to the explicit cultivation of the virtues requisite for the success of a republic." The "defect of better motives" was, plain and simple, not a defect of the founding. But Will is too hard on himself. Perhaps *Statecraft as Soulcraft* should be thought of as an early first draft for *The Conservative Sensibility*, which is more than three times as long. Some important differences and continuities between the two books reveal how Will has "refined and enlarged" his views, to borrow a phrase from *The Federalist*.

* * *

In particular, he has changed his mind about James Madison. In the earlier book Will blamed our supposed neglect of civic and individual virtue on Madison, who had founded a government on the low but solid ground of accommodating and checking the people's self-interest and passions. Will's heart belonged to Edmund Burke, the thinker cited most extensively in *Statecraft as Soulcraft*. "American conservatism needs a Burke, a Disraeli—a self-conscious practitioner who can articulate the principles implicit in the statecraft he practices," Will wrote 36 years ago. Furthermore, "The conservatism for which I argue is a 'European' conservatism.... It is the conservatism of Augustine and Aquinas, Shakespeare and Burke, Newman and T.S. Eliot and Thomas Mann." In calling for revisions to conservative rhetoric about government, Will argued that it should be "less Madisonian and [John] Marshallian." Like Russell Kirk's, Will's brand of American conservatism back then disregarded or disowned the distinctly American elements of our political life.

By contrast, Will's new book places the American Founding front and center:

Although it distresses some American conservatives to be told this, American conservatism has little in common with European conservatism,

167

which descended from, and often is still tainted by, throne-and-altar, blood-and-soil nostalgia, irrationality, and tribalism. American conservatism has a clear mission: It is to conserve, by articulating and demonstrating the continuing pertinence of, the Founders' thinking...reconnecting the country with the principles of the Founding [is] conservatism's core purpose today.

The Conservative Sensibility explicitly repudiates Burke:

Subtle and profound, [Burke's] works are rich in prudential lessons that remain germane. Nevertheless, his thinking is in the European tradition of throne-and-altar conservatism.... Burke's conservatism was, in large measure, produced by British premises and French events.... American conservatism is not only different from, it is at bottom antagonistic to British and continental European conservatism.

It is not so much that Will offers a sweeping revision of Madison as that he perceives more fully the virtues of the founders' thought. Now, he says, "properly understood, conservatism is the Madisonian persuasion," and "the fundamental political axis of our time is an argument between Madisonians and Wilsonians." Will joins the growing number of conservatives who, influenced by the work of Ronald J. Pestritto (Pestritto is cited more than any other scholar in Will's new book), regard Woodrow Wilson and Progressivism, not Franklin Roosevelt's New Deal, as the primary attack on the American Founding. Will does, however, include a good summary of how FDR built upon the Progressive attack.

* * *

Of equal significance, he also discusses extensively and admiringly the Declaration of Independence and its teaching about natural right. In *Statecraft as Soulcraft*, Will is equivocal, even skeptical, of the Declaration, especially its self-evident truths about natural right. He refers to its most famous sentences as a "highly charged declaration of a political philosophy" that ultimately amounts to a "rhetorical flourish" rather than a serious political theory. Will now says, however, that "the most important paragraph in humanity's political history [is] the second paragraph of the Declaration of Independence," precisely because it does embody serious principles that are the ultimate stumbling block to modern progressive ambitions.

168

And at the heart of the Declaration's principles is the central contested issue of our time: human nature. Progressives and their allies consider it unfixed, malleable, and therefore raw material that invites endless progressive social engineering. Will doesn't equivocate here: "If there is no sense in which there is an eternal human nature, there cannot be eternal principles—certainly no self-evident truths—of political organization and action." Throughout *The Conservative Sensibility*, he returns to human nature's centrality. "Civilization's enemies attack civilization's foundational idea," he writes, "the proposition that human nature is not infinitely plastic and therefore that people cannot be socialized to accept or do whatever those in charge of socialization desire."

Will still believes that "measures must be taken to make virtue less rare and more predictable," but whereas his earlier book treated our deficiency in promoting virtue as a political failure, his new one understands it primarily as an educational failure. His chapter on the wreck of American education today, a subject absent from *Statecraft asSoulcraft*, notes the continuity between the founders and the classics, a subject usually missing from the "low but solid" rendering of the founding. "[Madison] and his fellow Founders conceived of happiness as Aristotle did, as a durable state of worthy satisfaction with life.... Happiness, therefore, is an *activity*."

* * *

And what is the primary "activity" of America? Here Will pivots from Madison to Alexander Hamilton, and we see another significant revision. The commercial society that Will had mildly disdained in *Statecraft as Soulcraft* he now sees as an incubator of civility: "In fact, the nature of life in a commercial society under limited government is a daily instruction in the self-reliance and politeness—taken together, the civility—of a lightly governed open society." The subtitle of the chapter where this appears is "Capitalism as Soulcraft." Will doesn't neglect or deny the arguments of Harvard sociologist Daniel Bell and others that dynamic capitalism undermines some virtues necessary for ordered liberty and human flourishing, but regards the welfare state as social decay's more significant cause.

The subject of political economy displays one of Will's more important revisions. "If conservatism is to engage itself with the way we live now, it must address government's graver purposes with an

169

affirmative doctrine of the welfare state," he argued in *Statecraft as Soulcraft*'s brief chapter on "Conservative Political Economy." "A welfare state is implied by conservative rhetoric. A welfare state can be an embodiment of a wholesome ethic of common provision." Back then, Will wasn't much impressed with libertarians; he called them "ideological capitalists," and included a genial sideswipe at Milton Friedman just to make sure we got the point.

The difference between this and his much longer "Political Economy" chapter in *The Conservative Sensibility* can be summarized by a single name that never appeared in the earlier book: Friedrich Hayek. Today Will endorses the central insight that Hayek variously described as the "fatal conceit," "constructivist fallacy," or "knowledge problem": the coordination of human knowledge presupposed by socialism or central planning is epistemologically impossible. Will quotes one of Hayek's shorter formulas as the epigram for the chapter: "The curious task of economics is to demonstrate to men how little they really know about what they imagine they can design," and Will goes on to give an able summary of Hayek's seminal 1945 essay "The Use of Knowledge in Society."

Consequences ensue. Milton Friedman is rehabilitated, and Will calls as witnesses a number of contemporary thinkers who can be considered Hayek and Friedman's progeny, such as John Cochrane, Deirdre McCloskey, and Matt Ridley. In perhaps his most startling confession, Will thinks the Supreme Court's 1905 ruling in *Lochner v. New York* was correct: government regulations cannot violate individuals' constitutional rights to enter into contracts. His argument owes a great deal to David Bernstein's powerful revisionist history, *Rehabilitating* Lochner*: Defending Individual Rights Against Progressive Reform* (2011).

* * *

But if Will is now more friendly to classical libertarianism and notes that the welfare state is much more pernicious than consumerist capitalism as an acid eating away at family stability and bourgeois virtues, he has not embraced the hyper-libertarianism that disdains *any* political or policy role oriented toward both virtue and greater social equality. His richer understanding of the sensibility conservatives should bring to social policy can be revealed again by comparing parallel passages between *Statecraft as Soulcraft* and *The Conservative Sensibility*. In the former, Will argued:

But conservatives, in their eagerness to put government in its place (which they think is down, and far away), argue fatuously that "only people produce wealth; government does not." Government produces the infrastructure of society—legal, physical, educational, from highways through skills—that is a precondition for the production of wealth. The unlovely locution "human capital" reflects the impulse to reduce all social categories to economic ones, but it also reflects a recognition that investment must be made in people before they can be socially competent. And it is obvious, once you think about it, that government is, and must be, a major investor.

This formulation sounds uncomfortably similar to President Obama's claim, "If you've got a business—you didn't build that. Somebody else made that happen." Or, as Senator Elizabeth Warren had argued before him, "You moved your goods to market on the roads the rest of us paid for. You hired workers the rest of us paid to educate."

In *The Conservative Sensibility*, Will correctly discerns that for today's progressives, emphasizing the governmentally provided "infrastructure of society" is not intended to support the flourishing of individuals or to make greater individual achievement possible. Quite the opposite: Obama and Warren "both spoke in order to advance the progressive project of diluting the concept of individualism. Dilution is a prerequisite for advancement of a collectivist political agenda." The progressive appeals to "society" (or, to invoke former Representative Barney Frank's embrace of government, "the things we do together") serve as a sanctification of envy, and a justification for wealth confiscation and redistribution. Progressives are usually more artful than New York City Mayor Bill de Blasio, who says that "there's plenty of money in this country— it's just in the wrong hands." As Will warns, "government will not be a disinterested judge of what is its proper share of others' wealth."

* * *

With one simple distinction, Will's prior position on government's affirmative role can be squared with his current clarity about rapacious progressivism: It is conservatives, not progressives, who appreciate society and understand its complexity. And toward the family, the most important aspect of society, progressivism has been indifferent, if not hostile. "It is arguable," Will writes, "that the

171

most molecular word in political discourse, the noun that denotes something on which all else depends and builds, is neither 'justice' nor 'freedom' nor 'equality.' It is 'family.'" Whether the struggles of the family in recent decades should be attributed to progressives' mendacity (such as from feminists) or progressives' incompetence (such as from Great Society programs), the overall moral and cultural decay of our time is beyond the reach of conventional politics.

While pointedly rejecting the conventional narrative about income inequality that holds center stage for progressives today, Will explains in a roundabout way that conservatives should take inequality more seriously than the Left does, largely because conservatives do not avert their gaze from natural and deeply ingrained social causes of unequal outcomes. But he goes on to argue that conservatives should treat more seriously the barriers to equal opportunity. Again, there is a continuity with *Statecraft as Soulcraft*, in which Will argued that our growing understanding of "early childhood development suggests that 'equality of opportunity' is a much more complicated matter than most conservatives can comfortably acknowledge." He goes on in that book to suggest enhancing equality of opportunity by various forms of state action, family-friendly tax credits being one possibility.

* * *

In *The Conservative Sensibility* will expounds this subject at greater length, reflecting the insights and concerns of James Q. Wilson and, above all, Will's great friend Daniel Patrick Moynihan. "The depressing truth is that inequality has deeper, more complex origins than we have thought. And America's foundational promise of equality of opportunity is far more problematic and elusive than we, particularly conservatives, have thought." No mention of tax credits or other small-ball this time. To the contrary, channeling both Hayek and Burke, Will warns against the progressive hubris that we know how to fix complex social problems. Intuitive solutions "will be wrong most of the time," and when complex, undesigned systems such as the family "are unintentionally weakened to the point of disintegration, no one knows how to put them back together." What is most needed now is for "government to swear a version of the Hippocratic oath: 'Do no harm.'"

Will's capacious treatment of progressivism's threat to the republic, and robust revisions of his previous perspective on the

172

American Founding, would suffice to make this book interesting and important. But there's much more. His chapter on "The Judicial Supervision of Democracy" lays out the case for what is today called "judicial engagement" on behalf of protecting natural rights. Will unites the Declaration and the Constitution, consequently endorsing constitutional principles not necessarily in the document's text. He follows Harry V. Jaffa in linking Robert Bork and Antonin Scalia with the majoritarian positivism of Oliver Wendell Holmes. Will says that by criticizing the defective originalism that has facilitated the administrative state's relentless expansion, "Clarence Thomas becomes America's indispensable constitutionalist."

His chapter on foreign policy, "Going Abroad: A Creedal Nation in a World on Probation," is more theoretical than tethered to current events. Aside from a brief critique of George W. Bush's idealism, which manifested itself in the agonizing war and occupation in Iraq, Will takes the long view, revealing a geopolitical realism more harmonious with Thucydides than John Bolton. "Reflection about foreign policy, as about all other spheres of politics, should begin with the basic question: What is the essential, unchanging nature of human beings?" Applying Hayek's "fatal conceit" to the domain of foreign policy, Will finds our incompetence at nation-building has the same root as our incompetence at domestic social engineering.

He wants us to shed not only progressive romanticism about domestic social policy, but also our "temperamental optimism" about foreign policy—a trickier matter, precisely because America is founded on an explicitly idealistic creed. Will doesn't just want us to be realistic or prudent but properly pessimistic about the world. "In foreign policy, as elsewhere, one of conservatism's functions is to say some things that people do not want to hear, such as this: War, which always has been part of the human story, always will be." Offering no brief for isolationism, he merely thinks our departures from John Quincy Adams's declaration that we "do not go abroad searching for monsters to destroy" have lacked prudence.

* * *

The Conservative Sensibility's most idiosyncratic chapter concerns religion and science. Will describes himself as "an amiable, low-voltage atheist," for whom "[t]heism is an optional component of conservatism." His main object is to fix our emphasis on the first half of Jefferson's phrase in the Declaration about "the laws of nature" in preference to "nature's God," who was "not necessarily the God of the Bible." His respectful argument curdles only in his discussion of two figures—Whittaker Chambers and Russell Kirk—whose emphasis on the necessity of religious faith is, Will thinks, "politically ruinous" for conservatives.

After 30 pages of discussing religion, the chapter takes a sharp turn to science and cosmology, subjects rarely discussed in Will's newspaper columns. His Cook's tour from physics to biology contends that an entirely secular openness to transcendence is possible: who needs revelation when the awesome mysteries of the cosmos fire human contemplation and creativity? Or as he puts it, "Why speak of emptiness when our world is still filled with...astonishments, including the worlds Shakespeare created and peopled?"

* * *

Of course, a key aspect of modern cosmology is entropy: everything eventually runs down. *The Conservative Sensibility* concludes with a return to entropy in the political realm: "Conservatism's task is to urgently warn about what is perishable: Everything." The remedy is a return to the centrality of reestablishing respect for the principles of constitutional government, which in turn depends on one of the oldest and simplest of virtues: self-control or self-restraint. "[T]he Republican Party's intellectual pedigree traces directly to Lincoln's denial that Kansas could choose to have slaves."

Today's progressives promote a slavishness to the nanny state that doesn't just undermine self-control but debases politics itself. Although George Will can be said to have taken a libertarian turn in his late career, he does not have the anti-political attitude that often accompanies libertarian insights into government failure. He diagnoses a "protracted apostasy from principles that, by limiting the scope of government, protected the stature of politics" as the cause of our contemporary peril. His remedy is a "conservative sensibility [that] knows that the possibilities of politics, although limited, are not negligible."

—*Claremont Review of Books*, Summer 2019

Chapter 32

A Towering Achievement

Studying Thatcher through Charles Moore's eyes provides lessons about statecraft that will never stale.

Margaret Thatcher: From Grantham to the Falklands, by Charles Moore

Margaret Thatcher: At Her Zenith, in London, Washington and Moscow, by Charles Moore

Margaret Thatcher: Herself Alone, by Charles Moore

Leo Strauss described Winston Churchill's four-volume biography of his great ancestor, the duke of Marlborough, as "an inexhaustible mine of political wisdom and understanding, which should be required reading for every student of political science." With the recent publication of *Herself Alone*, the third, concluding volume of Charles Moore's biography of Margaret Thatcher, it is no exaggeration to place this epic work on the same plane as Martin Gilbert's *Winston S. Churchill*, Robert Caro's *The Years of Lyndon Johnson*, or indeed *Marlborough* itself.

A former editor of the *Spectator*, the *Sunday Telegraph*, and the *Daily Telegraph*, Moore masters details of the policy controversies that defined Thatcher's long political career while ably depicting the people and events that surrounded her. Some readers will get more information than they would prefer—such as Thatcher's purchases at the duty-free shop after a summit in Bermuda, or her apparel choices at various key moments—but the pace never drags. Moreover, this level of detail permits Moore to sort out discrepancies, mistaken accounts, and erroneous recollections to provide an undoubtedly accurate narrative.

* * *

Despite Moore's sympathies for Thatcher's politics and regard for her as a person, he criticizes her mistakes. As in Churchill's narratives, Moore pauses from time to time to observe the wider scene, offering wisdom and insight. Yet he conveys his judgments with a light touch, never lapsing into the mawkish sentimentality that frequently mars Caro's otherwise compelling LBJ biography. Along the way, Moore debunks many myths and misconceptions. For example, Thatcher did not say, "Don't go wobbly on us, George," to President Bush after Saddam Hussein's Iraq invaded Kuwait in 1990.

Moore presents the necessary analysis of Thatcher's character, the central factor in her (or any politician's) greatness, and explains why her political opinions were of secondary importance. From an early age we see Thatcher reaching heterodox views from her own reading and reflection as much as through formal education. Key elements of her outlook, formed at a young age, included: a core attachment to the rule of law; a hatred of totalitarianism and a corresponding opposition to leftist utopianism; an appreciation for a free-market economy (formed at a time when the enthusiasm for collectivism and central planning was running at flood tide); and, surely not coincidentally, a deep admiration for Churchill. Some of this orientation she acquired from her middle-class shopkeeper father, who was also a borough finance official in her hometown of Grantham. But much of her thinking was formed by reading the works of Friedrich Hayek, among others.

* * *

Thatcher was an apprentice lawyer. Her appreciation for the rule of law was deepened though her independent study of Roman law, and she was much taken with A.V. Dicey's neglected 19th-century classic, *The Law of the Constitution*. Throughout her entire adult life she supplemented her reading by interacting with authors and thinkers. After reading Allan Bloom's *Closing of the American Mind* (1987), for example, she hosted Bloom for lunch at Chequers. Robert Conquest influenced her latent anti-Communism, but she met, read, and kept in regular contact with Henry Kissinger, which didn't prevent her from becoming a vocal critic of détente. (In fact it was the Soviets, reacting strongly to an anti-détente speech she delivered in 1975 just after becoming Tory leader, who first called Thatcher the "Iron Lady," comparing her to Otto von Bismarck, Germany's "Iron Chancellor.") A 1975 meeting with Ronald Reagan, at that time a former governor and future presidential candidate, lasted twice the scheduled time and looms large in retrospect.

One of Moore's many invaluable services is explaining Thatcher's political philosophy, mischaracterized by her enemies and even many of her sympathizers and supporters. It has been commonly supposed, partly because of her stated affinity for Hayek, that she was purely a libertarian individualist or "economic" conservative. Even Roger Scruton criticized her on this ground in the 1980s, though he later retracted it. A core axiom of the Left's current obsession with "neoliberalism" is that Thatcher, along with Reagan, "gutted" the welfare state and unleashed the "cowboy capitalism" that led directly to the housing crisis and financial crisis of 2008. It is an exceedingly weak case for many reasons, but as Moore explains, Thatcher made few serious efforts to rein in social spending ("Public spending, as a whole, was never cut"), and "in truth she was more open to the very different charge that she shied away from serious reform" of the welfare system. In fact, Thatcher felt as early as the end of her first term that she should have been bolder in challenging the British welfare state.

* * *

Thatcher's critics treat her comment that "There is no such thing as society" as proof of unfeeling individualism, an unfair distortion that Moore corrects. Contrary to the common perception, he argues that Thatcher "instinctively disliked mere individualism: what she was searching for was liberty in a strong moral and social order." (He points to her strong opposition to proposals to institute a small charge for library books: "People must always have access to pull themselves up—that is why I will *never* have charges for libraries.") Individual persons, she explained in an early lecture, only exist in a rich social context of "family, clan, community and nation, brought up in mutual dependence.... '[L]ove thy neighbour as thyself' express[es] this."

To Thatcher, the welfare state's ideological defect was transferring responsibility from the individual and civil society networks to the state, expecting government to solve life's problems. She understood that "individual" is an adjective rather than a noun: "And you know, there's no such thing as society. There are individual men and women, and there are families. And no government can do things except through people.... It's our duty to look after ourselves and then, also, to look after our neighbours." "Far from advocating selfishness," Moore concludes, "she was

178

arguing against it, on the grounds of duty to neighbour." Predatory labor unions strangling the economy and robbing taxpayers were, Thatcher argued, a better example of selfishness.

* * *

Today we ascribe her outlook to a rebalancing between state and civil society, but Moore explains that Thatcher's view arose more from her religious sensibilities, a consideration most accounts overlook. Moore calls Thatcher a Methodist who "was not one of those who thought Christianity should be merely private, with nothing to say about the life of society." Indeed, one of Thatcher's pious private secretaries regarded her as "the most religious Prime Minister since Gladstone."

She took theology—and her interactions with senior Anglican clergy who were mostly critical or opposed to her—seriously. The religious component of her thinking owed much to Edward Norman, the Cambridge theologian who dissented from the prevailing leftward drift of the Anglican Church. Although appointing bishops to the Church of England was a mere formality by her time, she once chided Robert Runcie, the archbishop of Canterbury: "Why can't we have any Christian bishops?" "She had a preference for theologically orthodox bishops," Moore says, "whom she considered an endangered species." When school curriculum reform came up in her second term, she urged her education ministry to include explicit content about the religious (and specifically Christian) heritage of England. Predictably, Church leaders were opposed.

As a young woman Thatcher singled out the Acts of the Apostles as her favorite book in the Bible, which may explain her energetic practice of spreading a message. One surprising fact that emerges from Moore's account of her many policy battles is how she was much more flexible and compromising than ideologically dogmatic. The Thatcher who emerges is more cautious and deliberate than widely believed. "'Thatcherism' was never a philosophy, but a disposition of mind and character embodied in a highly unusual woman."

Key to that disposition of mind was her understanding that whatever compromises may be necessary as a practical matter, it was essential to keep the central principles and core ideas front and center before the public at all times. Like Reagan, she understood that persistent argument would shape compromises in your direction.

179

Thatcher delighted in drawing the sharpest distinctions between the Conservative and Labour parties, and welcomed conflict and confrontation. She hated appeals to "consensus" and "national unity," rightly regarding such watery terms as evasions of clarity and the necessity for decision. "No great party," Thatcher said early in her political career, "can survive except on the basis of firm beliefs about what it wants to do."

* * *

Nigel Lawson, one of her chancellors of the exchequer with whom she clashed sharply, said, "A key to understanding Mrs. Thatcher was that she actually said what she believed." Moore's own gloss is that "[s]he had the radical's total lack of embarrassment about arguing from first principles." In a speech she delivered in Canada in 1975, shortly after becoming Tory leader, Thatcher averred: "It is often said that politics is the art of the possible. The danger of such a phrase is that we may deem impossible things which would be possible, indeed desirable, if only we had more courage, more insight."

Thus, what emerges in Moore's treatment is that single most important virtue: courage. Beyond her natural political ability, evident very early when few women were recognized in British politics, Thatcher's raw courage explains virtually all of her success.

One startling aspect of her career that emerges from Moore's narrative is precariousness. Despite contrary perceptions, Thatcher's economic policy over her 11 years in office was often uncertain and halting. More importantly, she was never fully accepted by her own party establishment, and was effectively "on probation" for most of her first term. For long periods in all three of her terms she and her Tory Party were down in the polls and staring at electoral disaster. She turned things around twice to achieve landslide re-elections, even though internal conflict and uncertainty pervaded the Conservatives.

The ineptitude and hard-left lurch of the Labour Party helped, but her own steadfastness was decisive. Her three greatest triumphs— winning the Falkland Islands war, breaking the radical coalminers' union, and reviving the dynamism of the British economy through denationalization, deregulation, and tax reform—were all close-run affairs. But for her determination, each could have ended disastrously. Other major policy attainments resulted from traditional cabinet government at work. Moore explains that the famous industry

180

privatizations—a term Thatcher disliked as "a dreadful bit of jargon to inflict on the language of Shakespeare"—were almost entirely the work of her treasury department.

The Falklands War was crucial. Thatcher's first-hand memory of Britain's capitulation in the Suez crisis of 1956 left her determined not to repeat that humiliation and retreat, but she had to overcome the deep equivocations of her own foreign office, the U.S. State Department, and her military service chiefs. "It is not mere flattery to say that only she could have done it," Moore writes. "The Falklands War brought out Mrs. Thatcher's best qualities—not only the well-known ones of courage, conviction and resolution, but also her less advertised ones of caution and careful study."

* * *

Moore's account makes a compelling case that Thatcher deserves more credit than she gets for unwinding the Cold War, ending apartheid in South Africa, making progress on Northern Ireland, and for attempting, with less success, to make serious progress toward a settlement in the Middle East. One other foreign policy controversy remains highly salient—resistance to the metastasizing European Union. Europeans—and much of her cabinet—were horrified by her hostility to the "European project," most memorably expressed in her statement that "We have not successfully rolled back the frontiers of the state in Britain, only to see them re-imposed at a European level, with a European super-state exercising a new dominance from Brussels." The proximate controversy that caused a serious breach with her foreign minister and chancellor was Britain's entry into the nascent European exchange rate mechanism, the first step to the single currency that eventually appeared as the Euro. Thatcher was vehemently opposed, while her cabinet was in favor. She lost this battle in the short term, with cabinet resignations damaging her political standing and contributing to her eventual ouster. After 2016, however, it is clear that Thatcher's resistance to European integration helped make Brexit not only possible but necessary.

By her third term, as Moore's title *Herself Alone* attests, Thatcher was increasingly isolated from many leading cabinet officials and much of her party. Ultimately, her position as prime minister became untenable due to an attempt to reform local government finance. The so-called "poll tax"—which means a per capita tax in the British context, rather than one on voting as it does in the American—was hugely unpopular with the public and her own party, setting in motion the long train of party intrigue to oust her in 1990. This "political assassination," says Moore, amounted to "an unforgettable, tragic spectacle of a woman's greatness overborne by the littleness of men." His narrative of her downfall proceeds day-by-day and even hour-by-hour, a feat of forensic journalism producing a drama worthy of Hollywood.

* * *

Even with a restive party it was only by the narrowest margin that Thatcher was voted out, but she had lived and governed on narrow margins throughout her career. Moore thinks poorly of the cabal that ousted her—"The tribe acted largely by instinct against the leader whom it had never fully accepted"—but also assigns blame to Thatcher. She did not take the leadership challenge seriously and was absent from London while the intrigue gathered speed. Her rough personal relations with her male colleagues caught up with her. "Her victims could not have been expected to put up with it for ever," in Moore's judgment. "After more than eleven years, most colleagues were understandably sick to death of her.... As is often the case with great leaders—it makes them the subject of tragedy—her vices were inseparable from her virtues."

Beyond the Brexit legacy, Moore's three volumes have material relevant to 2020, such as Thatcher's remark that urban riots are "crime masquerading as social protest" and that most British people "regard the police as friends." The discussion of a proposed Tory campaign theme for the mid-1970s—"Who governs Britain?"—seems ideal for our present moment in the U.S. (The Tory leadership rejected the theme in favor of a bland campaign, which disgusted Thatcher and prompted her successful challenge to Ted Heath as party leader.) Thatcher's death certificate, Moore tells us at the end of the third volume, recorded her occupation as "Stateswoman (retired)." One of her favorite aphorisms was, "Time spent on reconnaissance is seldom wasted." Studying Thatcher through Charles Moore's eyes provides lessons about statecraft that will never stale.

—*Claremont Review of Books*, Fall 2020

Chapter 33

Can 'Darkest Hour' Avoid the Pitfalls That Have Plagued so Many Churchill Films?

It may well be impossible ever to make a film adaptation of *The Great Gatsby* that can successfully live up to the full majesty of the novel. Hollywood has tried it five times, each with disappointing results despite impressive casts including Robert Redford and, most recently, Leo DiCaprio. The soul of the great novel just doesn't translate to the silver screen. Not even 3-D can solve the problem; the story will always engage the imagination of a reader more than any celluloid version.

The same difficulty arises with nearly all film treatments of Winston Churchill, the greatest human being of the 20th century. His largeness of soul, his capacious intellect, his legendary wit, his soaring oratory, and the length, breadth, and heated controversies of his long career—including many disasters, mistakes, and personal setbacks—are hard to render in the compressed format of feature films while retaining the profundity and substance of the man. Most films or TV shows about Churchill, or containing a significant Churchill role, are disappointing. There are a few exceptions, all of which owe their success to combining three related challenges in the right proportion.

The first and most obvious is casting. The role has humbled some of the greatest actors of modern times such as Richard Burton, whose 1974 turn in <u>*The Gathering Storm*</u> is entirely forgettable. The question is freshly acute with the arrival of *Darkest Hour* with Gary Oldman in the starring role, which has become controversial even before its general theatrical release this week, and coming on the heels of two other Churchill depictions, last summer's *Churchill* featuring Brian Cox in the title role, and the prominent inclusion of Churchill's character in the Netflix series *The Crown*.

The less said about *Churchill* the better. This film took Churchill on the eve of the D-Day landing as its focus, and the result is a film that is not just ahistorical, but anti-historical. The summary judgment of Andrew Roberts, currently working on his own Churchill biography, is sufficient: "The only problem with the movie—written by the historian Alex von Tunzelmann—is that it gets absolutely everything wrong. Never in the

184

course of movie-making have so many specious errors been made in so long a film by so few writers." John Lithgow in *The Crown* plays a stooped-over Churchill who was borderline senile, a gross caricature of the reality of Churchill's second premiership. Part of the problem is a defective script, but at 6-foot-4, Lithgow would seem a poor physical match for the 5-foot-6 Churchill, if nothing else.

The second challenge for every screenwriter and director is what story line, or period of Churchill's life, should a film try to cover or employ as a character study? A person who was in office for more than 50 years, who switched parties twice, who was at the center of two world wars and the beginning of the Cold War, who saw combat as a young soldier on horseback (including the last full cavalry charge of the British army and a daring escape from a prisoner of war camp) and as middle-aged commander in the trenches, who was present in New York for the great crash of 1929 and later run over by a car on Fifth Avenue . . . you get the idea. And how can the many facets of Churchill's character and talents be conveyed—the soldier, the politician, the painter, the author of 50 books, the connoisseur of fine food and wine, the raconteur, the sportsman—even a turn as a bricklayer? There's good reason he was *Time* magazine's "Man of the Half Century" in 1950. At that time the magazine said "no man's history can sum up the dreadful, wonderful years, 1900-1950. Churchill's story comes closest."

The temptation is usually to cast Churchill at his peak, in his "finest hour" in World War II, but that is such a large story, involving other great figures such as FDR and Stalin, that Churchill usually ends up weakly defined. Most films attempting to portray Churchill against the wide canvas of the whole war, such as the 1994 made-for-TV movie *World War II: When Lions Roared*, are bland and forgettable, and capture the "roar" of Churchill at a very low decibel level and in monochromatic tones. *When Lions Roared* offers Bob Hoskins as Churchill, and is the weakest performance of the cast, which offers Michael Caine as Stalin and, ironically, John Lithgow turning in the best performance of the film as FDR. (Maybe someday Lithgow can be offered a Stalin film vehicle to complete the trifecta—he could do his own one-man Yalta show perhaps)

The more successful film renderings involve a shorter slice of Churchill's life, such as one of the earliest Churchill films, 1972's *Young Winston*, starring Simon Ward in a faithful adaptation of Churchill's memoir *My Early Life*. This winsome and utterly ingenuous film, based on the veteran screenwriter Carl Foreman's script (Foreman wrote the screenplays for *High Noon, Bridge on the River Kwai*, and *The Guns of*

185

Navarone) and directed by Richard Attenborough, featured a stellar supporting cast including Robert Shaw and Anne Bancroft as Winston's parents, Anthony Hopkins as David Lloyd-George, and Jane Seymour in one of her very first roles, as Winston's early love interest Pamela Plowden. The film holds up extremely well, and is notable for resisting the temptation to use Churchill's obvious ambition to make him into an ambiguous or grotesque anti-hero. The film ends just as *My Early Life* does—with a rendition of one of his controversial early speeches in the House of Commons in 1901 about the military budget, then meeting and marrying Clementine Hozier, with whom he "lived happily ever afterwards."

Sharp-eyed viewers may perk up at the early scene involving the stern school headmaster who caned the unruly 8-year old Winston excessively during his brief time at St. George's School. (The scene marvelously conveys Churchill's impertinence in his questioning of the Latin first declension vocative case.) The headmaster, with the unlikely name of Rev. H.W. Sneyd-Kynnersley, was played by Robert Hardy, who went on a decade later to turn in arguably the best performance of Churchill in the eight-part BBC TV series from 1981, *Winston Churchill: The Wilderness Years*, covering the long recovery from the low point in Churchill's career from 1929 to 1939. (Hardy also appears in the Richard Burton's *The Gathering Storm*, as Joachim von Ribbentrop.) Like *Young Winston, The Wilderness Years* hews faithfully to the source material, in this case the fifth volume of Martin Gilbert's magisterial official biography of Churchill covering that period, the longest of the Gilbert's eight volumes at 1,167 pages. Hardy turns in a brilliant and wide-ranging performance, capturing Churchill's intense energy and drive but also his emotional and romantic aspects with great effect, reaching a pitch-perfect climax in the eighth and final episode that contains a moving rendition of his speech attacking the disastrous 1938 Munich agreement. The very last scene, where a humbled Prime Minister Neville Chamberlain invites Churchill back into the Cabinet as First Lord of the Admiralty after the outbreak of war on September 3, 1939, shows Hardy inhabiting the role of Churchill with a couple subtle mannerisms that are easily missed if you're not watching closely.

A perfect case study in how Churchill films go wrong is seen in two HBO productions, *The Gathering Storm* in 2002, which also covers Churchill's "Wilderness Years" ending in 1939, and its sequel *Into the Storm* in 2009, which attempts to cover the entire sweep of World War II. Both films were produced by Ridley Scott and featured screenplays written by Hugh Whitemore, a veteran writer of many superb historical dramas (including most notably a 1984 PBS docudrama on the Hiss-Chambers case that remains strangely unavailable). Despite the common production teams, the different casts and different approach to the story line make the *The Gathering Storm* a success and *Into the Storm* a failure. Albert Finney fills the Churchill role (with Vanessa Redgrave as Clementine) in a rich performance that conveys every bit as effectively as Hardy Churchill's personal and political ups and downs during his Wilderness Years decade. *Into the Storm*, by contrast, cast Brendan Gleeson as Churchill, and though he looks and sounds the part decently enough, he puts in a flat and uninspiring rendition.

Part of the defects of *Into the Storm* can be attributed to the third challenge for all would-be Churchill filmmakers. Even when limiting the story arc to specific time period of Churchill's life, screenwriters can't resist the urge to work in or move around some of Churchill's "greatest hits," that is, some of his most famous witticisms, quips, or statements made at a different time or in a different context. *Darkest Hour* does this extensively, for example in a scene where Churchill barks at Lord Edward Halifax, "stop interrupting me when I'm interrupting you!" Most biographies attribute this illuminating comment showing Churchill's domineering side as directed against his son Randolph at the dinner table at home at Chartwell years before, not to a fellow Cabinet minister. *Into the Storm* commits a related mistake endemic to so many films today of playing with the timeline, telling the story as a series of flashbacks while repeatedly jumping back to an anchoring scene meant to convey a subtle theme—in his case showing a worn down and defeated Churchill at the end of the war, without, however, capturing the poignancy of what Churchill himself called the "tragedy" of the end of the war in the last volume of his war memoirs. Poor Brendan Gleeson was defeated by both the script and the direction.

Which brings us to the controversy over *Darkest Hour*. Director Joe Wright and screenwriter Anthony McCarten stick closely to the timeline of the crucial first three weeks of Churchill's premiership culminating in the intense battle inside the war cabinet between Churchill and foreign secretary Lord Halifax. This conflict, which was largely unknown to historians before the 1980s (largely because Churchill deliberately concealed and mistold it in his memoirs), reached its climax on May 28, with Churchill's "choking in our own blood on the floor" speech to the entire cabinet. But Wright and McCarten take great liberties with some facts, move around some of Churchill's statements, and invent some completely ahistorical scenes (especially Churchill taking a ride in the London underground), all in service of a revisionist narrative that on the whole gets more of the big things right than wrong. It is useful to compare *Darkest Hour* with *Into the Storm*. Both films offer a version of the Churchill-Halifax confrontation, but even with the objections that can be made about the inventions of *Darkest Hour*, its overall portrayal of this crucial moment is far superior.

Much more can be said, and undoubtedly will be, about *Darkest Hour*, and the controversy itself places it as a film apart from all the others, likely prompting fresh rounds of interest in Churchill. Maybe the semi-fictional inventions of *Darkest Hour* that in some ways understate Churchill's greatness are a grudging concession to the fact that Churchill's story, like *The Great Gatsby*, overwhelms the ability to render it on film straightforwardly, especially in our egalitarian age that resents this kind of magnificence. Nick Carraway's last words to Gatsby come to mind: "You're worth the whole damn bunch put together." Carraway's coda to this comment could just as easily fit Winston: "[H]is face broke into that radiant and understanding smile, as if we'd been in cahoots on that fact all the time."

—*Weekly Standard*, December 20, 2017

Chapter 34

The Other J.C.

Palestine: Peace Not Apartheid, by Jimmy Carter.

Right in the first sentence of Jimmy Carter's new book on the Middle East there is a seemingly throwaway phrase whose significance is easily missed en route to the web of distortions that follows: "One of the major goals of my life," Carter begins, "while in political office and since I *was retired from the White House by the 1980 election.* . . ." (emphasis added). Now, it is understandable that an ex-president would seek to couch his electoral humiliation in the least wounding terms, but is it really so hard to say, "since I lost the 1980 election?"

That Jimmy Carter–man of action, seeker of solutions, prophet of peace–would describe his electoral drubbing in the passive voice points to a persistent intellectual and character trait that has been evident throughout his long career: The presumption of his own self-evident superiority. This trait has led him to think that he could not possibly have been to blame when voters rejected him in favor of a B-movie actor. As *Time* magazine essayist Lance Morrow once wrote, Carter behaves "as if the election of 1980 had been only some kind of ghastly mistake, a technicality of democratic punctilio."

This presumption perhaps explains why Carter, in *Palestine: Peace Not Apartheid*, can go from outrage to outrage and never feel compelled to answer arguments or acknowledge gross errors of judgment or fact. This is not a new facet of Carter's character. One his earliest biographers, Betty Glad, noted that as governor of Georgia in the early 1970s, he "seemed to experience opposition as a personal affront and as a consequence responded to it with attacks on the integrity of those who blocked his projects. He showed a tendency to equate his political goals with the just and the right and to view his opponents as representative of some selfish or immoral interest."

Indeed, Carter has been able to get away with this for so long that he probably thought his immunity to criticism was unassailable. But with his latest book, he has finally gone too far. He willfully distorts facts; he

190

misrepresents the terms and conditions of treaties, United Nations resolutions, and diplomatic events; he traffics in dodgy anti-Semitic euphemisms. The book comes without any footnotes or source references, and Carter has never refuted the charge that he plagiarized maps that former President Clinton's Middle East negotiator Dennis Ross developed for his own book on the Middle East. *Palestine: Peace Not Apartheid* cannot be taken seriously as a commentary on the Middle East–and it has not been. But it is not useless. Properly understood, it reveals the tendentious and hostile mind of a man who has worked like few others to convince the world that he is a foremost repository of the very opposite traits: Objectivity and compassion.

It is Carter's presumption of his own great wisdom and judgment that has apparently led him to believe that the normal conventions of discretion that all ex-presidents have hitherto observed do not apply to him. He seems to suffer from Stockholm Syndrome when it comes to odious dictators who hate America–Carter admires, and has hugged almost every one of them. Hence he has globe trotted as a de facto shadow secretary of state, breaking bread with Hafez al-Assad, Fidel Castro, North Korea's Kim Il Sung (the last Stalinist, whom Carter inexplicably said North Koreans regarded "as almost a deity, as a George Washington, as a Patrick Henry, as a worshipful leader all rolled into one"), and, above all, Yasser Arafat. "There was no world leader Jimmy Carter was more eager to know than Yasser Arafat," Carter biographer Douglas Brinkley wrote. At their first meeting in Paris in 1990, they prayed and cried together, according to one account.

It has always been an interesting question whether Carter's credulity toward Arafat and the Palestine Liberation Organization (PLO) can be explained by simple gullibility, or something more sinister. In *Palestine: Peace Not Apartheid* Carter repeats verbatim from his prior Middle East book, *The Blood of Abraham*, a description of the PLO as a sort of Palestinian version of the United Way: "The PLO is a loosely associated umbrella organization bound together by common purpose, but it comprises many groups eager to use diverse means to reach their goals." As for Arafat, Carter depicts him as a beneficent statesman and humanitarian: "As chairman [of the PLO], Arafat turned much of his attention to raising funds for the care and support of the refugees and inspiring worldwide contributions to their cause." Carter also accepts, with stunning implausibility, Arafat's statement that "The PLO has never advocated the annihilation of Israel," instead endorsing his claim that "Zionist disinformation" and "differences among voices coming from the PLO" in truth perpetuate the idea of Palestinian hostility. (Carter even tries to absolve the other "voices" of their Israel-hatred, claiming in one recent interview that Hamas isn't committed to Israel's destruction.) Of course, it is tiresome to cite the nearly countless times Arafat declared the PLO's unambiguous intent to destroy Israel. Two examples will here suffice: "The goal of our struggle is the end of Israel, and there can be no compromise," Arafat was quoted in the *Washington Post* in 1970. A decade later he told a Venezuelan newspaper that "Peace for us means the destruction of Israel. We are preparing for an all-out war, a war which will last for generations."

The fallout from *Palestine: Peace Not Apartheid* has been volcanic, with widespread editorial-page denunciations and highly publicized rebukes from advisers of his own Carter Center at Emory University. The *Washington Post Book Review* called the book "cynical," while columnist Michael Kinsley called it "moronic." Fourteen members of the Board of Councilors at the Carter Center wrote an open letter deploring Carter's "false claims" and "malicious advocacy." The most substantial blow, however, came from Kenneth Stein, a distinguished figure in the field of Middle Eastern studies at Emory who had long collaborated with Carter on Middle Eastern issues and served as director of the Carter Center. In his letter of resignation from his affiliation with the center, Stein wrote: "Being a former president does not give one a unique privilege to invent information or to unpack it with cuts, deftly slanted to provide a particular outlook." Of course, Carter can't say Stein never warned him. In the early 1990s, Stein wrote to Carter of his growing concern about Carter's pro-Arabism: "If you continue on the course of only criticizing or minimizing Israel in your public presentations, you will be doing yourself a potentially devastating disservice, particularly if you want to be re-engaged in any capacity in future Middle East diplomacy." To this advice, Carter obviously paid no heed.

One of Stein's most damning charges against Carter's new book concerns the untruthful revision of the content of one of his exchanges with Syria's Hafez al-Assad in 1990. Stein is in a good position to know: He was Carter's note-taker at the meeting, and gave Carter a full set of his notes. In *Palestine: Peace Not Apartheid*, Carter says that Assad indicated his willingness to negotiate with Israel for the return of the Golan Heights, as well as to make the Golan a demilitarized zone. But Stein's notes unambiguously indicate that Assad rejected demilitarization as a violation of Syria's sovereignty. Stein writes: "These are intentional changes that Carter made for the apparent purpose of misrepresenting Israeli intransigence and Arab state flexibility."

To these and other charges, Carter has reacted as though he, in fact, is the wounded party. He has lashed out at critics for being under the sway of the "Jewish lobby," and, incredibly, denied that anyone has found any errors in his book. He says he wants to engage in debate and dialogue, but at the same time ducks every invitation to discuss the issues with informed interlocutors. His only concession so far has been to apologize for the most egregious formula of the entire book–his blatant endorsement of Palestinian terrorism. "It is imperative that the general Arab community and all significant Palestinian groups," he writes, "make it clear that they will end the suicide bombings and other acts of terrorism *when international laws and the ultimate goals of the Roadmap for Peace are accepted by Israel.*" (Emphasis added.) Carter is clearly saying that Palestinians need not give up terror until they achieve their political goals. At Brandeis University (where he agreed only to answer pre-screened questions), Carter said the phrase had been poorly and wrongly worded.

Is this explanation credible? Carter has a long habit of engaging in what was once described as "blurt and retreat," whereby he backs away from egregious statements when called on them. Yet circumstantial evidence suggests that this language was not mere verbal sloppiness, as Carter now wishes us to think. At the end of one of Carter's freelance Middle East peace conferences a few years ago, he let slip a comment that ranks up there with many racially tinged remarks from his various Georgia political campaigns: "Had I been elected to a second term, with the prestige and authority and influence and reputation I had in the region, we could have moved to a final solution." It is strange that an experienced politician would use that particular expression. Carter's secretary of state, Cyrus Vance, incautiously wrote years after leaving office that Carter's Middle East plan in a prospective second term was simple: Sell out Israel.

In another instance of "blurt and retreat," Carter has said he didn't mean to use the term "apartheid" in its South African, racial sense. But in the book, Carter says the Israelis are "imposing a system of partial withdrawal, encapsulation, and apartheid on the Muslim and Christian citizens of the occupied territories." He has also compared Israel's security fence to the Berlin Wall, glossing over the fact that the latter was intended to fence people in, while Israel's wall is intended to keep murderers out. The fence is necessary precisely because of the Palestinian intransigence that rejected the Clinton-brokered offer to settle once and for all the borders of the West Bank on terms advantageous to the Palestinians. Carter contradicts both Clinton and Dennis Ross (who were,

193

after all, in the room where the negotiations took place) in accepting Arafat's revisionist view of the terms of the deal, writing, "There was no possibility that any Palestinian leader could accept such terms and survive." Ironically, Carter is in a sense correct: Having nurtured the hatred of Israel for two generations, no Palestinian leader could make a serious peace deal with Israel, no matter the terms, without incurring the wrath of Palestinian militants. But this is Israel's fault?

Any number of character flaws may explain Carter's behavior and his statements. He may also suffer from living in the shadow of former President Ronald Reagan. Carter always thought Reagan an unworthy successor to him in the White House, and it must wound his pride to hear Reagan now lauded as the "great liberator" who set the stage for the peaceful end of the Cold War. Throughout his life, Carter's competitive streak has consistently led him to try to "one-up" the fellow next to him; the only possible way for Carter to match Reagan's achievement was thus to build on his one and only foreign policy success, the Camp David accords of 1978. Only the Middle East ranks close to the Cold War on the scale of world-historical conflicts that defy solution. Hence *Palestine: Peace Not Apartheid*, his last attempt to play grand-scale peacemaker in the twenty-first century.

Even if Carter were not so obviously unbalanced in his view of the conflict, it is evident that he does not have the sensitivity to address the matter clearly or effectively. One odd passage of *Palestine: Peace Not Apartheid* that several critics have noted with bewilderment concerns his preaching to Golda Meir during his first visit to Israel in 1973: "With some hesitation, I said that I had long taught lessons from the Hebrew Scriptures and that a common historical pattern was that Israel was punished whenever the leaders turned away from devout worship of God. I asked if she was concerned about the secular nature of her Labor government." Carter notes that Meir was taken aback by his "temerity," which of course did not prevent Carter from henceforth describing Meir, based on their one and only meeting, as his "good friend." Carter's use of this anecdote becomes even stranger when one considers that in Israel, the settler movement that Carter so vigorously deplores is in large part fueled by religious Jews who take seriously God's gift, in the Bible, of Israel to the Jewish people–including Judea and Samaria, more commonly known as the West Bank. If Carter were capable of taking ideas seriously, he would not unwittingly encourage the very faction of Israeli society that he most conspicuously detests.

The invocation of his faith in the advancement of his views was common for Carter. He famously "witnessed" (as evangelical Christians

194

call it) his personal faith to heads of state while president, including President Park Chung Hee of South Korea, whom he publicly chided over human-rights violations. South Korea's intelligence service apparently took Carter's disapproval of Chung Hee as a sign that they could get away with assassinating him, which they did a few months later. Yet Carter's theo-politics turn out to be highly selective. In Carter's previous book, *Our Endangered Values*, the tender concern over secularism that he expressed to Meir vanishes as he criticizes President George W. Bush for supposedly breaching the separation of church and state through the modest "faith-based initiative" that sought to encourage government cooperation with religious organizations that provide valuable social services. He also criticized Pope John Paul II's anti-communism, thinking it hindered the growth of the Catholic Church in the developing world.

These jejune contradictions reveal a miscellaneous intellect averse to consistent or compelling thought. Yet such is Carter's self-absorption that he is incapable of seeing "the mote in his own eye," as the New Testament reads, or of apprehending in himself the tragic flaw of pride. Carter revels in his status as an "elder statesman" and as America's "best ex-president," but with *Palestine: Peace Not Apartheid* he may have squandered the moral authority he so carefully burnished since leaving the White House, and pushed the scales from the eyes of many of his admirers. It is now likely that more Americans will come to understand the judgment of the late Murray Kempton, who wrote in 1994 that Carter "has no clear idea of the shrine he seeks except that it is built for him."

—*Azure*, Summer 2007

Chapter 35

Whose Declaration? Which Equality?

Our Declaration: A Reading of the Declaration of Independence in Defense of Equality, by Danielle Allen

It has always been the fate of the Declaration of Independence to bounce back and forth between the political equivalents of foster homes and orphanages. This owes to its ambiguous status in American political life. It is generally, though not universally, revered. But it is usually contested. Both Mitt Romney and President Obama quoted the Declaration prominently during the 2012 campaign (and Obama returned to it in his second inaugural address), but for contrasting purposes. Its formal legal status is doubted. Although it appears at the beginning of the U.S. Statutes, it is seldom — except, notably, by Clarence Thomas — cited as a constitutional authority.

The ideological character of the Declaration is even more diffuse. Many liberals and many conservatives are not sure they like it. Conservatives, following Tocqueville, worry that the emphasis on equality has eaten up, or will eventually eat up, liberty. The appeal to abstract principles of right is the kind of thing that Edmund Burke (who sympathized with the American cause) wouldn't approve. The ultimate insult from the right: It's *too French*.

Liberals have greater difficulty with the Declaration, because it is a stumbling block, as Lincoln promised it would be, to certain modern liberal purposes. Some liberals take notice of Thomas Jefferson's slaveholding, and disdain the Declaration as sheer hypocrisy, or denigrate the Founders by supposing the claim of equal rights was limited to white, property-owning males. Liberals of a more philosophical bent dislike the invocation of "self-evident truth" and especially natural right — "the laws of nature and nature's God" — because in this pillar of individual liberty is found the main justification for limited government. Hence Woodrow Wilson explicitly attacked the Declaration as obsolete. Wilson thought it best understood as a mere contract grievance against Great Britain: "If you want to understand the real Declaration of Independence," he wrote, "do not repeat the preface." Darwin and Hegel had overtaken Locke and Jefferson, Wilson thought, a view perfectly expressed in historian Carl Becker's otherwise excellent 1922 book *The Declaration of Independence*: "To ask whether the natural rights philosophy of the Declaration of Independence is true or false is essentially a meaningless question." Franklin Roosevelt didn't go as far as Wilson's filial impiety, but he did find it necessary to argue for separating the philosophy of the Declaration from the Constitution in order to prepare the ground for the New Deal's expansion of government to new and unknown places.

Danielle Allen has stepped into this tricky breach with an elegant book, deeply moving in many places, personal and conversational in style and yet also seriously philosophical and closely exegetical of the Declaration's text. (She spends 32 pages explicating just the first sentence of the Declaration.) Allen, a professor at the Institute for Advanced Study in Princeton, N.J., is a liberal, but not a leftist. (Actually, she was once an intern at National Review.) Even if some of her central arguments deserve strong engagement and criticism, taken in full the book represents a thoughtful celebration of the Declaration that will profit all readers.

The subtitle — "A Reading of the Declaration of Independence in Defense of Equality" — suggests the chief point of contention: What do we mean by equality, and does liberty inherently lead to unacceptable inequality? Allen treats the Declaration as "nothing less than a very short introduction to political philosophy," rather than a mere political tract. She is correct in arguing that "political philosophers have generated the view that equality and freedom are necessarily in tension with each other." In seeing equality and liberty as a tradeoff — a zero-sum game — Allen thinks "we have come, as a people, to choose liberty": "Equality has always been the more frail twin. . . . Under the general influence of libertarianism, both parties have abandoned our Declaration; they have scorned our patrimony."

It will surely come as news to libertarians to hear that the country is moving in a more libertarian direction (Obamacare, anyone?), and one might wonder whether reports of the rise of Elizabeth Warren, and of Obama's recent emphasis on income inequality, have somehow failed to make the Princeton newspapers. But Allen is more interested in exploring how we understand the subtle relationship between equality and liberty in the Declaration than in compiling a balance sheet of current public policy or income distribution. Like the Declaration, her full argument requires some careful disentangling.

The strongest aspect of Allen's argument is her implicit rejection of many left-liberal attacks on the Declaration, suggested in her title: "*Our*Declaration." Without minimizing or excusing the obvious contradiction of slavery, Allen by an elegant parsing of the text (especially her careful treatment of Jefferson's famous draft paragraph attacking slavery that was edited out by the Continental Congress) shows why the famous phrase "all men are created equal" meant everybody — not just property-owning white men. (Here she follows closely the understanding of Lincoln, who is largely absent from the book.)

Neither does Allen give much aid and comfort to simple-minded egalitarianism, or condone the modern liberal impulse to subsume individual rights under a general right to be made equal. She grasps that "equal" does not mean "same," and that still less should equality be measured by wealth: "It does not mean equal in all respects. It does not mean equal in wealth." Once again she derives these conclusions from a careful consideration of the text rather than through an imposition of her own preferences. From this careful reading she lays out five meanings of equality, several of which are recognizable but stated in contemporary language with an ever-so-slight liberal tinge. The first four are "freedom from domination, equality of opportunity to use the tools of government, the use of egalitarian methods to generate collective intelligence, and equality of agency achieved through practices of reciprocity."

While her textual constructions of these four understandings of equality are well-argued and plausible, the fifth and final one is where the mischief creeps in: "Equality as co-creation and co-ownership of our shared world." Allen derives this understanding from a less persuasive reading of the Declaration's closing passage, in which the signers mutually pledged "our Lives, our Fortunes, and our sacred Honor." "Each thereby claimed an equal ownership share," Allen writes.

Would this justify Krugmanesque 90 percent income-tax rates on the rich today? That conclusion would not square with, for example, James Madison's argument in the famous *Federalist* 10 that the first object of a government based on equal rights is to protect the unequal faculties of acquiring property. Allen goes nowhere near Krugmanland, however, and one of the virtues of her book is the complete absence of any Rawlsian turgidity about the mandates of egalitarianism.

In fact, her one specific suggestion for reducing inequality highlights a lingering confusion that the book does not resolve: "Perhaps the single most important thing we could do to reverse inequalities that abound in our society would be to repeal zoning laws and other measures that dramatically segregate people by income and ethnicity." The irony here is that most serious advocates of abolishing zoning and similar discriminatory regulation (such as restrictive occupational licensing) have been the libertarians Allen discounts. The one major American city without typical zoning — Houston — probably has the most social mixing and mobility of the kind Allen wants. It certainly has the greatest housing and job opportunities for lower-income minorities.

As the example of municipal regulation shows, the accumulation of more political power typically undermines both liberty and equality. Allen is on the verge of grasping this, noting briefly the recent empirical work of Larry Bartels, Benjamin Page, and Jason Seawright, currently very hot in political science, that finds that the richest Americans are dominating the political process and enjoying the most success in securing their public-policy goals, which differ from the preferences of the majority. Is this result purely because of wealth, or does the growth of government — and the flourishing of "crony capitalism" — explain some of it? Shouldn't it give egalitarians pause that five of the ten richest counties in America are clustered around Washington, D.C.? In this regard it is worth noting that Allen lingers only briefly on the complaint against King George III in the Declaration that perhaps best applies to our circumstances today: "He has erected a multitude of New Offices, and sent hither swarms of Officers to harass our people, and eat out their substance."

Allen, fortunately, doesn't venture into some of the usual prescriptions — e.g., campaign-finance reform — that are intended to equalize the playing field but in fact only centralize political power further in the hands of the bureaucratic class. This is to her credit, as she wants us to approach the Declaration as citizens rather than as policy wonks. If she isn't wholly successful or persuasive in harmonizing liberty and equality as they appear in the Declaration, it is chiefly because we shall never stop contesting the meaning of equality. By averting her gaze from the Founders' view that the harmony of liberty and equality requires strong limits on government power, Allen ends up framing her larger argument within the dichotomy she sets out to resist, leaving us still baffled by the problem.

But this is the book's only arguable major defect. I have dwelt on it at length here because it is central to the title and to the beginning and ending of her book, and it happens to be of most relevance to our current debate on inequality. She is not wrong to lament that our public discourse on equality is impoverished. There is much else in this book of great charm and substance. Her larger point that the Declaration is something every American should cherish is refreshing to hear from elite academia

199

today. This is an uncommon book for an uncommon document, and it contains many fine and fresh insights.

—*National Review*, September 22, 2014

Chapter 36

The Regressive Progressives

Illiberal Reformers: Race, Eugenics, and American Economics in the Progressive Era, by Thomas C. Leonard

Conservatives enjoyed extra helpings at the all-you-can-eat schadenfreude buffet when leftists at Princeton made the astonishing discovery that Woodrow Wilson was a racist and demanded that his name be struck from Princeton's well-known school of public affairs. Wilson's racism and other unappealing traits have long been well known among conservatives but came as news to the liberal ignorati.

The revisionist literature on Progressivism and the New Deal, once the near-exclusive province of conservative authors and a few eclectic economic historians, has been "going mainstream" for quite a while. The old narrative of brave and altruistic Progressive reformers' taking on "monopolist robber-baron capitalism" and government corruption, a narrative that dates back to the Progressive Era itself, has given way to a more spectral understanding that presents a complicated and mixed picture. This revisionism ought to, but somehow does not, prompt serious reflections about today's so-called progressivism, which in many respects departs significantly from its forebears but in other ways is a direct lineal descendant.

The latest entrant in the literature is Princeton economic historian Thomas C. Leonard's *Illiberal Reformers*. On the surface, as the subtitle indicates, the book is confined to the realm of economics, but Leonard captures very well how the various strains of Progressive thought — philosophy, political science, history, biology (especially Darwinian evolution), religion, law, and economics — were all amalgamated in the Progressive embrace of eugenics. "Hundreds, perhaps thousands of Progressive Era scholars and scientists proudly called themselves eugenicists," Leonard observes.

The idea of eugenics is thought to be wholly discredited or repudiated today; Leonard weaves in a number of useful reflections on Progressive ideas that have endured. What is now widely called "the administrative state" constitutes the central crisis of American government today, and Leonard nicely traces out the Progressive roots of this scourge. He concisely explains the core idea of Progressivism: that "science" should replace "politics" as the basis for government. This in turn gave license to the idea that "an industrialized economy should be supervised, investigated, and regulated by the visible hand of a modern administrative state." Leonard is equally clear, albeit brief in his explanation, that this new form of government entailed abandoning the classical-liberal philosophy of individual rights. He calls this "one of the most striking intellectual changes of the late 19th century, one with far-reaching consequences." He is especially good in clearing away many of the myths and misconceptions about "social Darwinism."

German historicism and Darwinian evolution provided the philosophical and scientific bases for abandoning natural rights and validating the presumption that expert administrators could guide the nation more wisely than elected politicians. Leonard notes the inherent contradiction of a movement that, on the one hand, called for more populist democracy but, on the other, wanted to govern more through expert elites isolated from direct political accountability — a contradiction that persists today. Leonard also briefly notes the Progressives' "extravagant" and "outsized" faith in their own scientific expertise and altruism. He notes that most Progressives' grasp of science was superficial, even for its time, and the same should be said for their grasp of German philosophy.

If Leonard's exploration of these central aspects of Progressive ideology is underdeveloped, it is because of his intense and thorough focus on the central question of eugenics in economic thought. To the extent that eugenics is thought about today, it is chiefly relegated to social and political enthusiasms, and it is Leonard's great service to have provided an exhaustive and detailed account of its centrality to advanced economic thinking and of the specific policies Progressive economists advanced in its name. And his exploration goes beyond simple issues of racial condescension to show how specific economic doctrines were vitally connected to eugenic ideology.

The most embarrassing idea was that the minimum wage could be a tool for discouraging immigration and promoting racial purity. (No one tell Paul Krugman.) "A minimum wage worked on two eugenic fronts," Leonard explains. "It deterred immigrants and other inferiors from entering the labor force, and it idled inferior workers already employed. The minimum wage *detected* the inferior employee." The Progressive economists a hundred years ago understood what progressive economists today have forgotten or willfully overlook: A minimum wage prices out marginally productive workers, who today as then tend to be young, unskilled, and minorities. The Progressives a century ago thought this would indirectly discourage immigration and reduce birth rates among immigrant populations. A number of other labor-union and liberal measures of the New Deal, such as the Davis-Bacon Act, also had eugenic underpinnings; they ironically remain totems of liberalism today, despite their nefarious origins.

Leonard fully traces out several other forgotten faces of Progressive illiberalism, such as the surprising connection of eugenics with religion and even conservationism. Eugenics, he writes, was "a keystone of the American conservation movement." Charles Van Hise, president of the University of Wisconsin and a prominent conservationist, "said that Americans must abandon individualism for the good of the race." Here we can see the seeds of the obsession with the "population bomb" of the 1960s and 1970s. There is one surprising omission from his vast catalogue of eugenic ideas and advocates: Margaret Sanger is barely mentioned.

Leonard also notes that Progressive economic policies were targeted not only against "inferior races" but also against women of all races, because women were either inferior or fragile, requiring the protection of the state. He correctly notes that, ironically, the only resistance to this paternalistic condescension came from the few conservative defenders of markets and individualism, such as Justice George Sutherland, who wrote the reviled Supreme Court opinions striking down sex-discriminatory labor laws.

The smug condescension of Progressives was of a piece with what Leonard describes as their "unstable amalgam of compassion and contempt," a trait that still very much afflicts today's self-described progressives. It hardly needs saying, but Leonard says it anyway: "American Progressive Era eugenics was anti-individualist and illiberal. . . . The original progressives' illiberal turn did not stop at property and contract rights. They assaulted political and civil liberties, too, trampling on individual rights to person, to free movement, to free expression, to marriage and reproduction."

An unstated implication of Leonard's conclusion is that a return to the principles of individual liberty and truly limited government might be in order, for even if it is true that eugenics is discredited, the undemocratic administrative state marches on, running roughshod with the latest pseudo-science in the same fashion as the eugenicists of a century ago. And while eugenics is gone certainly in name, has the idea of the "scientific" management of the human race been completely abandoned, in the age of increasing abortions for sex selection and disability avoidance, not to mention the coming age of genetically modified "designer babies"? *Illiberal Reformers* is a great achievement and an important contribution to the revisionist historical literature, but its tight focus on eugenics and economics avoids the deeper ethical ground on which we must confront this phenomenon.

—*National Review*, June 13, 2016

Chapter 37

A Premature Post-Mortem for Liberalism

The Strange Death of American Liberalism, by H.W. Brands

The Strange Death of American Liberalism is probably meant to recall George Dangerfield's 1935 classic, *The Strange Death of Liberal England*, which described the beginning of the slow-motion downfall of England's Liberal Party in the years immediately preceding World War I. Like the Democratic Party here in the 1960s and 1970s, the British Liberal Party buckled under the pressures from that generation's version of radical "new politics." As Dangerfield explained in his colorful prose, "the burden of Liberalism grew more and more irksome; it began to give out a dismal, rattling sound; it was just as if some unfortunate miracle had been performed upon its contents, turning them into nothing more that bits of old iron, fragments of intimate crockery, and other relics of a domestic past... [The Liberal Party] died from poison administered by its Conservative foes, and from disillusion over the inefficacy of the word 'Reform.'"

Dangerfield's description parallels the conservative view of the trials of liberalism in the U.S. since the 1960s, and at first glance it appears Brands is going to follow suit and offer a ratification of conservative triumphalism. "Liberals lost," Brands says on the book's fourth page, "not because they were wrong about American society, but because they were wrong about the world." Conservatives recognize that theirs is only a partial victory, for all the bruises and defeats liberalism has experienced over the past generation, liberalism remains entrenched in the media, higher education, and especially in bureaucratic government. Thus liberalism is still setting the political and cultural agenda of the country. Brands's real thesis, therefore, comes as a shock: American political culture is essentially conservative (or at least anti-government), and liberalism is an anomaly. The Cold War made liberalism dominant in the post-war decades; the passing of the Cold War, and liberalism's gradual embarrassment over the Cold War, led to the downfall of liberalism over the last generation.

Much of Brands's account is plainly right, and his book is filled with many shrewd observations and perceptions. (Nixon, he correctly notes, "was as much a liberal as John Kennedy or Lyndon Johnson.") But on close inspection there is mischief at work. The tacit premise of Brands's analysis is that the "national security state" necessary to prosecute the Cold War was the bulwark of big government in the post-war decades. Now the nefarious "national-security state" was a key theme of the New Left revisionism in the 1960s and '70s that sought to blame the Cold War on the United States, or at any rate to diminish the Cold War's seriousness. The benign end of the Cold War has given this argument a new lease on life—especially among the libertarian Right, which has converged with the isolationist rump of the Old Right (think Pat Buchanan) and the New Left on this point.

It is difficult to tell whether Brands sympathizes with one of these camps, or whether he is simply taunting liberals by ascribing their fleeting glory to the part of their legacy of which they grew to be most ashamed. The point of both Left and Right revisionism is that the Cold War was unnecessary, and Brand seems to share this point of view, though he does not say so explicitly. Here and there the reader will detect in Brands's prose the rhetorical tones of New Left revisionism, but New Left scholars such as Gabriel Kolko are missing from his bibliography; the figure Brands lauds most highly as a critic of the national security state is the original "Mr. Conservative," Senator Robert Taft.

* * *

The plot thickens when Brands introduces his back-story, a synoptic account of American political life since the Founding that emphasizes public distrust of centralized government. Brands has to perform some fancy footwork to lend verisimilitude to this argument. He portrays Woodrow Wilson's presidential victory as an expression of public preference for smaller government, and notes that in 1932 Franklin Roosevelt ran against deficit spending and centralized government. The New Deal was comparatively restrained in its reach, Brands argues. In all previous wars going back to the Revolution, government shrank in the aftermath. It wasn't until after World War II, he claims, that government remained large and growing, and this only because of the Cold War. "[I]t wasn't an accident that the high tide of liberalism coincided with the high tide of America's participation in the Cold War."

Ronald Reagan appears in Brands's account as a highly ironic figure. Reagan tried to revive 1950s-style fervor for the Cold war in the 1980s, which, it is implied, would have revived liberalism—Reagan's sworn enemy. Brands thinks Reagan failed to rally the public to his anti-communist banner, leading him to engage Gorbachev in his second term and bring the Cold War to its close. Clinton and Gore, Brands says, both kept a studied distance from the old-fashioned liberalism—remember, "the era of big government is over."

Brands is persuasive on many particulars—Americans' skepticism about centralized government is a legacy of the Revolution and Founding Era—but he elides the essential changes to out constitutional order that Progressivism wrought, changes that were instrumental in creating the administrative state that is the engine of perpetual liberalism today. Though Clinton and Gore paid lip service to the idea of small government, they pressed for every new government program they could. This appetite, like many others in the Clinton Administration, remained ungovernable. And for the far-left, the culture war serves as a nice substitute for the Cold War of their fathers, providing endless rationales for government growth.

If, in the end, Brands's thesis is wrong that liberalism was a short-run anomaly, still there is something in his claims worth taking to heart. His argument might be described as simply a fancy version of Randolph Bourne's famous phrase that "war is the health of the state." Brands finished his book before September 11, so it is ironic to read his closing judgments: "[A]nother serious threat to American security would be required to displace [public] skepticism...in the presence of a renewed security threat, the liberals will once again be called to power."

This is precisely the prospect that has cheered liberals since September 11, as polls have found public confidence in Washington at levels not seen in more than 30 years. Some liberals have forthrightly declared that they're back in business. Brands would not be so certain; the war on terror would need to be an unqualified success for public confidence in government to wax. Afghanistan may have gone well, but the government's bureaucratic approach to domestic security is likely to reinforce the skepticism of centralized government that has hobbled large liberal initiatives. Instead of effective security, we are getting the domestic equivalent of Vietnam, which was liberalism's undoing. Brands's book may be delightful mischief, but concerning the necessity of government to be effective in its objects, he is without illusion or contrivance.

—*Claremont Review of Books*, Winter 2002

Chapter 38

Hillary's Makeover

Living History, by Hillary Rodham Clinton

The Clinton Wars, by Sidney Blumenthal

Years ago I developed a standardized measurement for the agony involved in reading and reviewing tendentious books. I call it the "Donaldson Scale," after Sam Donaldson of ABC News, whose book I once had to suffer. "One Donaldson" means that a full bottle of scotch or its equivalent is necessary to grind out a review.

Hitherto few books have rated more than a Half-Donaldson, though the occasional effort of a French literary critic, or any John Irving novel, comes close to rating a Full-Donaldson. The memoirs of Hillary Rodham Clinton and Sidney Blumenthal have shattered the Donaldson Scale. To paraphrase one of Hillary's previous offerings, these books take a whole distillery.

Both Rodham-Clinton and Blumenthal have achieved new levels of groan-inducing banality. Consider this Blumenthal sample: "[Clinton] did not peer through a hazy lens into a nebulous future. Rather, he saw sharply defined problems requiring constant engagement to achieve practical solutions." Whoa! Stop the presses. Not to be outdone, Rodham-Clinton offers this profundity about the old Fleetwood Mac song that became the semi-official anthem of the Clinton years ("Don't Stop Thinking About Tomorrow"): "I had taken those lyrics to heart. It may have been a cliché, but the phrase that best summed up my political philosophy was: 'It's always about the future,' about what must be done to make America safer, smarter, richer, stronger, and better, and how Americans can prepare to compete and cooperate in a global community." More: "This [Bangladesh] was another country I had long wanted to visit, because it was home to two internationally recognized projects—the

International Center for Diarrheal Disease Research, and the Grameen Bank, a pioneer of microcredit."

Here and there, Rodham-Clinton manages to achieve some unintended wit in her banalities, usually in connection with her husband. "His ability to eat anything put in front of him is one of his many political talents," she writes, which may help explain his taste in women, too. Concerning the second most famous woman in Clinton's life, Rodham-Clinton offers this: "Bill told me that Monica Lewinsky was an intern he had befriended two years earlier when she was volunteering in the West Wing during the government shutdown. He had talked to her a few times, and she had asked him for some job-hunting help. This was completely in character to Bill. He said that she had misinterpreted his attention, which was something I had seen happen dozens of times before." Now that's funny. (But the biggest howler may be this one-liner: "I did my best to educate myself about cattle futures and margin calls to make it less frightening.")

It was not to be expected that either of these memoirs would be very good, though it is a mistake, as I shall argue, to dismiss them as mere self-serving propaganda. Presidential memoirs are notoriously bland and uninformative (with the notable exceptions of Dwight Eisenhower's and Richard Nixon's), and Hillary's ongoing political ambition circumscribes her derivative effort even further. Hillary calls the book *Living History*—though she and her (reported) six ghostwriters labor to make it as dead on the page as possible—thus resisting the tempting title *Rewriting History*. In fact, a deliberate anesthetic blandness serves her political purpose by making people think that perhaps she isn't so radical after all. It recalls Whittaker Chambers's description of how Alger Hiss would go about vindicating himself through endless professions of innocence: "What is vindication for him? It is the moment when one of the most respectable old ladies in Hartford says to another of the most respectable old ladies: 'Really, I don't see how Alger Hiss could brazen it out that way unless he were really innocent.'" Rodham-Clinton has already shown considerable political skill by seizing a U.S. Senate seat in New York, but she still has a lot of baggage to shed if she is to be a plausible presidential candidate. Many readers of this book will come away with the impression, "Gee, she doesn't sound so radical to me."

Thus *Living History* is a project to mask or soften Rodham-Clinton's massive will-to-power. Perhaps the most revealing moment of Rodham-Clinton's time in the White House was her famous 1993 speech on "the politics of meaning." In this speech she argued that we must "remold society by redefining what it means to be a human being in the 20th century," which will require "remaking the American way of politics, government, indeed life." This goes far beyond garden-variety liberal progressivism. The idea of "redefining who we are in this post-modern age" implies that there is no human nature, or that whatever human nature there is defines itself through sheer self-assertion. In other words, the human soul can be transformed at will. For Rodham-Clinton to say that we need to remake the American way of politics, government, and life is to imply that government has the right, even the duty, to change man into something he is not. (This effluvium prompted *The New Republic's* literary critic Leon Wieseltier, normally far-left in his politics, to offer a harsh judgment about the Clintonistas: "There is a certain sensibility, for which Mrs. Clinton's generation is famous, and which she perfectly exemplifies, that hates being preceded. Everything it experiences it experiences for the first time. When it sees, there is light; and when it fails to see, the whole world is covered in darkness.") Recalling Michael Oakeshott's axiom that "the conjunction of ruling and dreaming generates tyranny," Hillary's "vision" is truly frightening.

* * *

Rodham-Clinton attempts to de-radicalize this theme by attributing its inspiration to, of all people, the late Republican strategist Lee Atwater. Atwater, dying of brain cancer in 1989, understandably mused about his own spiritual deficiencies, and generalized them to the nation as whole in a magazine article published upon his death. Expunged entirely from Living History is the actual inspiration of Hillary's speech by the radical Jewish thinker Michael Lerner. It wouldn't do for Hillary's attempt to grasp the mantle of bipartisan moderation to advertise the real sources of her "politics of meaning." Her most brazen sanitizing effort is an early line paraphrased (without attribution) from Ronald Reagan to explain why she departed from her early political leanings as a Goldwater girl in 1964: "I sometimes think that I didn't leave the Republican Party as much as it left me."

She also dissembles about her senior thesis at Wellesley on radical community organizer Saul Alinsky. In *Living History* Hillary plays up her disagreements with Alinsky. She says she rejected the then-popular radical idea of revolution—even if there was one, she says she concluded in 1968, I wouldn't participate—and says she fundamentally disagreed with Alinsky that "the system" could not be changed through conventional politics. This is narrowly true, though Rodham-Clinton's thesis (I have read it) clearly sympathizes with Alinsky's radical viewpoint that the Great Society's liberal social policy didn't go far enough because it didn't redistribute power to the people. Hillary rejects Alinsky's "bottom-up" community organizing because she believes in "the role of centralized social planning in social change." She notes at the end of her thesis that many ideas considered "radical" at that time were mainstream policy in European social democracies. "Societal comparisons raise again questions about the meaning of 'radical' and even 'revolutionary' within a mass production/consumption state, particularly the United States." This is the Hillary of the health care fiasco of 1993, in which she brazenly declared that she couldn't be responsible for all the undercapitalized small businesses that could not afford health insurance for their employees.

* * *

Although Blumenthal's book is more explicit and honest in several ways, his well-known partisan hostility and paranoia warp the overall effort. There is an overwhelming tone of bitterness in both books—bitterness about Kenneth Starr, Republicans, Ralph Nader, the news media (in the Clinton-Blumenthal hall of mirrors, the media is a captive of the reactionary Right!), and especially Richard Mellon Scaife, who lurked behind every corner of what Hillary described as "the dark underbelly of the Republican Right."

Underneath this bitterness is a sense of unjustly insulted propriety. The Clintons and their circle are just such good people, with great ideas for America. The conservative attack machine prevented Americans from swooning before the Clintons' nobility and brilliance. The unworthy conservative opposition to the Clintons deprived America of the greatness they had to offer. "Had the proposals Clinton made for new legislation been enacted," Blumenthal laments, "the United States would now have universal health insurance, affordable prescription drugs for senior citizens, universal day care, more schools, higher teacher salaries and higher educational standards, more gun safety, greater voting rights, new civil rights laws against discrimination, and an even higher minimum wage." He adds that "If Gore had become president, undoubtedly progress would have been made on all these fronts."

The theme of the Clintons' essential goodness is carefully muted in Rodham-Clinton's book, but explicit in Blumenthal's. "Born in something like a log cabin," Blumenthal writes of Bill Clinton, "he was a member of a loose network that had grown up together politically since the 1960s…. The lingua franca of this network was the language of policy, the speci-fics of governmental activism. To be part of the network meant to be connected to its ongoing conversation. It was a large moveable feast, meeting at foundations, nonprofit issue-based organizations, universities, think tanks, journals, and the Democratic Party in all its manifestations." Jeepers, it sounds almost like a Vast Left-Wing Conspiracy.

The Manichean Blumenthal makes sure we understand that these are good people, while conservatives are bad people. Take, for example, his descriptions of the rival political consultants Lee Atwater (Republican) and Bob Squier (Democrat). "Atwater, then a thirty-eight-year-old South Carolinian, strutted as a Southern bad boy, masking his insecurities…. His pose as an electric-guitar-playing bluesman added to his image as a rebel…. Bush, the candidate who saw politics as unclean, hired Atwater to do the political dirty work for him." Not the sort of fellow you'd invite to dinner. Squier, on the other hand, "was unusual among politicos for his literary and epicurean interests. He had made PBS documentaries about Hemmingway, Faulkner, and Fitzgerald, and he had operated a wine press at his Virginia country home."

It is self-evident to Blumenthal that Al Gore was more worthy than George W. Bush to be president. "Gore had trained to run for the presidency…. Gore had command of an almost infinite array of intricate details and technicalities of science and social policy. He had mastered difficult fields, one after another, and arrived at innovative solutions to persistent problems." By contrast, "George W. Bush's advantages had been carefully arranged for him his whole life." In prep school, our author reminds us, "his chief distinction was as chief cheerleader." Hence Blumenthal isn't sated merely with refuting, in painstaking detail, the ethical charges against Clinton that culminated in impeachment; he ends his book with several chapters on the media unfairness to Al Gore and how Bush stole the election in Florida. "Whom the gods destroy," the ancient Greek lyric goes, "they first make mad." Blumenthal has written his own epitaph as a serious journalist, just as the Democrats, in their blind fury over George W. Bush, seem poised to drive over a cliff with Howard Dean, the perfect Blumenthal candidate.

It is a double mistake, however, to regard these memoirs as mere score-settling or self-serving revisionism. Blumenthal's book especially is built on a purebred progressivism that is rarely so clearly articulated from the Left today. One searches in vain in either book for a single mention of limited government, constitutional intent, or individual liberty. Rodham-Clinton supposedly channels Eleanor Roosevelt; Blumenthal channels Woodrow Wilson. "The presidency is the chief engine of progress in American history," he writes; "its leadership and power are central." Progressive presidents "seek to expand democracy by redefining the social contract.... Progressive presidents see themselves as the sole legitimate agent of the majority. In their mission to extend opportunity and rights, they constantly improvise their relationship with the people. They believe it is their unique responsibility and prerogative to reshape the country." Each progressive president, like Clinton, inherits the unfinished programs of the previous progressive presidents. Clinton "wanted to rebuild the inert executive branch and restore it as a progressive force, in order to turn the national government into an agent of change for American society as a whole. All these institutions were like bent, rusty tools that needed hammering and recasting."

Blumenthal goes on for pages in this vein. He attempts by sleight-of-hand (as does Hillary in a more cursory way) to deny the radicalism implicit in this unending progressive politics, by portraying Bill Clinton's object to be the "Third Way" between Left and Right, "neither statist nor *laissez faire.*" (Hillary calls it "the dynamic center.") Blumenthal unwittingly reveals Clinton's Third Way to be a fraud. He repeatedly describes Clinton's successful drive to the White House as being based on repudiating "the *perceived* failures" of the 1960s liberalism that shattered the Democratic Party. (Emphasis added.) Blumenthal's use of "perceived" failures, and his quotations from Clinton saying "We've got to turn these perceptions around," imply that liberal social policy was not mistaken. If this is their sincere belief, then the "Third Way" represents not an authentic moderate synthesis but a marketing tactic. Who's practicing Straussian concealment now? The substance and rhetoric of Clintonian progressivism represent a greater corruption of American government than either Whitewater or Monicagate.

* * *

Here it should be acknowledged candidly that Blumenthal, and to a lesser extent Rodham-Clinton, are correct that the intense focus on the Clinton scandals was a distraction from engaging the serious political argument that the Clintons represent. From time to time, especially during the health care debate of 1993-94, political argument turned on the clash between broader principles, which certainly contributed to the smashing Republican victory of 1994. (Both Rodham-Clinton and Blumenthal admit that the Clinton health care plan was a huge political blunder.) But once the Whitewater scandal cycle took over, serious political argument receded. Perhaps conservatives can't be wholly blamed for this in the way Blumenthal does; a media frenzy will always sweep away serious argument like a tornado does a trailer park. But at the end of the day the Clintons succeeded through an endless series of small gestures in shifting the political ground to the Left, such that George W. Bush was compelled to run for president as a compassionate conservative, similarly dedicated to policy gestures large and small that add up to an affirmation of big government.

Blumenthal tacitly underscores the failure of conservative argument during the second half of Clinton's presidency through his only substantive discussion of a conservative argument—the federalist jurisprudence of Chief Justice William Rehnquist. "The so-called original jurisprudence notion in which Rehnquist believes," Blumenthal writes, "that the United States is merely a compact of states, that state sovereignty nullifies national authority, that local control is more representative and expresses a superior 'majority,' harks back past John C. Calhoun, ideological forerunner of the Confederacy, to the anti-Federalists who campaigned against the Constitution in the early years of the Republic."

This is crude and incomplete, but essentially correct. Clinton, Blumenthal tells us, considered making a public speech before leaving office directly taking on Rehnquist, but ran out of time. (All those pardons required much burning of midnight oil.) Had Clinton done so he would have bored in on contemporary conservatism's weakest point.

As dreadful as these books are in a literary sense, they are politically instructive, even though in a manner not intended by their authors. *Living History* reminds us about the cleverness and determination of Rodham-Clinton. One fears that she has learned only too well from her mistakes. And Blumenthal's narrative reveals that the Right's concentration on the Clintons' scandalous behavior distracted from the real game—a game conservatives are losing in too many places.

—Claremont Review of Books, Fall 2003

Chapter 39

A Progressive's Progress

Love, Poverty, and War: Journeys and Essays, by Christopher Hitchens

I wake up every day to a sensation of pervading disgust and annoyance," Christopher Hitchens explains at the outset of *Love, Poverty, and War*, his new collection of essays. In due course, he offers a corollary: "There can be no progress without head-on confrontation."

Contrarianism is not a bad way to approach the modern world, because you will seldom be wrong. Hitchens has refined contrarianism into a high art that transcends mere iconoclasm, though one may doubt whether his name will be made into an adjective after the fashion of his hero, George Orwell. Hitchens would be among the first to admit that the cadences are incommensurate: "Hitchensian" doesn't roll off the tongue as neatly as "Orwellian." He shares two important traits with Orwell, nonetheless: his loving skill with the English language, and his revulsion at the smelly little orthodoxies of the Left.

As successful as this combination is, he may not be entirely well-served by channeling his disgust and annoyance into a confrontation with the first person or idea he sees over his morning coffee. Yet he seems to advance from triumph to triumph. What's the secret of his success? He offers a clue in the middle of the book: "No serious person is without contradictions." Sure enough, Hitchens's affection for the United States redeems his chronic indignation and makes his overall project worthy of deep admiration.

Many of the pieces included in this collection are either literary essays from *The Atlantic* or miscellany from *Vanity Fair*. As such they might be considered his hackwork. The world could use more such hackwork. In fact, Hitchens's real calling may be literary rather than political. His *Atlantic* essays, mostly new encounters with old books and authors such as Joyce, Borges, Proust, Kingsley Amis, and Waugh, read surprisingly fresh. But like Orwell—and Lionel Trilling, Joseph Epstein, and Norman Podhoretz—one suspects that Hitchens's literary sensibility is closely related to his political pilgrimage, which now finds him allying himself mostly with the Right after a generation's fealty to the Left.

But it is not easy to put sail to Hitchens's whirlwind. His strong dislikes include Henry Kissinger, Mel Gibson, Bill Clinton, Michael Moore, Noam Chomsky, Pope John Paul II, and, most notoriously, Mother Teresa. (The case of Winston Churchill will be considered in a moment.) He could probably find a dark side to Mary Poppins. The book is filled with acerbic gems. New York City Mayor Michael Bloomberg gets a well-deserved pasting: "And petty is not just Bloomberg's middle name. It is his name.... Who knows what goes on in the tiny, constipated chambers of his mind? All we know for certain is that one of the world's most broad-minded and open cities is now in the hands of a picknose control freak."

Sandwiched between his literary and political pieces are sterling examples of that time-tested genre, the travel essay. While the writing is first-rate, Hitchens indulges some of the typical Euro-Northeastern prejudices about heartland America. His journey across Route 66 in a borrowed Corvette brings him to Texas:

You hear a lot about the standardization of America, the sameness and drabness of the brand names and the roadside clutter, but you have to be exposed to thousands of miles of it to see how obliterating the process really is. The food! The coffee! The newspapers! The radio! These would all disgrace a mediocre one-party state, or a much less prosperous country.... Happening upon a stray copy of USA Today seems like finding Proust in your nightstand drawer instead of a Gideons Bible.

One wonders whether Hitchens isn't consciously playing to the *Vanity Fair* bleachers, since most *Vanity Fair* readers can only understand—or want to understand—the nation's nether regions through red-blue glasses. I've grinned at the same oddities along Route 66, including the largest cross in North America near Groom, Texas, and the Cadillac Ranch outside Amarillo. (Somehow Hitchens missed my favorite Route 66 landmark, Amarillo's Big Texan Steak Ranch, which will serve you a 72-ounce steak for free—*if* you can eat the whole thing, including side dishes, in under an hour.)

* * *

That Hitchens may be playing the rube card to fool the provincials back in Gotham and the Hamptons is suggested by his enduring admiration and affection for America, which have grown larger in the aftermath of September 11. Let him explain it:

Then there is the rather awkward question: Can one love a country? In the England of my youth, this would have come under the heading of the superfluous: some things just don't need to be affirmed publicly and there is something suspect about those who get too strenuous on the point. I'll go this far, though. The United States of America has been very kind and hospitable to this immigrant, and I would calmly affirm that, in case things should ever become desperate enough for anyone to have to care, my adopted country has found a defender in me. This necessarily broad allegiance came to a tungsten-sharp point in the fall of 2001, when my favorite city in all the world—and a favorite city of the world—was foully assaulted, as was my hometown of Washington D.C., by barbaric nihilists.

In one of the collected essays, written for *Vanity Fair* shortly after September 11, Hitchens was even more elemental, making clear that he would stand with America without equivocation: "one has to be able to say, My country after all.... Shall I take out the papers of citizenship? Wrong question. In every essential way, I already have."

Consequently, Hitchens has trained his lacerating invectives on several of his old allies—in some cases, co-authors—on the Left, such as Noam Chomsky and Edward Said. But no one fares worse than Michael Moore and his squalid film. "To describe [*Fahrenheit 9/11*] as dishonest and demagogic would almost be to promote those terms to the level of respectability. To describe this film as a piece of crap would be to run the risk of a discourse that would never again rise above the excremental.... *Fahrenheit 9/11* is a sinister exercise in moral frivolity, crudely disguised as an exercise in serious thought." And Moore himself has become "one of the sagging blimps of our sorry, mediocre, celeb-rotten culture."

Hitchens has no patience with the moral-equivalence, we-had-it-coming Leftists. He wrote on *The Nation*'s website in October 2001: "I have no hesitation in describing this mentality, carefully and without heat, as soft on crime and soft on fascism. No political coalition is possible with such people and, I'm thankful to say, no political coalition with them is now necessary. It no longer matters what they think." After carrying on in this way for several more weeks at *The Nation*, Hitchens was, in his own words, "excommunicated," ending a more than two-decade association with the Left's flagship journal. He hasn't looked back.

The final essay of the collection, from *Vanity Fair*'s October 2003 issue, describes the fall of Saddam. At the time he wrote the article, the missing WMDs in Iraq were becoming an issue, and the insurgency was starting to escalate. Hitchens has some deserved criticisms of George W. Bush and Tony Blair for insufficiently defending the war to the public, but he does not wring his hands or come within shooting distance of the Q-cliché ("quagmire"). On the contrary, Hitchens argues that Iraq "is emerging from a period of nightmarish rule to which anything would be preferable. So dare to repeat, in spite of everything, the breathless question: What if it works?" Right now it looks like it might, but only because Bush didn't lose his nerve. Perhaps Hitchens's relative silence about Bush—put it this way: he hasn't tossed barbs at Bush the way he has at just about everyone else—is a sign of grudging respect from a critic who isn't accustomed to showing any to political figures.

This defect shows itself fully in the opening essay of the book, which attempts to cut Winston Churchill down to size. Hitchens spends most of the essay disputing what he calls the "consecrated narrative" about Churchill—the "cult" of Churchill. He tempers his massive debunking effort with what he admits is the man's one redeeming quality. He was right about the Nazis:

Some saving intuition prompted Churchill to recognize, and to name out loud, the pornographic and catastrophically destructive nature of the foe. Only this redeeming x-factor justifies all the rest—the paradoxes and inconsistencies, to be sure, and even the hypocrisy.... He excoriated [Nazism] as a wicked and nihilistic thing. That appears facile now, but it was exceedingly uncommon then.

This won't do. Even if one concedes, for the sake of argument, that all Hitchens's criticisms are correct, it is remarkably superficial to attribute Churchill's one redeeming virtue to an unintelligible "x-factor" or "intuition." Hitchens seems incapable of pondering whether the qualities that led Churchill to his clarity about the Nazis were on display in the other controversial chapters in Churchill's career. Hitchens confuses supreme ego and magnanimity with dangerous or contemptible megalomania. Indeed, he more than once interprets Churchill as a Hegelian figure, more lucky than good.

222

Rather than a serious examination of Churchill's character strengths and weaknesses, we get an appalling catalogue of errors and myths about Churchill, starting with the chestnut that actor Norman Shelley read several of Churchill's key 1940 speeches to the British people, "perhaps because Churchill was too incapacitated by drink to deliver the speeches himself." This myth has been thoroughly recycled and debunked over the years, but Hitchens falls for it, probably because its most recent incarnation came from his friend, fellow leftist columnist Alexander Cockburn, in 2001. (Hitchens's essay originally appeared as a cover story in *The Atlantic*, and when the letters poured in wondering what happened to basic fact-checking at the magazine, Hitchens beat a partial, chagrined retreat.)

But that is only the beginning of the errors and recycled slanders. Another familiar charge that Hitchens revives is that Churchill knew of the coming German bombing of Coventry, but did nothing to stop it for fear of compromising the British code-breaking efforts. "The allegation has been in print for fifteen years [closer to 25 actually], and I have never seen it addressed by the Great Man's defenders, let alone rebutted." This merely shows that Hitchens hasn't read everything, despite the impression he likes to give. At least four British historians—Norman Longmate, Ronald Levin, Harry Hensley, and David Stafford—have refuted this widely held myth, as far back as 1979. Likewise, Hitchens alleges, Churchill possibly knew about Pearl Harbor in advance but declined to tell FDR—also disputed by numerous historians. He endorses the view that Churchill was complicit in a conspiracy to bring about the sinking of the *Lusitania* in World War I, a charge that has been chewed over and generally rejected for decades.

Hitchens accepts credulously every criticism and denigration of Churchill, and reads very superficially overall. This problem, especially, comes to light in an aside about William Manchester's unfinished Churchill biography. "In an extraordinary gesture," Hitchens writes, "Manchester rendered Churchill's wartime speeches as blank verse, with carefully incised line breaks and verse settings." But this is no "gesture." Manchester's books, like Martin Gilbert's, faithfully reproduce the format Churchill employed to give speeches—a fact Hitchens would have picked up had he read either author with any care, thus sparing him embarrassment.

* * *

In the Introduction to *Love, Poverty, and War*, Hitchens betrays his low opinion of politics: "Did politics always seem to be a sordid auction between banal populists?" One lesson he took from September 11 is that "there *is* no refuge from political engagement, and that if you try and hide from public life, it will assuredly come and invade your precious private sphere." Hitchens's vague anti-political temperament is a residue of his days on the Left, where the denigration of political greatness is an essential aspect of radical ideology. His artful critical faculty cannot ultimately disguise his cyncism. As Churchill once said of another grand weakness (appeasement): "It is too easy to be good."

An equally apt summation of the problem comes from British historian Geoffrey Elton, who wrote:

When I meet a historian who cannot think that there have been great men, great men moreover in politics, I feel myself in the presence of a bad historian. And there are times when I incline to judge all historians by their opinion of Winston Churchill—whether they can see that, no matter how much better the details, often damaging, of the man and his career become known, he still remains, quite simply, a great man.

Hitchens fails Elton's test. We might say then that Hitchens's progress since September 11 has brought him halfway to a sensible understanding of politics. He knows who the bad guys are, and while he seems to know who the good guys are and why, his old reflexes are against them. If he gets over this, he'll have at least a fighting chance to establish his place as an essayist alongside Orwell.

—*Claremont Review of Books*, Summer 2005

Chapter 40

The Liberal Republicanism of Gordon Wood

Reassessing liberalism's favorite historian.

Gordon Wood is the favorite historian of America's liberal establishment. His essays appear regularly in the *New York Review of Books* and the *New Republic*, and liberalism's leading intellectuals—from Michael Sandel to Morton Horwitz to Bruce Ackerman to Cass Sunstein—regularly cite him with approbation. What virtues do they see in his work? In Wood's books, particularly his *Creation of the American Republic, 1776-1787*, they see a hammer with which to bash American individualism and capitalism, and to support an ever-growing administrative state.

Wood says that the American Revolution was a "republican" revolution. By that he means that it had intellectual roots ranging from ancient Greece and Rome to the English Commonwealth, and that it was more communal than capitalistic. "Ideally," he writes, "republicanism obliterated the individual." He explains that

republicanism was essentially anti-capitalistic, a final attempt to come to terms with the emergent individualistic society that threatened to destroy once and for all the communion and benevolence that civilized men had always considered to be the ideal of human behavior.

Given that belief, we should not be surprised that America's liberals look to Wood to find an image of America that suits them. In his interpretation of the American Revolution, they find support for their belief that what is good about the American past is a certain communitarianism, which they wish to marry to the modern state. As Mark Seidenfeld wrote in the *Harvard Law Review*: "I view the civic republican conception as providing an essential justification for the modern bureaucratic state.... Moreover, given the current ethic that approves of the private pursuit of self-interest as a means of making social policy, reliance on a more politically isolated administrative state may be necessary to implement something approaching the civic republican ideal."

Wood's work has been particularly important to liberal legal theorists. They have embraced key aspects of his argument in *Creation of the American Republic* as the foundation of a renewed attack on the Constitution's few remaining restraints on government power. Law reviews are packed with articles touting the "revival of civic republicanism" as the new theoretical justification for welfare-statism, and as a substantive alternative to the historical dead-end of modern individualism. Mindful of the defects of Marxism, legal positivism, and Progressive era-style economic regulation, and facing the need to overcome the formidable arguments of constitutional originalism, civic republicanism enables the Left to turn the tables and claim an original intent argument of its own. The Left's enthusiasm for Wood's ideas took off, not coincidentally, in the late 1980s in the aftermath of Attorney General Edwin Meese's elevation of the controversy over original intent. As University of Wisconsin-Milwaukee historian J. David Hoeveler, Jr., observes,

What is at stake is nothing less than a contemporary liberal version of original intent.... These reconstructions of republicanism apply with varying specificity to the role of the Supreme Court in American society. They constitute a liberal original intent providing an ideological outline, or cultural value system, that has direct applications to law and the interpretation of law.

Wood's *Creation* is invariably the principal source offered as historical support.

The eager extrapolation of Wood's argument is seen not merely among obscure, tenure-seeking adventurists, but also among the leading celebrities of the legal academy. Horwitz, who teaches at Harvard Law School, cites Wood to give effect to his view that "republicanism was a truly coherent political alternative to liberalism in American thought." Sunstein, a leading light at the University of Chicago Law School, is explicit about the project of finding a non-Lockean, non-liberal narrative for America, writing in the *Yale Law Journal* that

it is no longer possible to see a Lockean consensus in the founding period, or to treat the framers as modern pluralists believing that self-interest is the inevitable motivating force behind political behavior. Republican thought played a central role in the framing period, and it offers a powerful conception of politics and of the functions of constitutionalism.

Sunstein adopts the postmodern formula that property rights are a "social construction," adding that "republicans are hardly hostile to redistribution or to collective efforts to reassess the existing distribution of wealth and entitlements." And he is clear that civic republicanism, as he understands it, involves the negation of natural right: "What is distinctive about the republican view is that it understands most rights as either preconditions for or the outcome of an undistorted deliberative process." In sum,

[R]epublicans see the private sphere as the product of public decisions, and deny the existence of natural or prepolitical entitlements.... The creation of such a sphere, based on a theory of natural rights, coexists uneasily with republican conceptions of politics.

In Sunstein's hands, civic republicanism would entitle the judiciary—especially the Supreme Court—to be more political than it already is, and provide the theoretical basis for radical policy prescriptions, such as a "New Deal for speech" in which access to the media would be "redistributed" to make American politics more "democratic."

Uncommon Liberal

Two questions come to mind: is this a reasonable interpretation of Wood's work? And beyond that, is Wood's interpretation of the American Revolution itself reasonable?

It is not clear that Wood himself would go as far as Sunstein, Seidenfeld, or the other legal scholars who use his work as a prop. He is no typical lefty academic, though he has taught American history at Brown University for many years. He assails postmodern multiculturalism in spirited terms: "multiculturalism," he wrote in the *William and Mary Quarterly*, "not only falsifies our past; it destroys our future." He deplores relativism's "insidious" attack on the idea of objectivity in historical research and writing. He rejects the victimology inherent in the class- and group-based obsession with

227

"oppression"—taking special aim at the prominent oppression-studies specialist Gary Nash (who criticized Wood for not paying more attention to the Left's anointed victim classifications). Wood comments: "What is extraordinary about the American Revolution is not, as Nash suggests, the continual deprivation and repression of the mass of ordinary people but rather their release and liberation."

In 1991, five years after Wood wrote this, he published *The Radicalism of the American Revolution*, perhaps the most thorough, engaging inventory of the astonishing democratic social changes the Revolution unleashed. "[T]he American Revolution," he declares, "was not conservative at all; on the contrary: it was as radical and as revolutionary as any in history." The Revolution upset social hierarchies and accelerated the social mobility that has always been one of the cornerstones of American character. He suggests that between 1776 and the early 1800s, American culture and society went from republican to democratic. In *Revolutionary Characters*, his latest book, he affirms that the founders were an extraordinary and admirable group of political thinkers.

One suspects that Wood's conclusions changed between 1969, when he published *Creation*, and 1991, when he published *Radicalism*. In both books, Wood argues that democratic nationalism triumphed over republican ideology. In that sense, they tell the same story—the one by describing an ideological change, and the other by describing a cultural and social transformation. Even so, his evaluation of the shift to democratic nationalism alters from one book to the other. In the 1960s, Wood, like many others, believed that individualism had ruined America. By the 1990s, however, he thought middle-class democracy was not half bad. So it is not surprising that academic liberals tend to quote the former and not the latter book. In the penultimate chapter of *Creation*, "The Relevance and Irrelevance of John Adams," which Wood reprints in *Revolutionary Characters*, he suggests that America rests upon a false foundation: "for too long and with too much candor [Adams] had tried to tell his fellow Americans some truths about themselves that American values and American ideology would not admit." By the time he wrote *Radicalism*, Wood had grown less hostile to the American regime.

Even if Wood might not like all the uses to which *Creation* is put, that does not mean that liberals are interpreting it incorrectly. Wood's account of republicanism *is* fundamentally communitarian. Yet by citing Wood as they do, Sunstein, Ackerman, and the others neglect

228

something essential in his work. In particular, they ignore the book's conclusion. In*Creation*, Wood argues that an anti-capitalist concern for civic virtue and some idea of the "public good" lay at the heart of the 1776 revolution. That's what liberals like about it. Yet to win ratification of the Constitution, he argues, the Federalists had to pretend it was rather more democratic than in fact it was, with results both ironic and tragic. The Federalists wrote the Constitution, according to Wood, to insert republican checks on American democracy, and upon democratic individualism. But to get the people to ratify the Constitution, the Federalists had to appeal to the sovereignty of the people. As a result, they secured the triumph of the very democracy they were trying to contain. Necessity and events put republicanism onto the trash heap of history. In the most frequently cited passage from *Creation*, Wood becomes the heir to, and modifier of, Charles Beard and Louis Hartz:

[T]he Federalists helped to foreclose the development of an American intellectual tradition in which the differing ideas of politics would be intimately and genuinely related to differing social interests. In other words, the Federalists in 1787 hastened the destruction of whatever chance there was in America for the growth of an avowedly aristocratic conception of politics and thereby contributed to the creation of that encompassing liberal tradition which has mitigated and often obscured the real social antagonisms of American politics.... [T]he Federalists fixed the terms for the future discussion of American politics...and created a distinctly American political theory but only at the cost of eventually impoverishing later American political thought.

After 1789, Wood argues, there was no longer any room in America for classical thinking about the common good, or for the ideas that sustained it. Wood laments the loss.

Unlike today's liberals who quote his magnum opus, Wood does not think that America can return to its republican roots. He may be crying over spilled milk, but he has the fortitude to admit it. On that ground, he criticizes some of the uses to which his work has been conscripted. In a symposium on civic republicanism in the *Chicago Kent Law Review*, Wood wrote that

the idea that we today can restore some sort of classical politics to our public life strikes me as utterly chimerical.... All of [the legal scholars] seem to speak and write as if we had more freedom and choice in the matter than we do. They seem to suggest that people can actually be talked into restoring classical politics or even aspects of classical politics to American political life.

According to Wood, any effort to return to past ways of life is futile. History moves relentlessly onward. Wood's point is not that America's founding was republican, but that America was founded as part of a historical process that soon rendered republicanism obsolete.

The Virtues of History

If Wood does not quite teach the lessons that liberals often draw from his works, what does he teach? He is correct that America's founders read classical political thinkers with attention and learned from them, particularly about the connection between liberty and virtue. It is also true that, when it was founded, the American regime was something new and distinctive in history. And it is hardly unreasonable to find, as he suggests in *Radicalism*, that there was something noble in the founding, and something good in American society from the start. In that sense, it is not such a bad thing that Newt Gingrich regularly quotes him, or that Wood's latest book appeared on President Bush's summer reading list.

If one reads Wood closely, however, his work becomes less sound. Consider his treatment of classical virtue. Wood defines virtue simply as submission to the public good—that's why it "obliterated the individual." In other words, he collapses the classical virtues of individuals—wisdom, courage, justice, moderation—into a crude notion of civic virtue. His seemingly exhaustive exegesis of the classical republican sources of American political thought is deficient, too. Critics have impeached his use of sources, noting that he sometimes wrenches quotations out of context in order to bolster his interpretation.

Wood's discussion of liberty in the American Revolution is similarly inadequate. In the hundreds of closely argued pages of *Creation*, a book that is supposed to cover the years 1776 to 1787, the Declaration of Independence barely receives a glancing nod, while Locke and social contract theory are shunted aside perfunctorily. Wood does not think it is important to explore the ideas of the Declaration in any detail. In his short book *The American Revolution*, the Declaration fares slightly better. Here he echoes Lincoln: "The

230

Declaration of Independence set forth a philosophy of human rights that could be applied...to peoples everywhere. It was essential in giving the American Revolution a universal appeal." Wood does not grasp, or does not think it possible to compare, the difference between the founders' understanding of rights and that of contemporary liberalism. Consider this animadversion on Jefferson from the same volume: "Jefferson stood for the rights of individuals, and these rights have been carried to extremes in recent years. So Jefferson and his Declaration of Independence are at fault." (To be fair, it is not clear whether he is speaking for himself here, or describing the views of others with the historian's pose of critical detachment. This is a recurring ambiguity in his writing.) Wood's disregard of the Declaration and Locke's influence is akin to an account of Christianity that left out St. Paul or omitted the doctrine of salvation by grace.

By misreading both the classical understanding of virtue and the modern understanding of liberty, Wood misconstrues the nature of the American Revolution and the republic it helped to create. His readers don't get the tools with which to understand Jefferson's famous remark that the American mind drew, *inter alia*, upon the principles of the elementary books of public right, such as "Aristotle, Cicero, Locke, Sidney, etc."

Wood's vices are born of his virtues. He is a good historian who recognizes that the past is fundamentally different from the present, and for that reason, must be understood on its own terms. He takes that idea to such an extreme, however, that it damages his achievement. The fundamental difficulty in Wood's approach to the founding is that he is closed to the possibility that the founders might have discovered some political truths that transcend time and place. The ideas of the founding cannot guide us today, he suggests, because they are ideas from the past, and the past, being different from the present, is irredeemably alien.

This belief animated his full-throated attack in the *New York Review of Books* in 1988 on the "quasi-religious view of the Founding" and the "fundamentalism" of what he called "the Leo Strauss bicentennial." The Straussians "are wrong to see the Constitution as having timeless and universal meaning embodied in the philosophical aims of the Founders and discoverable through textual exegesis.... [H]istorically there can be no real 'original intention' behind the document." This makes one wonder why Wood ever devoted such extended attention to the Constitution.

231

"In the end all the Founders created something that no one of them ever intended," he writes. For him, that conclusion is a truism. According to his premises, historical figures cannot really know what they are doing; and historians who can know, but only in retrospect, cannot *do* anything with their knowledge. In short, one can learn about the past, but never from the past. Perhaps that goes too far, but only a bit. The deepest truth Wood sees in history is that history never ceases to move. From history, one cannot learn wisdom but at best a certain Romantic longing to be part of the communal whole that is in motion. This is watered-down, very watered-down, Heidegger.

Another way of saying all this is that the same dramatic irony—that the readers know truths about the founding that the founders could not possibly know—which makes the story Wood tells in *Creation* so compelling, also limits Wood's insight into the era. Thomas Pangle argues that Wood and his emulators read republican political thought "in a spirit which is not only alien, but also inferior in seriousness to the spirit of the eighteenth-century readers." Historian Edward Countryman observes that "Wood comes very close to writing as if a single intelligence lay behind the numerous quotations that make up his book." John Patrick Diggins is more blunt, charging that

Wood has allowed himself to be convinced that the mind is so much the product of social interaction that the ideas that derive from its cognitive operations cannot tell us anything about historical reality.... If one were to follow Wood's advice to its logical conclusion, intellectual history would become not the history of ideas but of opinions and interpretations, and the historian would have no way of judging the accuracy or rightfulness of such opinions and interpretations.

Yet Wood gets angry when his own premises and interpretations are attacked—as though he were somehow in the right. He might deny that John Adams could learn the same things that Cicero or Marsilius did from reading Aristotle's *Politics*. Yet Adams thought that he could. In short, Adams and the other founders disagreed with Wood's bedrock historical premise. As a result, his assumptions limit his vision, disabling him from giving a full account of the American Revolution and the ideas that animated it; disabling him, indeed, from giving a consistent defense of his own laudable researches.

The Future of the Past

232

These difficulties make interesting Wood's more recent expressions of dismay over multiculturalism and postmodernism. His own commitment to seeing political ideas as transient products of historical and social context leaves him, finally, no grounds of resistance to the intellectual corruption of our time. He arrives unarmed at conferences and faculty meetings. He betrays this here and there with a throwaway phrase. In a 1981 review of Oscar Handlin's *Truth in History*, Wood writes: "[A]s we wait for modernism to engulf us, we can only carry on our historian's business as best we can, clinging to Handlin's belief that 'truth resides in the small pieces that together form the record.'" But Wood never gives the sense that these small pieces will ever fit together into a larger whole, which could correct or instruct us about our present circumstances. For him, political thought remains not even a large jigsaw puzzle, but an ever-changing kaleidoscope. His criticism of multiculturalism is thus of a piece with his dismissal of natural rights. He dislikes the former because it suggests that a culture cannot, or should not, cohere as a historical whole. He scorns the latter because it implies that rights are beyond culture. He has no truck with either conclusion. For him, cultures are comprehensive wholes, and they are constantly evolving.

The most important reason for Wood's wide, enduring appeal is that he cast a much-deserved spotlight on the ways in which classical republican thought infused the founding. Such an inquiry was a needed corrective to the view of America as a wholly modern, wholly liberal regime indifferent to public considerations of virtue. His approach might yield a new synthesis or at least combination of ancient and modern strands of political thought. But though his work raises the question, he does not, and cannot, answer it. In Wood's recreation of the political thought of the founding, the idea of natural right (whether understood in ancient or modern terms) goes missing in action.

As a historian, Wood has many virtues. He writes with becoming modesty. As much as possible, he lets his sources do the talking. But that is what makes the limits of his vision all the more frustrating. His "objective" approach to history simplifies the past in order to make it more susceptible to interpretation. His historicism leads him to affect an apolitical posture when writing about deeply political things. An "objective" historian is not supposed to make value judgments. That is partly what he has in mind when he writes that historians cannot pay attention to philosophers if they are to do their work. This is a pity, for the political philosophers he disdains agree with him to a large extent that the tension between classical republican virtue and modern liberalism is a crucial question for understanding—and preserving—America. Yet those scholars of philosophy speak of moral reason and moral argument, not "value judgments."

By its ambition and scope, Wood's body of work will remain preeminent for some time in the historiography of the American Founding. But it begs to be superseded by an equally large-scale treatment that does not shy away from treating the founders as thinkers and statesmen, rather than as 18th-century ideologues.

—*Claremont Review of Books*, Winter 2006

Chapter 41

Reading Up on the Right

The Conservatives: Ideas and Personalities Throughout American History, **by Patrick Allitt**

The Conservative Century: From Reaction to Revolution, **by Gregory L. Schneider**

Reappraising the Right: The Past and Future of American Conservatism, **by George H. Nash**

The Death of Conservatism, **by Sam Tanenhaus**

We Are Doomed: Reclaiming Conservative Pessimism, **by John Derbyshire**

With the stunning victory of Scott Brown in Massachusetts it appears the long night of the soul for conservatives may be over. The last two years have been tough for the Right. In terms of political power, conservatism is at its lowest point in more than 30 years. A radical president and a willing Congress have expanded the size and reach of centralized government in ways that Lyndon Johnson and Bill Clinton never dreamed of. Although Barack Obama may be stymied on health care, cap and trade, and other large ambitions, conservatives should not suppose the tide has turned decisively in their direction. Conservatives appear confused or less than fully confident about their understanding of the economic crisis. The Tea Party movement, though reflecting a healthy populist backlash against Obama's program of governmental gigantism, lacks the programmatic focus of the tax revolt of the late 1970s, which quickly joined itself to supply-side economics. Polls reveal a public increasingly uneasy with Democratic policies, but the public also continues to hold the Republican Party in low regard.

235

This low pass is leading to a lot of stock-taking. Conservative intellectuals, in particular, are in eclipse at the moment. The leading public figures on the Right today tend to be the media celebrities of talk radio and cable TV, who make up in decibels what they lack in rigor and depth. We've traded Bill Buckley for Glenn Beck, Irving Kristol for Ann Coulter. The intellectual generating the most enthusiasm on the Right these days is Ayn Rand, the once-marginalized figure whose books have been selling like Shamwows since Obama took office. Neoconservatives remain in the doghouse—and not only among liberals (the Cato Institute's Ed Crane wants them thrown "under the bus"). The Religious Right is said to be a spent force.

The fraying and infighting on the Right partly revolve around whether America is still a "center-right" nation, as was confidently asserted when Ronald Reagan thumped liberals in the 1980s and Bill Clinton was compelled to move right to preserve his presidency in the 1990s. While independent voters are swinging sharply against Obama, opinion polls only show a slight uptick in the proportion of Americans who describe themselves as conservative. Reaction to Obama's overreaching should not be confused with a sea change in bedrock political sentiment. The fractiousness of the Right, rooted in conflicting intellectual principles in its different camps, is nothing new, and has always been a source of conservatism's dynamism in ways few liberals perceive. The Left, in the suggestive simile of Joe Sobran, is like a hive, uniformly swarming in support of more collectivism as if by insect instinct. The analogous simile for the Right might be a soccer or basketball team, where the players move independently of the ball in seemingly chaotic fashion.

But even if the diversity and fractiousness of the Right is a sign of health, there are still fundamental tensions that the Right has been unable to resolve. Conservatives have been observing and commenting on their intramural intellectual divisions for more than 50 years now, searching for a stable synthesis along the lines of Frank Meyer's famous "fusionism." Rather than making progress in defining a synthesis, the Right seems to be inventing still more subdivisions for itself, nowadays including "crunchy-cons" (conservatives with green lifestyles) and, if John Derbyshire has his way, what might be called "grumpy-cons," to join the ranks of neocons, paleocons, and libertarians. The good news is that conservatism is no longer the orphan of historical scholarship that Alan Brinkley described over a decade ago. To the contrary, there are perhaps more books about the Right than the Left over the past few years (partly because with only a few exceptions the Left is largely uninterested in its intellectual patrimony). But there are still some crucial blind spots in this burgeoning literature, along with some plainly wrongheaded analyses.

Conserving a Revolution

Patrick Allitt's *The Conservatives: Ideas & Personalities Throughout American History* has the great virtue of treating conservatism as an *American* phenomenon rather than as a transplant or mere derivation of European thought. It would be an excellent book to assign in any survey course on American political thought. And instead of beginning the story, as so many recent histories do, in the post-World War II decades, Allitt starts with the American Founding, though a case could be made for giving a small nod to the early colonial and Puritan settlers. Like most other observers, Allitt finds it difficult to offer a unified definition of conservatism. "[W]hy is it internally divided?" Allitt asks at the outset. Chiefly because conservatism is more "an *attitude* to social and political change" and hence "there is no consistency in conservatives' beliefs about what should be conserved."

Allitt is on the right track, though, in insisting that understanding the founding is central to any reckoning with American conservatism: "American conservatism has always had a paradoxical element, entailing the defense of a revolutionary achievement." The American Revolution has been a stumbling block for some conservatives, who deny its revolutionary character and try to portray it as continuous with British or European political thought. (Hence Russell Kirk's dislike of the Declaration of Independence, for example.) James Madison and Thomas Jefferson, both rightly considered 18th-century liberals, emerge in Allitt's account as "conservative innovators"— only in America would such a phrase not be considered an oxymoron—and *The Federalist*, according to Allitt, should be considered "the new nation's first conservative classic," even though it laid out, if not a *new*, at least an improved science of politics. Here we come across the first major difficulty. Allitt says that "conservatives have generally taken an antitheoretical approach to their world," but the politics of the founding relied heavily on theoretical insights.

Despite this, Allitt's generally unbiased and objective treatment of conservative thinkers and ideas through the decades is one of the best ever produced, even though it is still uneven in spots. He gets Lincoln largely right, while noting the Southern conservatives who vehemently hate Lincoln, but he gets Theodore Roosevelt mostly wrong. T.R.'s large and admirable personality should not distract us from his anti-conservative and often demagogic Progressivism that manifested itself in a cavalier attitude toward the Constitution, which helped prepare the transformation of the presidency and the birth of the modern administrative state.

Like most recent surveys of the Right, Allitt's narrative really gets hopping in the postwar years, with the emergence of free-market intellectuals such as Friedrich Hayek, Ludwig Von Mises, and Milton Friedman, and the sensational arrival of William F. Buckley, Jr., and *National Review*. At this point, Allitt recognizes, the Right graduated from being an attitude to being a self-conscious movement. Allitt also makes a nod to a few important conservative activists and activist organizations such as Phyllis Schlafly and the Young Americans for Freedom, and notes the centrality of the *Roe v. Wade* (1973) decision to the shape of modern American politics.

As good as Allitt's account is, Gregory L. Schneider offers a more thorough one in his new survey, *The Conservative Century: From Reaction to Revolution*, precisely because it is limited to the 20th century. Like Allitt, Schneider confronts at the outset the problem of defining conservatism: "The focus on factionalism demonstrates that American conservatism possesses a protean character and that self-definition has been an elusive, and fascinating, conservative quest for a century." Noting successive attempts to cobble together a definition, he throws up his hands: "It might be time to move beyond such efforts."

While Schneider's copious account of the post-war conservative movement is superb, his brief summary of conservatism in the decades before World War II, like Allitt's, leaves some important questions unexamined. They both offer good surveys of the few American conservative thinkers of the Progressive and New Deal eras such as Albert Jay Nock, Irving Babbitt, Paul Elmer More, Ralph Adams Cram, and the Southern Agrarians, but do not explore why there was not a more robust conservative critique of the constitutional deformations of Progressive ideology. Schneider notes that except for a few spasms in the 1930s, "The Old Right lacked the institutions necessary to confront the New Deal political revolution." But of course the problem goes back further than FDR. Schneider writes elsewhere, "The Old Rightists never were effective in addressing the central tendencies of liberalism and remained, as historian George H. Nash described them, 'scattered voices of protest, profoundly pessimistic about the future of the country.'" Not until after World War II, admits Schneider, did conservatives understand that they needed to "plunge into politics," define their principles, spread their ideas, and seek electoral majorities via a necessarily more populist appeal: "The answer was not the conservatism of Cram, Irving Babbitt, or the Southern Agrarians."

Conservatives and Progressives

Which brings us to George H. Nash, the author of one of the first major treatments of conservatism, his 1976 classic *The Conservative Intellectual Movement in America Since 1945*. (It is tempting to paraphrase Albert North Whitehead's comment about Plato and philosophy, and suggest that most histories of modern conservatism are footnotes to Nash.) Nash updates his previous work with a new essay collection, *Reappraising the Right: The Past and Future of American Conservatism*. He is also the biographer of an important pre-war figure—Herbert Hoover—and Hoover casts into particularly sharp focus the anemia of pre-war conservatism.

In his new collection Nash notes Hoover's "idiosyncratic blend of progressivism and antistatism," which pleased no one. Hoover "showed the influence of pre-1914 Progressivism" that made him both a "modernizer" and a "technocrat." Hoover's dilemma points directly to the twin problems of pre-war conservatism: the inability to reckon fully with the real social and economic problems of industrialization, along with the slowness to perceive and react to the Progressives' wholesale overturning of the Constitution—amounting to refounding the country—that occurred during these decades. Hoover appears to have staked out a position midway between Hamilton's and Jefferson's famous disagreement about whether large-scale national commerce or individual, small-scale agrarianism was the best form of political economy for the preservation of the republic. As Nash writes,

we must not lose sight of the fact that for all of Hoover's reforming and modernizing impulses, he also had a conserving purpose: the preservation, in an urban, industrial society, of the American tradition of equal opportunity.... The purpose of Hoover's limited governmental regulation was to strengthen and preserve American Individualism, not to subvert or supplant it.

Here we see Hoover embracing the decent or rightful purposes of Progressivism—we might say Hoover was the original "compassionate conservative" —while lacking Calvin Coolidge's insight into the deforming premises of Progressive political thought. (Nash's collection, by the way, includes a terrific essay on the complicated relationship between Coolidge and Hoover when the latter was Coolidge's secretary of commerce, though Nash doesn't contrast their constitutional views—chiefly because Hoover didn't seem to have any.) Conservative thinkers—mostly in the libertarian camp—have only begun in recent decades to confront the genuine problems (child labor, workplace safety, labor markets, concentrated market power, and so forth) the Progressives sought to tame.

One reason for this lacuna in conservatism is that the so-called Social Darwinists of the late 19th century, usually counted as conservatives, lustily attacked the natural right ideas of the founders and essentially paved the way for the formal rejection of the founding by Woodrow Wilson and other Progressives. This problem is still not widely recognized today in the chronicles of conservative thought. Conservatism has also been ambivalent about the Hamilton-Jefferson argument. Allitt recognizes both Hamilton and Jefferson as conservatives, though acknowledging that the case for each is not ironclad. But here we note that one strain of Progressivism—the Herbert Croly variety—was thought to be a synthesis of the Hamilton-Jefferson argument: endorsing Hamiltonian means to Jeffersonian ends.

Even if Croly's prose were clear, the idea would still be muddled. Yet it raises one of the central questions in any attempt to define conservatism: is conservatism merely a branch of the liberal tradition, or is it a fundamental alternative to liberalism? Allitt fumbles this question at the end of his treatment. Having argued that conservatism is more an "attitude" than a coherent doctrine, he briefly dismisses Louis Hartz's thesis in *The Liberal Tradition in America* (1955) that Lockean liberalism is the sole political philosophy defining the American experience. "Individuals whose ideas I have here described as conservatives [Hartz] treated merely as the inhabitants of one end of the liberal spectrum," Allitt writes. Hartz's book "was an artifact of its time," Allit concludes. "Fifty years later…it would be perverse to voice an argument like Hartz's." Well, one post-Hartz figure who embraced his view was Ronald Reagan, who Nash points out liked to argue, "Today's conservative is, of course, the true liberal—in the classical meaning of the word."

Leftward Ho?

Yet Nash also notes that by becoming a self-conscious political movement with its own national establishment, conservatism would seem to have absorbed Croly's framework of using national, Hamiltonian means for individualist, Jeffersonian ends. In other words, contemporary conservatism in practice is not far removed from Hooverism, despite Reagan's robust voice and actions. "[I]n practice if not quite in theory," Nash laments, "American conservatism today stands well to the left of where it stood in 1980."

The leftward drift of American conservatism will come as a surprise to Sam Tanenhaus, who argues in *The Death of Conservatism* that what ails the Right today is precisely its drift to reactionary "revanchism." He charges that the conservative movement has not accommodated itself *enough* to the leftward end of the liberal continuum of which it is a part. Instead, the "revanchist" Right today is "committed to a counterrevolution, whether the restoration of America's pre-New Deal *ancien régime*, the return to Cold War-style Manichaeanism, or the revival of premodern 'family values.'" Today's conservatives, Tanenhaus says, "seem the heirs of the French rather than of the American Revolution," and are the true Jacobins of American politics, rigidly attached to "orthodoxy." (Tanenhaus finished his book before the tea parties broke out; there's no telling how many more odious comparisons these would have summoned forth.)

Tanenhaus earned for himself a large portion of respect from conservatives for his masterly biography of Whittaker Chambers nearly 15 years ago, and although he writes with grace and attempts to treat conservative ideas seriously, with*The Death of Conservatism* he has squandered his goodwill with the Right. Despite his professed sympathy for conservatism, his depiction of it in this book will be unrecognizable or seem badly distorted to most right-wingers. *The Death of Conservatism* offers yet more evidence that the *New York Times* (Tanenhaus edits the Sunday *Times Book Review* and "Week in Review" sections) exists in some kind of twisted parallel universe.

A properly oriented or "realist" conservatism, Tanenhaus thinks, exists to make liberalism better. A plausible argument, perhaps, but Tanenhaus's model of realist conservatism is mostly the *National Review* of the 1950s and '60s—especially the outlook of Whittaker Chambers, James Burnham, Willmoore Kendall, and Kendall's protégé, Garry Wills—along with certain practical men of the Right, particularly Eisenhower and Nixon. There is a delicious and almost comical irony in Tanenhaus's embrace of the old *National Review*. On the surface his argument would seem to be a repudiation of Dwight Macdonald's dismissal of *National Review* at the time of its founding: "We have long needed a good conservative magazine.... This is not it.... It is neither good nor conservative." Macdonald's complaint against *National Review* was, on closer inspection, nearly identical to Tanenhaus's complaint against conservatism today, namely, that *National Review* was merely "anti-liberal" rather than conservative, that is, not properly deferential to liberalism. Buckley's response reveled in exactly what Macdonald (and Tanenhaus) scorned: "[*National Review*] does not consult Arthur Schlesinger, Jr. to determine the limits of tolerable conservative behavior." Yet that is more or less exactly what Tanenhaus thinks conservatism needs to do today. Tanenhaus's argument turns out to be a restatement of G.K. Chesterton's quip that the business of Progressives is to go on making mistakes, while the business of conservatives is to prevent the mistakes from being corrected. No thanks.

History and Its Discontents

But there is a more serious core to Tanenhaus's embrace of Chambers, Burnham, and "realistic" conservatism that explains the defects of his analysis and reveals a serious problem for conservatism. Consider the astounding conclusion of this passage:

Once again the American right must 'face historical reality,' as Whittaker Chambers advised half a century ago.... It is also why David Souter, who in his nineteen years on the Supreme Court infuriated so many on the right by his refusal to advance the movement's pet judicial causes—instead immersing himself in the study of history, partly to uncover in the past 'some relevance to a constitutional rule where earlier judges saw none'—may well endure as the most authentic conservative in the Court's modern history.

242

Resist the urge to snort coffee out your nose at the endorsement of Souter as the age's "most authentic conservative," or write off Tanenhaus for a lame attempt at deadpan humor. We see here in his evocation of "history" that modern liberals—or Progressives as they more accurately refer to themselves lately—presume, without any longer having to adduce a reason, that history is moving purposely in a direction in conformity with their ever-expansive social vision. Within this bubble of presumption it is natural to suppose that only a hidebound reactionary wedded to an unthinking orthodoxy could believe otherwise. In other words, if thinking conservatives would only look more seriously at the flow of history, as Souter did, they'd realize they are on the wrong side of it and get with the program.

While the stiff and formal Hegelian theories of History or Progress have faded into the mists, the sentimental residue lingers on. The progressive-historical attitude has become so embedded in the liberal mind that its pedigree is no longer recalled; thus liberalism presumes the illegitimacy of conservatism without having to argue the matter. This defect of the liberal mind finds its parallel in the conservative mind, however, which Tanenhaus unknowingly reveals in his approving citation of Whittaker Chambers's counsel that conservatives need, however distasteful it may be, to accommodate history. Tanenhaus writes: "To Chambers, an avid student of history, well schooled in Marxist argument, it was obvious that the growing dependency on government was a function of the unstoppable rise of industrial capitalism and the new technology it had brought forth.... And the Right had better adjust."

Chambers was of course a pessimist, noted for thinking he was joining the losing side of history. (One wonders what Chambers would have made of Ronald Reagan, let alone the fall of the Berlin Wall and the collapse of the Soviet Union.) His pessimism was rooted partly in what he saw as the asymmetry of each side's moral strength: the Communists and the radical Left were determined and ruthless; the West was decadent and weak. But his pessimism was really informed by the fact that although he traded his Communism for Christianity, he never really shed his Marxist historicism. Ditto for James Burnham, also cited in Tanenhaus's narrative. This lingering fatalism represents a self-inflicted debilitation for conservatism.

Neither Chambers nor the conservative movement as shaped by Buckley ever explicitly challenged the Left's idea of progress, or the terms in which the Left understood human advancement. This may

243

have had something to do with why Buckley ultimately abandoned his "big think" book about a conservative vision of the world; it will be interesting to see what Tanenhaus has to say about that in his eventual WFB biography. But remember the *National Review* rallying cry: to stand athwart history yelling "Stop," rather than grabbing hold of history and sending it in a different direction.

Chesterton reminded us, "All conservatism is based upon the idea that if you leave things alone you leave them as they are. But you do not. If you leave a thing alone you leave it to a torrent of change." But Chesterton also noted, "We are fond of talking about 'progress'; that is a dodge to avoid discussing what is good." Tanenhaus is right that pre-war conservatives did a poor job of understanding and responding to the changes that were taking place as a result of industrialization and urbanization; but is a return to Burkean conservatism the answer, as Tanenhaus suggests? The trouble with a generic "Burkean" approach to understanding change and progress is that it is a weak reed against the Left, as can be seen by Woodrow Wilson's easy fusion of Burke and Hegel in the service of reinterpreting the Constitution. (If any more evidence were needed, consider David Brooks's report that Barack Obama is an admirer of Burke; one looks forward to a future Obama memoir in which he will provide a Burkean veneer to Saul Alinsky's little platoons of union goons.)

Tanenhaus, who professes to admire Willmoore Kendall, would have done well to think through Kendall's critique of Russell Kirk's Burkeanism. In Kendall's unfinished *Sages of Conservatism*, he writes: "Let us ask, rather: Is the [Burkean] teaching *sound*, that is, a teaching that contemporary American conservatism would be well-advised to let the Benevolent Sage of Mecosta talk it into accepting? And let us give at once the only possible answer, which is No." Kendall scorned "Kirk's writing and thinking with an eye too much to Burke and not enough to the Framers, so that he addresses himself to, for Americans, the wrong topics in an inappropriate vocabulary." A return to the founders, rather than Burke, ought to provide us with a means of seriously and explicitly contesting liberalism over the meaning of progress.

The Audacity of Hopelessness

On the other hand, we could just resign ourselves to the thought that liberalism is inevitable, unstoppable. Such is the advice of John

Derbyshire's *We Are Doomed: Recovering Conservative Pessimism*. Derb, as his friends and fans on *National Review Online* know him, might seem to be the Dr. House of the conservative movement— acerbic, abrasive, sarcastic, but usually right; but a better comparison is to Albert Jay Nock. Seldom has doom and gloom been expressed with so much style and laugh-out-loud prose. In fact, Derb appears in places to offer a more plainspoken version of Nock's famous essay on the "remnant": "We pessimists, you see, are not only wiser than the smiley-face crowd; we are *better people*" (original emphasis). For all of his acerbic grumpiness, one can imagine Derb going down on the Titanic with a relentless stream of mordant wit about the whole thing. *We Are Doomed* is simply a great read, and will have an oddly cheering effect on some readers.

Conservatives of all types will find much to agree with, and much to be troubled by, in Derb's tour of the horizon. Most will be in emphatic agreement with his critique of the diversity mongers and money-grubbing educrats. "Education," he writes, "is a vast sea of lies, waste, corruption, crackpot theorizing, and careerist logrolling," for which there is little or no chance of serious reform. More problematic is his chapter on culture and human nature, where he dilates on recent findings on genetic and biological determinism that undermine a central tenet of conservatism, that culture shapes human character. He may well be right or partly right about this, and he is certainly right that "culturism" (as he calls it) is the premise for leftist social engineering. He recognizes that the implications of his speculations in this area would require "a new conservatism."

Derb also thinks the U.S. is fated to follow the example of Europe by becoming even more secular: "America's religious exceptionalism is doomed, and American conservatism with it." He is against "the damn fool Iraq war" (though he initially supported it as a punitive raid, akin to gunboat diplomacy), along with the "conservative utopianism" that thinks we can implant democracy in the Arab world. It is the foreign policy cousin, he argues, of "compassionate conservatism" at home. He refreshingly omits the usual animadversions against the dreaded neocons, but wishes the George W. Bush who spoke against "nation-building" in the 2000 campaign had stuck to this position.

In advocating that conservatives embrace "the audacity of hopelessness," Derbyshire does not offer political prescriptions or strategies for the conservative movement. To the contrary, he says near the end, "I fully expect to pass the rest of my life as an

American without ever seeing any major conservative legislation passed by Congress, or any major executive action drawn from conservative principles, or any Supreme Court ruling that will do more than slow the advance of state power by a percentage point or two." In his last chapter he attempts to conform to convention by offering some hope, though this might be subtle parody on his part (note the juxtaposition of Samuel Beckett's stage play *Happy Days* with the television sitcom *Happy Days*). His "hope" is pretty forlorn and antipolitical: through pessimism "we can still transmit something of value to the future, while seeking for private contentment in the present while the earth-pile rises."

Here one arrives at the odd, unintended convergence between Tanenhaus and Derbyshire. Tanenhaus thinks the conservative movement would be better off if it ceased to think of itself as the self-conscious political movement it has been since the 1950s. Implicitly Derbyshire's privatization of conservatism would have us do the same thing. While the prospects for conservative "revanchism" may still seem daunting in the Age of Obama, it is nonetheless surprising that Derbyshire never raises the obvious question: without the conservative movement of the past 50 years, how much worse would things be? The revival of conservatism, drawing upon the richness of American exceptionalism, probably explains most of the political variance between the United States and Europe in the postwar era—explains, in particular, why America has refused to make peace with the modern welfare state, why we remain a military superpower, and why Americans remain a religious people. With Obama faltering and a resurgence of conservative energy evident, even Derb might want to don his armor, draw his sword, and enter the fray once more.

—*Claremont Review of Books*, Winter 2009

Chapter 42

Up From Liberalism

I Am the Change: Barack Obama and the Crisis of Liberalism, by Charles R. Kesler

The only thing worse for liberalism than President Barack Obama's defeat might turn out to be his re-election. After Mitt Romney's dispiriting loss in November, conservatives may at last move beyond the comfortable thesis that the United States is an essentially "center-right" nation. They do not need to rend their garments that the country is irretrievably lost, but nor should they settle for debates about tactical adjustments over immigration and other social issues. Conservatives must finally understand and duly repudiate the modern American liberalism Obama champions. His narrow victory does not represent a decisive point-of-no-return so much as one more step in a long train of significant turning points.

Clarity about Obama's liberalism is especially important because of his enormous success, abetted by a sympathetic and uncurious media, in obfuscating it. Liberals and the media (but then, I repeat myself) say he is just another "pragmatist" like Franklin Roosevelt— or as Cornel West derisively put it after the election, "a Rockefeller Republican in blackface." Some on the Right, on the other hand, think they behold a real-life Manchurian candidate. Obama's trendy educational background, dubious company (Bill Ayers, Derrick Bell, Reverend Jeremiah Wright), and past work as an Alinskyist agitator seem to bespeak radical designs to bring the nation down. But these furies and confusions on both the Left and the Right have missed the ways in which the president is a kind of culmination of the modern liberal project, and what his "audacity of hope" means in practical terms for the future.

This bigger story behind and beyond Obama is the subject of Charles R. Kesler's superb new book, *I Am the Change: Barack Obama and the Crisis of Liberalism,* which aims right for the heart of the Left's revolution in American politics. Readers of the *Claremont*

Review of Books will not be surprised to learn that Kesler, the journal's editor and a distinguished professor of government at Claremont McKenna College, carries off his argument with insight, learning, and wit.

* * *

Far from being something alien to American politics, Obama fits comfortably into the tradition of the 20th-century Progressive Movement—and is a real-time working out of the contradictions and weaknesses building in liberalism since Woodrow Wilson first won the Oval Office exactly 100 years ago. Though the title *I Am the Change* might suggest a narrow excursion into Obama's personal narcissism, the president's overweening self-regard is not merely a personal conceit, Kesler argues, but a *political* conceit with deep philosophical roots that suffuse the modern liberal mind. To understand Obama, then, is really to answer the question "what does it mean anymore to be a liberal?"

Obama may have thought more about the meaning of contemporary liberalism than most denizens of the American Left, but it's a low bar to reach. He shares modern liberalism's essential laziness arising from its philosophical presumption, which helps explain not only his own *hauteur* but also his surprise at Romney's robust performance in the first debate. (That same lazy presumptuousness explains some of the bizarre liberal reaction to this book, as we shall see.)

In order to understand Obama and what he reveals about today's liberalism, it is necessary to put him in the context of what Kesler calls the "three powerful waves" of liberal reform—inaugurated by Wilson, FDR, and Lyndon Johnson—to which Obama hopes to add the fourth. This masterly tour through 20th-century liberal thought is essential to piercing Obama's rhetorical conceit that he is a "postpartisan" political figure out to transcend the bitter political divide of the Baby Boom generation. Unlike Bill Clinton, whose politics Obama didn't think bold enough, "Obama assumes the Reagan Revolution is not here to stay," Kesler writes, "because the Obama Revolution is just beginning.... [It aims] to prove that the era of big government is *not* over." Obama believes that liberals can win the debate over the size and scope of government, in part because he believes liberalism's lasting victories of the past century, despite the Reagan-Gingrich-Bush interlude, provide the high ground from which to march further. And liberals, Kesler wryly reminds us, "are very fond of marching."

The arc of liberalism Kesler traces is not merely the tale of more and bigger and costlier central government, it is the story of a shift in our governing principles regarding individual rights, the meaning of constitutionalism, and, above all, the new idea of unending Progress with a capital P, which made bigger government not simply possible but supposedly *necessary*. The changes liberalism wrought over a century, though radical in substance, proceeded by slow, subtle steps, gradually amounting, as Kesler has written in the *CRB*, "to a prescription for an American character increasingly unfit for self-government."

* * *

In many ways Obama is the uncanny epigone of Woodrow Wilson, whose political philosophy was a strange amalgam of Hegel, Burke, Darwinism, and that home-grown American ideology, Pragmatism, all of which congealed into a doctrine that made historicist assumptions the philosophical core of modern liberalism. Kesler disentangles Wilson's often convoluted prose and confusing concepts to see through to the essentially radical ideas cloaked in a moderate, even slightly conservative, disposition.

Wilson saw Darwinian evolution as an alternative to socialist revolution. His embrace of the "living constitution" went beyond jurisprudence to include all three branches of government, and his self-conscious inflation of the idea of presidential "leadership" has transformed the way every candidate and president has conceived the executive office ever since—and not for the better. It was Wilson who bestowed "the vision thing," as George H.W. Bush once ironically but correctly disparaged it, as a prerequisite for all subsequent presidents. The American Founders would have been wary of Wilson's conception of the popular presidency, if not outright appalled by its demagogy. From elevating the president into the one man with both the "vision" of the future and the will to lead the American people to a collective destination of which they themselves are unaware ("men are as clay in the hands of a consummate leader" was Wilson's famous formula), it is a straight line to Michelle Obama's 2008 comment that "Barack will never allow you to go back to your lives as usual, uninvolved, uninformed."

Wilson's seemingly moderate bearing disguises the other profound consequences of his radical break with the founding's natural rights philosophy. He eroded if not completely eliminated the older liberal suspicion of state power: 18th-century liberalism overthrew the divine right of kings; 20th-century liberalism celebrated the divine right of the State. He championed administrative expertise, which led to the continual expansion of unlimited, unelected bureaucracy. Above all, Wilson's deprecation of the founders' understanding of just government arising from individual natural rights set the stage for drastically altering the relationship ever since between American citizens and their government.

* * *

This last point remains difficult to grasp largely because of the second wave of liberal reform that Franklin Roosevelt accomplished through the New Deal. Kesler rejects the standard view of FDR as a pragmatic politician with no firm governing philosophy, a superficial reading of the New Deal's erratic lunges and Roosevelt's own rhetorical embrace of experimentation. "To many historians and biographers," Kesler notes, "Roosevelt was hardly worth taking seriously as a thinker." Nevertheless, he "was the second great captain of liberalism," with "successes so lasting that liberal public policies and, even more important, the assumptions behind those policies, became ruling elements in our public life.... Roosevelt's own political genius may have owed more to insight than reflection, but it has been underrated regardless."

FDR recognized that Wilson's more or less open filial impiety toward the American Founding was politically ill-advised. Roosevelt anchored the new progressive liberalism in an affirmation of the founding that upon closer inspection revealed deep affinities with Wilson's critique of it. (See, for example, FDR's 1932 Commonwealth Club address). In 1938 Roosevelt said in a radio address: "Think of the great liberal achievements of Woodrow Wilson's New Freedom, and how quickly they were liquidated under President Harding. We have to have reasonable continuity in liberal government in order to get permanent results." In order to achieve that permanence, FDR claimed for liberalism sole possession of the founding's "title deeds." He did this by slyly severing the Constitution from its grounding in the natural rights doctrine of the

250

Declaration of Independence. By separating rights from nature, he turned our understanding of rights upside down, paving the way for so-called economic rights and the government programs to secure them. He spoke openly of "redefining rights" and establishing a new social contract. Under this contract, Kesler summarizes, "when the central government is on the side of the people, then according it more power will not diminish but enhance the people's rights. One could call this the First Law of Big Government: the more power we give the government, the more rights it will give us."

Although the New Deal was a staggering political success, Kesler argues that it set up serious long-term problems for liberalism. The programmatic nature of economic rights fractured Americans into more and more grasping special interest groups, diluting the New Deal's high idealism. Kesler concludes his treatment of FDR with a premonition of trouble ahead:

But rather than permanently lifting the moral tone of American life, the welfare and regulatory state plunged our politics into an amoral scramble for power, benefits, and influence that looked all the more tawdry next to the high hopes Roosevelt had raised. This interest-group or social-welfare Darwinism proved a lasting part of liberalism, and helped spur the greater disillusionment to come in the 1960s.

* * *

That disillusionment arrived on the heels of Lyndon Johnson's Great Society, when liberalism was undone by a pincer movement of its own making. The Great Society represented a substantive leap beyond the New Deal for liberal social policy—a graduation from civil engineering (think Works Progress Administration) to social engineering (Community Action Program, Head Start, etc). Kesler's formula is that the *quantitative* liberalism of social insurance and pro-labor measures gave way to a *qualitative* liberalism that promised not just a chicken in every pot but "self-actualization" (a favorite buzzword of the time) itself. With his expansive rhetoric, Johnson abetted a strain of thought present in liberalism since Wilson but not very far advanced before the 1960s-personal fulfillment, which manifested itself in what came to be known as "lifestyle liberalism" or the exaltation of "the self-creating Self." As Kesler explains, *the Great Society accepted and encouraged—how consciously is a different question—the New Left's inclination to base politics increasingly on issues of personal identity, gender, and sexuality, and 'postmaterialist' concerns like environmental activism.... Mainstream liberalism found it hard to confront the radicals because so many of their premises were its, too.*

* * *

Between the rise of a more radical New Left born of qualitative liberalism's own insatiability and the Baby Boom's demographic bulge, which magnified the social unrest, LBJ was soon engulfed by a civil war between the political Left and the cultural Left. It ended with Johnson's abdication, and "the long whimper of white liberal guilt." "The deepest truth," Kesler observes,

is that the Great Society destroyed the Great Society. Its soaring expectations, its utopian promises, could not be fulfilled in ten years or a hundred years. What it proffered was the satisfaction, in principle, of all material and spiritual needs and desires.

Liberalism shuffled along through the 1970s as a spent force, with Jimmy Carter unable to end the malaise or revive the creed. The salient aspect of liberalism in its terminal phase is that its increasingly programmatic and bureaucratic character—"big government" in the vernacular—transformed government itself into "a cynicism-generating machine." As Kesler puts it, "The Sixties' more enduring legacy was the strange combination, still very much with us, of a more ambitious State and a less trusted government than ever before." The way in which Ronald Reagan swept in to pick up the ruins of exhausted liberalism had to come as a surprise to those whose historicism and celebration of willful passion (i.e., "commitment") had caused liberalism to abandon sustained self-reflection.

* * *

Which brings us to Barack Obama, whom supporters and media cheerleaders insist on portraying as another non-ideological pragmatist with only modest ambitions (though none of them can explain why he didn't emulate Bill Clinton's successful

252

"triangulation" strategy in the face of a resurgent GOP after the 2010 election). This theme does an injustice to Obama's own large ambitions and his place in modern liberal thought, both of which are not hard to tease out of his writings and speeches. Although he is no deep thinker, he doesn't need to be, given how fully liberal assumptions of unidirectional progress and unending reform have become the basic furnishings of modern politics. Still, he is clever, purposeful, and more rhetorically deliberate than Clinton ever was.

The three former waves of liberal reform provided ample political capital when electoral fortunes finally smiled again upon the Democratic Party in 2008. The object of the fourth great wave of liberal reform—for that is clearly what Obama aspires to—is to revive unapologetic liberalism as a governing creed. Rather than patching it up and trimming to fight another day as Clinton had, Obama doubled down on liberalism. He has not been content with poll-tested, short-term personal success. Instead of addressing the stagnant economy, his desire to play the long game drove him to pass at all cost the Patient Protection and Affordable Care Act (to which Kesler gives ample and expert attention). "We did not come here just to clean up crises," Obama told Congress; "We came to build a future."

Despite his re-election, Obama's vision of the future still faces three problems: 1) the combined weight of Obamacare's unpopularity, our protracted economic doldrums, and a continuing conservative opposition; 2) the internal tensions and attenuation building in modern liberal thought over the past century; and 3) an unsustainable and soon-to-be bankrupt welfare state that must contract. To the book's central question—"is liberalism on its last legs, or about to be reborn?"—Kesler's own answer is the former. It remains to be seen not just whether Obamacare—the administration's central achievement—will thrive and become accepted by the American people, but whether liberalism itself can survive the looming fiscal catastrophe that is unraveling what Walter Russell Mead has called "the blue state model" of governance. James Piereson recently argued in the *New Criterion* that Obama is destined to take his place alongside John Adams, James Buchanan, and Herbert Hoover as the last president of a dying political order and mode of governance.

* * *

Though Kesler doesn't put it this way, his argument suggests conservatives should cheer up: the future is slipping away from liberalism. Despite the successes over the past century, liberalism's philosophical hollowness and actuarial imbalances are catching up to it. "Liberalism can't go on as it is, not for very long," Kesler writes; "[i]t faces difficulties both philosophical and fiscal that will compel it either to go out of business or to become something quite different from what it has been." He points to the irony of liberals deciding to call themselves "progressives" again: "liberalism is in a bad way when it has lost confidence in its own truth, and it's an odd sort of 'progress' to go back to a name it surrendered eighty years ago." Obama is the apotheosis of all of progressive liberalism's worst traits, including the penchant for willed "visions" from the top, an impatience with ordinary politics and constitutional forms, a disdain for the American Founding (Kesler's exegesis of how and why Obama fundamentally agrees with Reverend Jeremiah Wright's "God damn America!" is not to be missed), and the unquestioned assumption that "progress" culminates in him personally. (This, by the way, is why Obama will eventually become a much more obnoxious and irritating ex-president than Carter.)

Though this might seem willfully optimistic after the long catalogue of liberal success that comprises much of the book, Kesler reminds us that if Communism could "collapse of its own deadweight and implausibility, why not American liberalism?" He acknowledges that more than gravity will be required to bring it down. American statesmen and the American people need to do their part, too. Liberalism's wager—and Obama's ambition in particular—is that no Republican who wins the White House again can overthrow or even pare back the massive and still evolving state apparatus put in place by a century of liberalism. This is why the question of Obamacare's repeal or unwinding is so crucial. Never mind taking Big Bird off the dole, rolling back Obamacare, argues Kesler, would shatter the superstition that liberal "progress" moves inevitably in one direction. Moreso than an Obama defeat, it would have shaken liberalism's confidence. Although a second term makes that outcome much more remote, the flaws that will emerge as Obamacare is implemented mean that its sustainability is not assured.

* * *

254

The fate of Obamacare aside, that such a shakeup is necessary is evident from the liberal reaction to Kesler's book, especially by Mark Lilla in the *New York Times Book Review*. Lilla, an able and provocative intellectual historian and critic, dismisses *I Am the Change* because its author takes Obama's stated ambition seriously. It is an odd criticism to say that your argument should be rejected because you think *too well* of your opponent. To hear Lilla tell it, Obama is "a moderate and cautious straight-shooter," and there isn't much of a progressive tradition to draw upon in thinking about the president—or anything else. More embarrassing is the tacit premise that Obama doesn't deserve comparison to, or placement within, the grand tradition that preceded him, chiefly because his modest achievements (including the holy grail of universal health care) don't rise to the canonic level of the liberal giants of old. Whether Obama agrees with or wishes to build upon the Progressive tradition is regarded as unworthy of consideration, as though Progressivism itself is something best regarded as a Smithsonian Institution curiosity. It is an odd thing for someone to profess to take political ideas seriously but not to take statesmanship seriously.

Liberals are understandably riding high after Obama's dramatic re-election. But after the party will come the hangover. Twenty-five years ago Harvey Mansfield wrote about "a liberalism that is politically exhausted and bored with itself." The way in which so many liberals like Lilla have dismissed as meaningless rhetorical flourishes Obama's self-proclaimed "audacity" and ambition to "transform the country" reveals a liberalism that increasingly disdains the purposeful ambition and public argument it once championed, even as it cheers on every possible incremental enlargement of the modern State. The ultimate irony of Barack Obama—as the indispensable *I Am the Change* makes plain—is that he has been regarded more seriously by a conservative than by almost any liberal intellectual. That can't be a good sign for liberalism's future.

—*Claremont Review of Books*, Fall 2012

Chapter 43

The Road to Freedom

Masters of the Universe: Hayek, Friedman, and the Birth of Neoliberal Politics, by Daniel Stedman Jones

The Great Persuasion: Reinventing Free Markets since the Depression, by Angus Burgin

Ever since the collapse of the housing bubble became a full-blown banking crisis in the fall of 2008, the Left has been reveling in *Schadenfreude* at this "market failure." It matters not that most of the causes of the crisis should be laid at the feet of *government* failure rather than market failure. The aftermath of the crisis found the defenders of free markets in disarray, as they lost control of "the narrative" to their critics.

It is hard to blame the Left for the new spring in its step. For almost 30 years liberals were in retreat before market ideas that spread far beyond the successes of the Reagan and Thatcher administrations—to the vast privatizations and market liberalizations in the former Soviet empire and in the developing world. Libertarians owned the most successful branch of conservatism during this period, with monetarism, sensible anti-trust policy, de-regulated markets, and their critique of central macroeconomic planning accepted almost everywhere in speech if not always in deed. By the 1980s, Keynesianism seemed as vanquished as Lamarckian biology. With free marketeers' near-monopoly on the Nobel Prize in economics (Milton Friedman, Friedrich Hayek, James Buchanan, and many more), the collapse of the Soviet Union, the rout of Hillarycare, and the willing embrace of market logic by the Clinton and Blair governments, the Right by the mid-1990s reveled in a triumphalism (remember the End of History?) that became complacency—the first step to hubris.

Perhaps it was so much success after so many decades of being the pessimistic opposition that lulled the Right into overestimating its position going forward. At any rate, a number of early warning signs

257

were missed. The welfare reform of 1996 did not breed similar reforms of other welfare state programs. The disaster of California's misnamed "electricity restructuring" cast public suspicion on "deregulation." And the passage of the onerous, counter-productive Sarbanes-Oxley law after the bursting of the internet bubble and the Enron accounting scandal should have been a warning that we were backsliding into the kind of policies that clotted our economic arteries from the 1930s to the 1970s. From there it was a straight line to the massive interventionism of Dodd-Frank after the housing-banking collapse.

* * *

Around the time of Sarbanes-Oxley, Milton Friedman tried to warn us:

> After World War II, opinion was socialist while practice was free market; currently, opinion is free market while practice is heavily socialist. We have largely won the battle of ideas (though no such battle is ever won permanently); we have succeeded in stalling the progress of socialism, but we have not succeeded in reversing its course. We are still far from bringing practice into conformity with opinion.

I'm not sure Friedman was right even a decade ago that we had won the "battle of ideas," but his admonition that practice wasn't really following our self-congratulatory narrative was correct. As long as Friedman was on the scene a certain confidence seemed reasonable; he was unquestionably the most formidable champion of the cause of free markets in our time. (Just check out any of the numerous YouTube videos of him in action back in the 1970s and 1980s and you'll get an instant sense of the overpowering confidence of resurgent free market thinking in that era.)

It may not be a coincidence that the onset of the housing crash, beginning the year following Friedman's passing in 2006, saw his heirs seemingly unable to gain public attention for their admittedly more complicated account of the real causes of the crisis. (For one thing, there is just enough truth to the Left's "market failure" narrative—such as reckless risk-taking by banks—to render a pure market-friendly counter-narrative problematic.)

* * *

The crisis created a huge opening for liberals to do what they do best—roll out a revisionist narrative that the free-marketeers were wrong all along. We shouldn't have been surprised to see the corpse of John Maynard Keynes exhumed, and the pop culture zombie fad of the moment may explain the seeming acceptance of the zombie-like economy that revived Keynesianism has delivered. But the Left is not content with an excuse to spend more money; it wants to go in for the kill.

The previous generation of books about the revival of free market thinking, such as Daniel Yergin and Joseph Stanislaw's *The Commanding Heights: The Battle for the World Economy* (1998), or Richard Cockett's superior but less well known *Thinking the Unthinkable: Think Tanks and the Economic Counter-Revolution, 1931-1983* (1995), generally followed the "heroic" narrative of the role and consequences of the free market counter-revolution. While respectful in significant ways, Daniel Stedman Jones's *Masters of the Universe* and, to a lesser extent, Angus Burgin's *The Great Persuasion* discard the heroism and cast subtle and not so subtle aspersions on free market thought. Stedman Jones, a barrister in London who was educated at Oxford and the University of Pennsylvania, aims to take Friedman, Hayek, and their peers down several notches, while Burgin, a history professor at Johns Hopkins University, situates them within a subtle historicist frame that downgrades their achievement more than he probably intends.

The Great Persuasion is the more thorough and readable of the two, and goes a long way toward explaining why Hayek is the more important figure in the long run than Friedman, despite Friedman's greater fame and policy influence. Like other accounts of the postwar rise of "neoliberalism" (as it came to be called) Burgin's centers on the founding and crucial role of the Mont Pelerin Society (MPS), which Hayek was instrumental in founding in 1947.

* * *

The strength of Burgin's recounting is how it brings back into view two aspects of the story not well recalled in most of the heroic narratives. First, what became the Mont Pelerin Society in 1947 had its origins, and a dress rehearsal, back in the late 1930s, meaning that the critique of the defects of Keynesianism and central planning was beginning to percolate earlier than usually supposed. Burgin is

259

especially thorough in reclaiming the importance of earlier figures such as Frank Knight, Henry Simons, Karl Popper, Wilhelm Röpke, Albert Hunold, and several other now-obscure Europeans. As the scattered remnant of free market thinkers in the U.S. and Europe struggled to mount a more vigorous and popular defense against the rising tide of collectivism, an unexpected ally came into view: Walter Lippmann. His 1937 book, *Inquiry Into the Principles of the Good Society*, marked a significant departure from his earlier support of Progressivism in the pages of the *New Republic*. In this book, Lippmann aligned himself with the critics of the New Deal and sketched an outline for a revival or reform of capitalism. Much of his argument presaged the one Hayek would offer a few years later in *The Road to Serfdom*.

The nascent Chicago School and its European allies saw Lippmann's fame as the ideal vehicle around which to organize a larger effort, which would involve founding a new journal as well as an organization to carry out a public education effort. Hayek and others struck up an extensive correspondence with Lippmann, proposing a meeting of minds to develop the idea. The dry run for what would become the Mont Pelerin Society occurred in Paris in 1938 and was entitled *Le Colloque Walter Lippmann*. The first meeting produced some papers but no clear plan for moving forward. The coming of war in Europe the following year interrupted any sequel to *Colloque Lippmann*, and by the time of the crucial Mont Pelerin gathering in 1947 Lippmann disdained the effort and declined to participate. The absence of Lippmann or other political thinkers (Karl Popper, for example, dropped out after the initial MPS meeting) meant, second, that the effort to create neo-liberalism, and the Mont Pelerin Society itself, would come to be dominated by economists rather than represent a broader, interdisciplinary effort to recover classical liberalism. Here emerges a major irony: the original inspiration behind the Mont Pelerin Society aimed at a "third way" between the old purebred *laissez faire* capitalism and collectivist socialism. Wilhelm Röpke in particular can be seen as an early advocate of what would come to be known as fusionism (Frank Meyer's great cause); but the idea immediately ran into a buzz saw of resistance from the economists who regarded such talk as an untenable halfway house.

* * *

The final nail in the coffin of a broader interdisciplinary effort came in 1956 when Hayek lobbied successfully to block Russell Kirk's proposed membership in the Mont Pelerin Society. After being initially enthusiastic about Kirk's *The Conservative Mind* (and even offering a dust jacket blurb at the time of its publication in 1953), Hayek had a change of heart, and his famous essay "Why I Am Not a Conservative" was in part a response to Kirk. Hayek also had little appreciation for William F. Buckley, Jr., or the *National Review* circle, even though *NR* offered consistent editorial support and coverage for the MPS. Röpke resigned from the MPS shortly after the Society completed its turn to a libertarian, economics-dominated body. As Burgin puts it, "The foundational tension of postwar American conservatism had begun to emerge."

Burgin brings out the ways in which Hayek regarded *The Road to Serfdom*, his most famous book, as defective, but he fails to discuss how Hayek's thought developed in *The Constitution of Liberty*, published in 1960, and later works (this is covered well in Bruce Caldwell's excellent 2005 biography of Hayek). Even after his turn against Kirk, Hayek still retained some sympathy for an interdisciplinary approach to reclaiming the liberal tradition, but the MPS solidified its economics focus with the ascension of Milton Friedman as its dominant figure in the 1960s, who differed from Hayek in several important ways (especially about central banking). Even John Kenneth Galbraith, Burgin reminds us, would admit in 1987 that in "the history of economics the age of John Maynard Keynes gave way to the age of Milton Friedman." Burgin makes clear that without Hayek the MPS would never have been established. But by the end of the 1960s, he had been eclipsed and had begun to experience periods of deep depression.

Burgin's concluding chapter provides a brief tour of the critics like economist Jeffrey Sachs who used the housing bubble and crash of 2008 to discredit the entire free market enterprise and proclaim once again the end of *laissez faire*. He thinks the critics on the left are too hasty, that free market thought is more solidly established than it was at the time of the Great Depression and therefore poised for a comeback. But Burgin displays the typical historian's weakness for historicism, by rendering neoliberal ideas as mere epiphenomena of the "spirit of an age" (the subtitle of his conclusion, in fact). This is unfortunate and detracts from the respect that he obviously has for the MPS circle.

That respect is missing from Stedman Jones's *Masters of the Universe*, as can be seen in the very inaptness of its title. The core of Hayek's thought was the rejection that anyone can master any large-scale social or economic activity, let alone "the universe." Stedman Jones follows the lefty line that the financial crisis of 2008 discredits free market principles: "The crisis was the direct result of a culture that had endowed the free market with a divine status it has never merited.... [T]he financial crisis was the direct result of neoliberal policies.... These were the terrible effects of uncritical deregulation and market liberalization, bred by the Chicago faith in untrammeled markets."

His narrative begins at the conventional starting point of the immediate postwar years and the founding of the MPS, and includes brief glances at ancillary organizations such as the Heritage Foundation, the American Enterprise Institute, and the Liberty Fund, which "runs reputable workshops," he notes in his clunky prose.

The author rightly notes that "neoliberalism" began infiltrating both major parties in Britain and the United States in the 1970s, though its half-hearted versions under Democrats and the Labour Party in the U.K. were ultimately supplanted by the real thing with the arrival of Margaret Thatcher and Ronald Reagan. He offers several strong accounts of the clash of monetarism and Keynesianism and other economic debates of the era, but the essential strangeness of his book is revealed in the one application of neoliberalism that he singles out in a chapter for major attention: housing policy. This chapter has the feel of a wholly different book, or a journal article that never found a home. *Housing policy?* Thatcher's privatization of public housing in Britain—a substantial achievement—was never matched in the United States, and in any case housing policy, aside from scattered attention to rent control, was hardly an important preoccupation of American neoliberals.

* * *

Neoliberalism in Stedman Jones's hands is always "radical" if not extreme. If Hayek were alive, he'd note that today's would-be "masters of the universe" are the same types they've always been— that the true radicals are the Obamanauts who think they can fix American health care with tens of thousands of pages of regulations from the Department of Health and Human Services, solve the eternal problem of bank risk with the ministrations of Dodd-Frank, and generate a "green energy revolution" with a combination of subsidies, mandates, and regulations.

This is why Hayek is enjoying more of a revival than Friedman in the Age of Obama. Friedman's successors are divided over whether Ben Bernanke's Federal Reserve is following a Friedmanite path or is sowing a future of disastrous monetary instability. But Hayek's epistemological critique of economic planning and regulation is suddenly salient again in the face of contemporary liberal hubris. The "neoliberals" of the MPS era may never succeed in reclaiming the rightful understanding of liberalism, but their critique of government power remains more urgent than ever and does not depend on the spirit of any age.

—*Claremont Review of Books*, Spring 2013

Chapter 44

Practical Wisdom

Trying to reconcile Burke's apparent inconsistencies, let alone trying to harmonize him with Lincoln on a theoretical level, is a mistaken enterprise.

Old Whigs: Burke, Lincoln, and the Politics of Prudence, by Greg Weiner

If someone had to come up with a bumper sticker encapsulating Edmund Burke's political philosophy, it would probably read: "Against metaphysical abstractions!" If Burke had lived to the 1850s, he might well have expressed private reservations about Abraham Lincoln's use of the Declaration of Independence. Burke might especially have disputed an 1859 letter to the Boston politician Henry L. Pierce, in which Lincoln characterized the Declaration as "an abstract truth, applicable to all men and all times." Burke embraced prudence as the highest object of political thought and the most important quality—probably the sole qualifying trait—of the statesman. But even had he accepted Lincoln as a model of prudence and high statesmanship (as is likely), it is not easy to square Burke's understanding of "abstract truths" and their place in political practice with Lincoln's. Fortunately we have associate professor Greg Weiner of Assumption College on the job with his compact but rich new book, *Old Whigs: Burke, Lincoln, and the Politics of Prudence*.

On the surface, it is not easy to nail down either man's account of how abstractions such as natural rights play out in reality. The paradox of Burke is that he supported natural rights in the abstract but (mostly) opposed appealing to natural rights in practical deliberations. This has been a puzzle to readers of Burke ever since his *Reflections on the Revolution in France* first appeared in 1790. For example, take this declaratory judgment from the *Reflections*: "Government is not made in virtue of natural rights, which may and do exist in total independence of it." Yet in a 1783 debate over the governance of India, Burke argued, "The rights of men, that is to say,

265

the natural rights of mankind, are, indeed, sacred things; and if any public measure is proved mischievously to affect them, the objection ought to be fatal to that measure, even if no charter at all could be set up against it."

But trying to reconcile Burke's apparent inconsistencies, let alone trying to harmonize him with Lincoln on a theoretical level, is a mistaken enterprise for two reasons. First, the prudence of the statesman cannot be understood purely theoretically, much less scientifically—which means modern political science cannot understand it at all. In fact, Weiner points out early on that "scientific politics" is inherently imprudent. Second, Burke explicitly argued that the ability to understand the circumstances of the moment is at the heart of prudence. As he put it in a debate in the House of Commons in 1792, "A statesman, never losing sight of principles, is to be guided by circumstances; and judging contrary to the exigencies of the moment, he may ruin his country forever." Weiner thus concludes that understanding true statecraft requires "genuine instruction in the unapologetic histories of great and prudent statesmanship."

* * *

As Weiner reminds us at the outset of *Old Whigs*, even those who understand that the statesman's prudence is an art acknowledge it to be an art that is poorly understood. This is why there are so few public figures today deserving to be regarded as true statesmen. "No lines can be laid down for civil or political wisdom," Burke wrote in a 1770 pamphlet on abuses of royal power; "They are a matter incapable of exact definition." In one of his more enigmatic pronouncements, from his 1777 "Letter to the Sheriffs of Bristol," Burke wrote that prudence is "the god of this lower world." Weiner connects this with Burke's well-known critique of ideological and utopian politics, but the analogy to godhead is equally apt because the divine is ultimately impossible to comprehend. It may be going too far to ascribe godlike attributes to the supremely prudent statesman, though perhaps Lincoln came close when he observed in his 1838 Lyceum Address that "men of ambition and talents" with a "ruling passion" for glory belong to "the family of the lion, or the tribe of the eagle." Burke would likely have approved of Lincoln's careful efforts to modulate such passion through dedication to the rule of law, which binds both citizens and statesmen alike. "The

Lyceum Address was a model of Lincolnian prudence," Weiner writes. "He sought to calibrate actions to circumstances, such that calm times, like those he wrongly foresaw continuing, elicited calm leadership."

* * *

Aristotelian moderation is the heart of prudence and enables the prudent statesman to avoid or fend off extremes. But the paradox is that the potential or actual arrival of extreme circumstances warrants a kind of intransigence which, *in the abstract*, seems highly immoderate. So it was with Lincoln as the 1850s wore on, but Weiner also reminds us of the more felicitous comparison to Winston Churchill, whose central perception in the late 1930s was that "compromise with evil was not only wrong but also imprudent.... Churchill...did not make an idol of daring for daring's sake. The moment—which is to say the circumstances—demanded it."

Weiner notes that "One suspects Burke would see some of Lincoln's early rhetoric about the power of reason as intemperate," most especially the climax of his Lyceum Address: "Reason, cold, calculating, unimpassioned reason, must furnish all the materials for our future support and defense." But if Lincoln was more Platonic while Burke was more Aristotelian, still a Burkean defense of Lincoln is possible: Lincoln was, after all, drawing on the "tried and true" tradition of the American Founding to ground his statecraft. Burke was sympathetic to American independence. But his assertion in a 1775 speech about the colonies that "[a]bstract liberty, like other mere abstractions, is not to be found" presaged the problem America would pose for him. Still, it is easy to imagine Burke discerning that Lincoln's attachment to "an abstract truth, applicable to all men and all times" did not constitute a utopian vision or threaten a new American Jacobinism. Prudence, after all, counsels all things in their time—and even idealism has its place.

—*Claremont Review of Books*, Fall 2019

Chapter 45

Reading Bill Clinton

Amidst all the fuss about Bill Clinton's co-written (with James Patterson) thriller novel and his agonies over having the new liberal standards of the #MeToo movement applied to him, everyone has passed over the **short interview** he gave to the *New York Times* about his favorite books. His list sounds like something he ran through a focus group a long time ago, as he did so often when he was president. The neediness of liberals to appear both eclectic and serious never ceases to amaze. Ronald Reagan used to go out of his way to conceal the serious books he was reading as president, and would only cop publicly to reading the latest Louis L'Amour western.

But I take Clinton at his word on most of these, and you can add this to the pile of reasons we'll never entirely figure out Clinton. Let's start here:

NY Times*: What books over the years have most influenced your thinking? Has a work of literature ever affected your policy positions?*

Clinton: *These books had a profound impact on my thinking: "The Evolution of Civilizations," by Carroll Quigley; "Politics as a Vocation," by Max Weber; "The Denial of Death," by Ernest Becker; "Imitation of Christ," by Thomas à Kempis; "Meditations," by Marcus Aurelius; "The Cure at Troy," by Seamus Heaney; and "The Guns of August," by Barbara Tuchman.*

I don't know that any specific book affected my policy positions, but books by Richard Wright and Ralph Ellison made me want to do more about civil rights. I read "America: What Went Wrong," by Donald L. Barlett and James B. Steele, in 1992, and it strengthened my determination to try to reverse trickle-down economics and achieve a fairer and more prosperous economy.

You can almost see the check boxes in Clinton's mind as he unspools this list and thinks about his claim for connection with each author or author's ideas. Clinton didn't know his father, just like Marcus Aurelius! Is *The Imitation of Christ* meant to be a joke? More fitting for Slick Willie, given his slick willy, would be Augustine's *Confessions*, especially Augustine's famous prayer, "Lord, make me chaste—but not yet." And not much needs to be said about his fondness for the Barlett and Steele book, which was one of the shoddiest and most partisan works on current affairs ever published. (Among other things, income inequality actually widened as much under Clinton as it did during the supposed "decade of greed" under Reagan and Bush.)

But two of Clinton's titles stand out for a closer look. We know from previous biographies, and a direct shout out from Clinton in his 1992 nomination acceptance speech, that historian Carroll Quigley was one of Clinton's favorite professors during his undergraduate years at Georgetown in the 1960s. But the book Clinton cites, *The Evolution of Civilizations: An Introduction to Historical Analysis* (published in 1961) is a work one can easily imagine Steve Bannon embracing. Indeed, one of Quigley's other obscure titles, *Tragedy and Hope*, is popular among the quack global-banker-conspiracy theorists—an application of his work that Quigley disavowed during his lifetime. (Quigley died in 1977.)

Quigley's *Evolution of Civilizations* is a synoptic framework for understanding what he saw were typical cycles of civilizations and culture, emphasizing cultural and technological change. Quigley's book is intended not as history, but as an exercise in prescriptive historiography. He explicitly disclaims any originality, acknowledging that he builds on Arnold Toynbee and allowing that other historians might come up with equally useful frameworks for historical interpretation. He anticipates some of the themes of civilizational competition determined by technological asymmetries explored in Jared Diamond's bestseller *Guns, Germs, and Steel* among other more recent works.

But it is no mere reconfiguration of "rise and fall" theories. "I have sought to go beyond the mere recognition of 'rise and fall' to seek to find the mechanism of the process," Quigley wrote. He identified seven stages of civilizations, the key stage being *conflict* (both internal and/or external), during which a civilization or culture will either renew itself and begin a new phase of expansion, or enter

270

a phase of terminal decay. Yet Quigley's book, besides being dated in many ways, would be nearly impossible to assign in a college course today, because it would be blasted as "Eurocentric." The climax of the book is his treatment of Western civilization, which has enjoyed the longest and most successful run of any civilization in human history, and notably having survived and overcome repeated crises and conflicts to renew itself and expand its reach and influence further. Quigley's analysis makes clear that the reason for the dominance of European civilization for more than a millennium is that it simply outcompeted all rivals both technologically and intellectually. "No culture has ever exceeded Western civilization in power and extent," Quigley wrote. "Western ideology is optimistic, moderate, hierarchical, democratic, individualistic, yet social, and dynamic."

There is no triumphalism in Quigley's treatment of the West, but it is comparable to Niall Ferguson's *Civilization: The West and the Rest*, or several of Rodney Stark's books such as *How the West Won*, not to mention Samuel Huntington's body of work. Even without a pro-Western attitude, though, you're not allowed to say such things today, unless it is done with the premise that the West's success was due primarily to oppression and exploitation, and therefore was unjust and irredeemable. Someone might even use the word "deplorable."

Quigley thought the West had been in "an Age of Conflict" since at least the late 19th century. Past such ages of conflict have experienced a rise in "irrationality," which manifest themselves in "Religious organizations [that] no longer linked men to God but adopted diverse mundane purposes. Our intellectual theories no longer explained anything or made us at home in the universe. . . Our political organizations increased the burden of their demands on our time, energy, and wealth but provided with growing ineffectiveness the justice, public order, education, protection, or incidental amenities we had come to expect from them." Does Bill Clinton perceive that cosmopolitan leftism is primarily responsible for this trend?

It is an open question at the end of Quigley's book whether the West would once again reform and renew itself or whether this time the West would succumb and decay to the point that it is eventually knocked over by a more willful competing civilization. Islam wants to, and China might someday be capable. In the classroom Quigley was apparently more optimistic about America's chances. In 1992

271

Clinton said that "As a student at Georgetown . . . Carroll Quigley . . . said to us that America was the greatest nation in history because our people had always believed in two things: that tomorrow can be better than today and that every one of us has a personal moral responsibility to make it so."

But Quigley's account is notably silent or weak on the importance of formal political and legal institutions and the role of statesmen, seemingly offering little of practical use for an ambitious young pol. Exactly how Quigley's idiosyncratic teaching filled out Clinton's political being remains murky. Maybe Quigley was just fun and interesting in the classroom, and had Clinton merely encountered the book instead of the man, nothing would have come of it. Or maybe he just confused Quigley with a lyricist for Fleetwood Mac: Don't stop thinkin' about tomorrow.

Which brings us to the second of Clinton's curious picks:

NY Times: *If you had to recommend one book to a student of government, what would it be?*

Clinton: *"Politics as a Vocation," by Max Weber.*

It is hard to imagine an analysis of history and politics more starkly different from Quigley than this notable work of Weber.

Let's start with a minor quibble. "Politics as a Vocation" is not a book. It's a long lecture Weber gave in January 1919, hard on the armistice of World War I when Germany was in a revolutionary situation, especially in Munich where the lecture was held and where several political assassinations had recently taken place. To be sure, the lecture is nearly 23,000 words long and is often printed in book form along with another famous Weber lecture from the time, "Science as a Vocation," but it's not quite a book. And it is a matter of some interest that Weber didn't want to give this lecture, but did so at the insistence of his students and for some other complicated political reasons.

It is significant that in the very first sentence Weber declares that this lecture "will necessarily disappoint you," suggesting that he was not going to tell students what to think or what to do, which is what his students wanted from him in that moment of high anxiety. Much of the essay is sobering if not morose. It is relentlessly hostile to the idealistic romanticism of modern politics, and ends with his famous paragraph about how "Politics is a strong and slow boring of hard boards." Weber's lecture would have made a depressing commencement address.

There is a lot to be said about Weber, who seems ever so slowly to be receding from the pre-eminence he once held as a first-rank thinker of modernity. Despite his often turgid writing, I have always found Weber to be interesting and worthy of study for his honesty and openness that you don't find in very many thinkers aligned on the left, and also for his defects. He was an atheist who nonetheless had great respect for religion and religious people; he was sympathetic to socialism but he knew that socialism was probably unworkable in practice, for reasons that anticipate some of Hayek's later critique about the "fatal conceit" of perfect synoptic knowledge; he was a key figure in developing social science methodology but was uneasy about the fact-value distinction that arose from it; he was a theorist of why bureaucratic government was essential and necessary for modern government, but at the same time he acknowledged that it was really going to suck. (Those weren't his literal words.) At some level Weber was genuinely concerned that replacing the statesman with the bureaucrat, and replacing ambition with "science," wouldn't work out very well, and this concern is the subject of both "Science as a Vocation" and "Politics as a Vocation."

I am curious to know what Clinton takes away from Weber's famous but little-read lecture, because I assign "Politics as a Vocation" to students in my course on statesmanship. When read and discussed patiently there are profound insights to be gleaned from Weber's confrontation with the fundamental dilemmas of political life. Yet I never ask students to read the entire lecture because it is disjointed. The first two-thirds are a dry and ponderous treatment of party and organizational forms of modern government, an effective substitute if you are out of sleeping pills (or copies of old Clinton State of the Union speeches). It is in this opening section, however, that Weber discusses the possibility of "charismatic leadership" as a legitimate basis for political life, and it is possible to see Clinton grabbing on to this well-known Weberian theme. Otherwise there is little to recommend in this forgettable bulk of the lecture.

"Politics as a Vocation" takes a sudden and dramatic turn in its last third, however, adopting a more personal tone that is moving and poignant in places, especially if the full context of the lecture is known. It is almost is if Weber wanted to reserve his most serious and important thoughts for the smaller number of students and readers with the fortitude and seriousness to stick it out. Weber understands "vocation" not as a profession or specialty, but in the biblical sense of a "calling" by God. Only certain kinds of human beings are suited for putting "his hand on the wheel of history." Yet he understands crucially the limits of politics. "He who seeks the salvation of the soul, of his own and of others, should not seek it along the avenue of politics." Good counsel, that, though one wonders whether Bill ever suggested the essay to Hillary Clinton before or after her infamous and grandiose "Politics of Meaning" speech in back in 1993.

With his students whipsawed between the extremes of Christian pacifism on one side and revolutionary Communism on the other, Weber confronts the ethical dilemmas of politics and the nature of individual political commitment. Weber lays out a treatment of what he called "the ethic of responsibility" and the "ethic of ultimate ends." The former operates in the familiar mode of practical compromise, but at the sacrifice of principle and idealism that Weber acknowledges is necessary for the forward movement of the human story. The latter too easily lapses into the mentality of "the ends justify the means," and anyone who does not recognize that such a commitment means contracting with "diabolical forces" often leading to extreme violence and counterproductive reaction is "a political infant."

While Weber admits that his two "ethics" are not absolute contrasts but supplements to the genuinely political person, he declares that he is unable to provide any guidance or rules as to when someone should follow the one or the other. Here Weber comes close to describing what an older political thinker—Aristotle comes to mind—would call the quality of "prudence," which is the art of the statesman. But in his inability to derive any rational ends of human society, Weber cannot embrace prudence as an intelligible idea, nor a statesman as a real specimen of political being, even if he does think political life is not something for the romantic dilettante.

Weber's setup might lead you to think he tilts at least implicitly toward the "ethic of responsibility," but he is unable to do so because of his fundamental premise that violence—and the State's legitimate monopoly on violence—is the decisive means of politics. He is too much of a Machiavellian to think this effectual truth can be avoided, but he is also unable to escape the undertow of Nietzsche and argue that reason can find answers to these dilemmas in real time. The best Weber can offer is that a serious political person must combine "passion, a feeling of responsibility, and a sense of proportion." An

274

older political science might call this "prudence," but Weber was unable to escape the positivist chains of modernity to recommend Aristotle or Burke. He gives no guidance on how an aspiring political leader would acquire or balance these traits.

Thus for all of its deep interest and occasional glimpses at the profound problems of political life, "Politics as a Vocation" leaves us at a dead end—sort of like the Clinton presidency and Clinton himself. Probably, though, Clinton's fondness for the lecture derives not from any subtleties and depths of Weber's rich discussion, but from the final two sentences, which offer what sounds like a comforting justification for the stubborn ruin of Clinton's life and reputation: "Only he has the calling for politics who is sure that he shall not crumble when the world from his point of view is too stupid or too base for what he wants to offer. Only he who in the face of all this can say 'In spite of all!' has the calling for politics."

—*Claremont Review of Books* online, October 2018

Made in the USA
Las Vegas, NV
15 September 2024